## "IN ALL AFRICA THERE IS NO MORE VIVID SIGHT, NO MORE ELECTRIFYING EXPERIENCE FOR MOST VISITORS THAN THAT OF ELEPHANTS . . .

"Until Iain Douglas-Hamilton, a young British zoologist, decided to live among them, . . . African elephants were known through little more than myth and misunderstanding.

"Until Mr. Douglas-Hamilton and his wife, Oria, wrote their book *Among the Elephants,* the remarkable discoveries he made about elephant behavior and the prospects for the animal's survival in a rapidly changing Africa remained inaccessible to most.

"*Among the Elephants* is . . . full of life and warmth . . . [It] offers colorful descriptions of the sights and smells of life in the African bush and chilling accounts of brushes with danger . . .

"Mr. Douglas-Hamilton, though a serious and skilled scientist, is not afraid to write his story with obvious feeling . . . That feeling plus dozens of excellent photographs by Mrs. Douglas-Hamilton should give most readers a vivid idea of what it is like among the elephants."

—*The New York Times*

"[AN] AFFECTING PORTRAIT OF THE LIFE OF THE PLANET'S LARGEST LAND ANIMAL."

—*Chicago Tribune*

---

"DR. DOUGLAS-HAMILTON HAS BROKEN NEW AND FASCINATING GROUND. There have been few books on elephant behaviour and, until Mr. Douglas-Hamilton developed the obsession that kept him at Lake Manyara in Tanzania for four and a half years, no large-scale, systematic study of their social system and way of living. With its pictures by his wife, Oria, who also wrote some of the chapters, it reads more like an adventure story than a text book, and is written with the passion of a Karen Blixen, with much of the excitement of *Out of Africa* . . . Quite an achievement."

—*London Sunday Times*

---

"INVALUABLE SCIENTIFIC INFORMATION IN THE CONTEXT OF HIGH ADVENTURE AND RARE POETIC VISION."
—*Los Angeles Times*

"A WORK TO RANK WITH JANE GOOD-ALL'S ON THE CHIMPANZEE . . . Fascinating . . . A book of great humour, empathy and delight."

—*The Observer Review*

---

"AN EXTRAORDINARY CLOSE-UP VIEW OF ELEPHANT LIFE, from birth to death, enhanced by photos . . . that are among the most vivid and intimate ever taken in Africa."

—*Boston Sunday Globe*

---

"THE DOUGLAS-HAMILTONS HAVE MADE SOME IMPORTANT AND MOVING BREAKTHROUGHS in human understanding of these beautiful animals . . . Iain and Oria, narrating in turn, earnestly convey the sense of mutual concern, loyalty, and tenderness that dominates the huge creatures' relationships. It may not be too farfetched to insist, as they do, that man has much to learn from this mode of social organization."

—*Kirkus Reviews*

# AMONG THE ELEPHANTS

Iain and Oria Douglas-Hamilton

*Foreword by Niko Tinbergen, F.R.S.*

This low-priced Bantam Book
has been completely reset in a type face
designed for easy reading, and was printed
from new plates. It contains the complete
text of the original hard-cover edition.
NOT ONE WORD HAS BEEN OMITTED.

AMONG THE ELEPHANTS
*A Bantam Book | published by arrangement with
The Viking Press*

PRINTING HISTORY
*Viking edition published June 1975
2nd printing .................... August 1975
3rd printing ................. October 1975
A selection of the Macmillan Book Club and
Reader's Digest Condensed Books
Literary Guild edition published July 1975
Condensations appeared in* ANIMAL KINGDOM MAGAZINE
*and* GRIT *Magazine*

*Bantam edition | October 1976*

All rights reserved.
Copyright © 1975 by Wytham Publications Ltd.
Copyright © 1975 Foreword by Niko Tinbergen, F.R.S.
This book may not be reproduced in whole or in part, by
mimeograph or any other means, without permission.
For information address: The Viking Press,
625 Madison Avenue, New York, N.Y. 10022

ISBN 0-553-02667-4

Bantam Books are published by Bantam Books, Inc. Its trade-
mark consisting of the words "Bantam Books" and the por-
trayal of a bantam, is registered in the United States Patent
Office and in other countries. Marca Registrada. Bantam
Books, Inc., 666 Fifth Avenue, New York, New York 10019.

PRINTED IN THE UNITED STATES OF AMERICA

*for our parents*
PRUNELLA, MARIO AND GISELLE
*and in memory of*
LEE LYON

# Contents

## III Iain Douglas-Hamilton

# AMONG THE
# ELEPHANTS

# Foreword

*by Niko Tinbergen, F.R.S.*

This is a truly remarkable, fascinating book by an equally remarkable, indeed unique couple. Written in a charmingly natural style, it reveals not only the deep involvement of the authors with the subjects of their studies, and their love of East Africa; it also relates a story of scientific discovery, of courage and adventure, of perseverance, and perhaps above all of *joie de vivre.* Their text reads deceptively like the narrative of one long, light-hearted, jolly safari, one that so to speak ran itself and in which the incidents merely added spice to their experience. But because I have been involved, though in a minor role, in their odyssey among the most magnificent wild creatures to be found in Africa, I know only too well that their lives have not run all that smoothly, and I am glad to have this opportunity for saying a few words about the story behind their story, about the curious course of events that brought this young Scotsman and his French-Italian wife together in the joint enterprise of which this book presents a condensed, lively yet modest, almost diffident report.

For me, the experience of having watched Iain Douglas-Hamilton set out on his unconventional career as a research graduate, of having seen him feel his way into his research problems, of having witnessed his

long struggle with obstacles that at times seemed insurmountable, and of having myself worried for years
about his chances (which at first seemed slim) of
producing a report that could satisfy two critical
examiners of a doctor's thesis—for me, this experience
has been a signal lesson. Of course, when one has to
act as an academic supervisor one often lives in doubt,
and one always heaves a sigh of relief when the pupil
succeeds. But Iain Douglas-Hamilton's story has a
special significance for me, because it drove home to
me how extremely difficult it can be to assess correctly a young man's true potential; how easily, by failing
to notice a youngster's hidden abilities (and by at-
taching too much weight to his weaker points) one
could fall short in one's duty of giving him the moral
support that might be crucial to his success.

Iain's remark, that during his undergraduate days in
Oxford I "had been a . . . distant figure in the department with whom (he) had little contact" is embarrass-
ingly correct. Having been more involved with the
guiding of graduate research than with the teaching
of undergraduates, I had not been perceptive enough
to see in him anything but just another face. Nor did
his diffidence allow him to take the initiative to approach me, although it became clear enough later that
we were kindred souls. And, to be fair to myself, the
Zoo Department had undoubtedly fewer attractions for
him than mountaineering in Scotland.

It was not until he returned, together with two
friends, from a spell as temporary assistants to Dr. John
Owen's research team in the Serengeti, that I became
more aware of him. Bubbling over with enthusiasm,
the three of them visited us one day in our Oxford
home, told us of their exciting holiday in a country
that I had so far known only from hearsay, and
showed us their color slides of the habitat on which
they had all become thoroughly imprinted. It was
clear that each of them was determined to return to
Africa. But they still faced the awesome prospect, which
none of them exactly relished, of having to spend

another year in Oxford to prepare themselves for the hurdle of our zoology finals—an examination of pretty frightening exactitude.

When Iain had successfully taken this hurdle, he came to see me, and I must confess that I felt somewhat apprehensive when he told me of his plans, so seemingly unattainable, to go back to East Africa and to start working, all on his own, on a research project for a doctor's degree. Typically, he was not as yet certain what project he would tackle—it was East Africa and its large mammals that drew him; almost obsessed him. How on earth could I help satisfy this ambition? And should I even try to? The Serengeti Research Institute had by then already been established, and suitable, experienced field workers had been appointed. There seemed to be neither a niche nor the funds for the realization of his dreams.

As Iain relates, it was John Owen and the Royal Society who gave him a start. And it is equally clear from his account how many others have given him support and guidance, and how well he appreciates how vital this help was.

A Royal Society Leverhulme scholarship gives a man a one-year trial period. After that, the dual problem arises of acceptance by the home university and of the finding of further funds. Both depend wholly on the scholar's performance in this one year. Having worked in the isolation of his carefully selected, breathtakingly beautiful base near the lower waterfall of the Ndala River, Iain could at the end of his first year show no more than moderately promising results. But there was an indefinable something, a strong urge, a charming obstinacy that, somehow, inspired confidence, and (we can now say, fortunately) he was given the means to continue. There is no denying that at home we were worried. At times the adventurous side of his nature seemed to gain the upper hand. Would he not (as rumors suggested) be too daring and even reckless, and were we justified in accepting responsibility for what we considered a risky and dangerous enterprise?

Would he get down to the systematic hard slog that would be required? Would he be able to bear his self-inflicted isolation? Would he retain enough scientific contact with his colleagues in the Serengeti? The severe attack of bilharzia that he suffered; his near-lethal adventure with two irritated rhinos; the dangerous charge by the four "Torone sisters"—an ill-tempered quartet of powerfully tusked female elephants; his habit of stalking his elephants on foot ("there was no greater pleasure than to walk silently down a well-padded elephant trail") —all this added to our apprehensions. But partly by luck, partly by his good judgment, Iain survived it all. He also proved himself a good listener, who took advice from experienced scientists; he showed technical inventiveness (witness his ingenious photographic method for recording the size, and so the age, of individual elephants); he learned how to utilize to the full his remarkable ability for recognizing individual animals by their slight natural differences; above all, he soon became "hooked" on his elephants, and literally lived with and among the several "family units" that he had learned to recognize. Dr. Hugh Lamprey and I myself, who had been appointed his joint academic supervisors, stayed with him several times, and he himself used to visit Britain for discussing his results, and for working out further plans. And gradually his work began to grow into a fascinating story. Sections one and three of the book describe the gist of what he discovered. Step by step he shows how much he found out, by "mere" but prolonged intelligent observation, about the remarkable social life of the African elephants; about their relations with their habitat; about their intelligence and the amazing knowledge that they build up during the long years as young members of their family units; and also how much could be learned about the many factors that have to be taken into account for the planning of sound management of the protected populations—for the problem of their conservation soon became one of his main concerns.

Yet, however well his field work developed, his senior friends never forgot that, in order to get his degree, and ultimately to make the results of his work available in the form of a publication, Iain would have to take yet another hurdle. He would have to go back to Oxford; to sit down at a desk in the laboratory and force himself to go through the long grind of working out his data, of putting them in their proper perspective, and of arguing, in writing, their biological relevance. But Manyara rather than Oxford had by now become his real home; he loved the place, and the carefree life. Once, when we had been struggling for five long hours, in the hot sun, to retrieve the Land-Rover out of a hole of sticky black mud, the four of us had sat down, stark naked, in the cool, clear Endabash River. While we were happily splashing about like babies in a bath, a group of elephants emerged noiselessly from the bush nearby, walked slowly down the bank to have a good look at us, and (perhaps concluding that we were nothing but some rather odd baboons) continued their leisurely way across the river bed to have a good shower themselves. Iain's delighted comment was "This is the Garden of Eden!" I agreed profoundly, but I also wondered: "Will he ever be able to stick it in Oxford?"

However, we need not have worried. When the time came, he did come, and he did see it through, however much he hated working out his innumerable data, drawing his graphs, plotting his maps; and however strong was all the time his longing for his Ndala home. Throughout these endless, strenuous months he was admirably supported by his wife, Oria.

Finally the day came when he had to submit to the grilling by the statutory team of two examiners—both of them men who required high standards. During the two hours of searching questioning his many friends lived in suspense. But, not really unexpectedly, the examiners approved of his work and accepted it as "an original contribution to knowledge." Iain emerged from the room a full academic fledgling, a "Doctor of

Philosophy (Oxon)" pending confirmation by the Faculty Board; a man who had proved himself. After a jolly party at their Wytham home the Douglas-Hamiltons quickly packed, and within a fortnight they were back in Africa.

Dr. Douglas-Hamilton would be the last to claim that his work is the final word, even on his four hundred-odd Manyara elephants. His work is clearly of the descriptive and interpretative kind. It provides many valuable data, but it also raises many new questions. He describes for instance the pronounced differences in the personalities of the different elephants, and he gives fascinating details of the frequent, almost continuous interaction between the young calves and their mothers and their older siblings. He rightly draws the inference, even though he cannot prove it, that the long years of dependence of the calves and of their association with their experienced elders must teach them a great deal. One of his remarkable discoveries is that adults and sub-adults give the youngsters so much help and guidance. The elephants emerge, even more clearly than in the famous book *Elephant Bill,* as highly intelligent and highly cooperative animals, on a par with, for instance, whales and dolphins. How vital the association with the family unit is to the young becomes clear when one reads for example the story of the orphaned calf that was killed by a lion. The work described in this book and documented in detail in his thesis will take its rightful place among the growing number of large-mammal studies that have been published in the last ten years, and it provides a firm basis for further work. The authors also show us how important it is to combine the purely intellectual curiosity of the scientific observer with an emotional, personal involvement. "I profoundly disagreed with Parker's view that sentiment can have no place in the policy of the National Parks" Iain writes; and further on, when he describes the behavior of one cow (whom he had aptly named Boadicea and who consistently met him with a mixture of hostility and fear) he muses: "I often wondered what terrible experience Boadicea must have suffered at the hands of man for her to hate and fear us so much." It is worth emphasizing that without the emotional involvement revealed by such remarks no man could have had the perseverance to carry out this type of study.

So far I have spoken mainly of one of the two authors. Without belittling the achievement of the man who initiated and carried through this work, I should like to stress how much Iain—as other men of his stamp—owes to the life partner who gave him so much support and encouragement when many others might have considered him a mere eccentric. Those of us who have followed Iain's life and work in his Manyara years know that section two, written by Oria and describing so vividly and naturally how she came to join him, is restrained and does not tell the full story. But this girl with long dark hair, so exuberantly posing in the last photograph of the book, is entitled to her full share in our admiration. With her husband she has taken her place among the biographers of Africa's most imposing and at the same time so very endearing mammal.

I would also like to draw attention to the book's illustrations, most of them taken by her. All of us who have visited East Africa have come back with numerous snaps—some of them beautiful, the majority commonplace mementoes—and we have entertained (and at times bored) our friends at home with the glimpses that our color slides give of that distant paradise, so utterly different from our own habitat. And the Douglas-Hamiltons describe how they too were bitten by the bug of "shooting away" whenever they had the chance. But the very carefully selected series reproduced here tells a *story;* in fact they form an integral part of the book. Without them the text alone would be interesting enough, but the pictures make it infinitely more vivid. (And they give a tantalizing preview of the film *The Family that Lives with Elephants.*)

Finally, this foreword would not be complete without a serious word of warning. There is a real danger in making public the evidence of the authors' astonishingly friendly relations with some of the wild elephants. The touching pictures showing how trustingly they introduced their own child to Virgo should on no account give the impression that anyone can approach wild elephants anywhere without serious risk of life and limb. The warning in South Africa's Kruger Park "Pas op!—olifante is gevaarlik" (caution!—elephants are dangerous) remains as necessary as ever. The very fact that this warning is required drives home the extraordinary achievement of the Douglas-Hamiltons: to have patiently won the confidence of the world's largest land animal, and through this to have discovered so many details of the way they really live—a way so much more dignified than the rather pathetic, almost humiliating way in which we see them, or at any rate their Asian relatives, perform in circuses, and even on occasion in zoos. May this book succeed in alerting readers all over the world to the need to give active support to the attempts at carrying out the intentions laid down in President Nyerere's Arusha Manifesto, which has so clearly inspired the Douglas-Hamiltons in their work and in writing this evocative account.

# Author's Note

In this book Oria and I have tried to convey the sense of exploration, the excitements and the rewards of our venture into the world of elephants. In 1965 I was invited, as an inexperienced zoologist fresh from university, to study the elephants of Lake Manyara, for they were believed to present an "urgent problem" there. A study of their ecology—their relationships with their environment—soon compelled me to immerse myself in details of their social behavior, about which very little was known at that time. But when I came to ponder the keys to their survival, the field widened, and I realized that elephant ecology and survival can only be considered in relation to what men believe and how they behave.

Part I of this book develops the ideas which were in my mind when I arrived at Manyara. These soon became woven into a network of questions, some of which I hoped to answer during my study. For the first three years I lived alone among the elephants; then Oria joined me.

In Part II Oria describes her arrival at Manyara, and the life we led in the bush, with a vivid immediacy denied to the inhibited pen of a cautious scientist. She carries our story on to the end of our time at Manyara.

In Part III I set out the answers to many of the questions I faced in Part I and which Oria and I examined further in Part II.

Our book is a personal story and does not attempt to be a comprehensive guide to elephant behavior and biology. I have mentioned the work of others where it touched on mine but I have not been able to do justice to all the studies that have been made on African elephants. The basic facts underlying our account have been recorded in my thesis, designed for scientists and now deposited in the Bodleian Library at Oxford (currently being published in the East African Wildlife Journal). *Among the Elephants* is written for the general reader.

Admittedly only an exploratory study, I feel that my four-and-a-half years' work at Manyara, together with the work of others, narrowed the areas of uncertainty and helped to reduce the atmosphere of crisis which prevailed in early discussions of elephant problems and provided guidelines which could steer future work into effective channels. Although I only began to scratch the surface of elephant social life, I believe we clarified a few of the major features of their social organization and came to recognize a little of the astonishing variety of their individual characters and temperaments.

IAIN DOUGLAS-HAMILTON

# I

## Iain Douglas-Hamilton

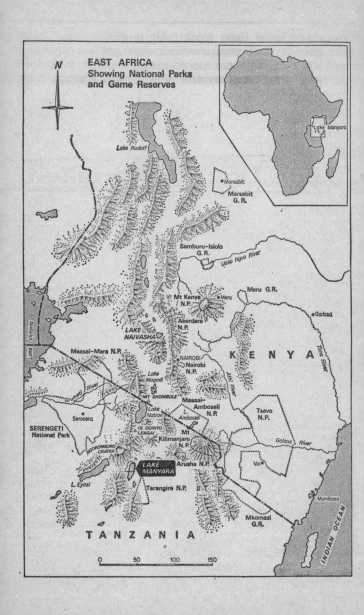

EAST AFRICA
Showing National Parks
and Game Reserves

# 1

# Serengeti Prelude

It all started in 1963 when I stood outside the National Park Headquarters in Arusha, waiting to meet John Owen, the Director of the Tanzania National Parks.

Before long he came down the office stairs. A powerfully built man with grey hair and steely blue eyes, he was dressed in green corduroy shorts, a green pullover and green woolen stockings, neatly gartered at the knee.

"You must be Douglas-Hamilton," he said. "Come to my office."

It was the summer vacation of 1963 and I had arrived in Africa from Oxford, where I was studying zoology. Owen had invited me to work for a brief spell as an assistant in the newly formed animal research project on the Serengeti Plains, where there is the largest concentration of wild animals in Africa.

I had always wanted to work with animals in Africa ever since I can remember. The old accounts I read as a child told of vast horizons in little-explored lands, adventures with wild beasts, hairbreadth escapes and tough, resourceful men who survived by their bushcraft.

We went up to his office where he showed me maps of the five great National Parks: Serengeti, Manyara, Arusha, Ngurdoto and Mikumi. Altogether, their area

3

totaled 10,000 square miles. The Parks were controlled by a Board of Trustees, who had recently appointed John Owen as Director; and John Owen had realized that the conservation and management practices of Wardens who worked under him should be based on detailed ecological studies. With enthusiasm and determination he had established the Serengeti Research Project, later to become the Serengeti Research Institute. The scientists were entirely funded from abroad.

In the rest of Tanzania, outside the National Parks, wildlife was looked after by the Game Department, who not only had to suppress poaching, but also had to protect crops by shooting any wild animals that conflicted with human interests. However, newly independent Tanzania placed a very high value on its natural assets and new parks were being planned. In the decade following independence, more was done for wildlife than in the previous fifty years.

"You will be assisting Murray Watson," John Owen said. "He is our scientist working on the wildebeest. The life is pretty rough and ready, but I am sure you won't mind that and I don't think you can fail to enjoy yourself."

The green lorry which next morning drove up to the hotel where I had spent the night was painted with the Tanganyika National Park's emblem: an impala leaping over a thorn tree. The driver greeted me with a warm smile. I was glad to find that he spoke a little English. We set off on the first seventy-five mile leg across wide plains where we saw occasional herds of Masai cattle. Then we reached the village of Mto-wa-Mbu, on the northern edge of the Lake Manyara National Park. Here we stopped to buy freshly picked bananas. The driver told me that this park had many elephants and that they often came out and damaged the banana and maize crops inside the village.

We drove on through lush, cool, green forest on either side of the road for about a mile before climbing up a steep escarpment. The lorry ground up in low gear over the corrugated dusty road, pushing a wave of heat into the cabin.

At the top of the hill the driver stopped at a lay-by. He asked me if I wanted to get out and look. I did and immediately exulted in the magnificence of the scenery. A sheer drop fell several hundred feet to a rubble slope covered in vegetation, below that the crowns of huge trees rolled away to the distant Lake shore, where the forest changed to open grassland and palm trees. The Lake itself seemed to stretch forever until the horizon of the water was lost in the sky. This was Manyara.

Further on the road climbed slowly up to the Ngorongoro Crater where colder air ventilated the burning cabin. On the lip of this huge natural bowl we passed a simple stone pile with an inscription which read,

MICHAEL GRZIMEK
12.4.1934—10.1.1959
He gave all he possessed for the wild animals
of Africa, including his life

I had read of the adventures of Michael Grzimek and his father Dr. Bernhard Grzimek in the book *Serengeti Shall Not Die,* which told of their plane painted with black and white zebra stripes, in which they had made the first counts of the Serengeti herds, before Michael's tragic crash.

Edging around the rim of the Crater we started our descent to the famous Serengeti Plains.

As we reached the bottom of the escarpment, the main road branched out into a series of white dusty tracks. From here onwards there was no road, and each vehicle made its own way across the plains. Clouds of white volcanic dust filled the air, coming through the floorboards like smoke, and we were soon covered with it.

We arrived at Seronera in a red sunset to find a handful of concrete houses, some square, some round, standing where the vastness of the plain merged into scattered trees, silhouetted against a blazing sky. These marked the Park HQ and the Rest Houses. Here we were to spend the night. The following morning, in a Park's Land-Rover, we would drive on to Banagi, which was the Research Center, and my destination. My memory of that first night is filled with all the thrilling sounds of Africa. I lay listening to calling lions, laughing hyenas and the distant sound of galloping hooves, until I fell asleep.

At Banagi, I met Murray Watson, the scientist with whom I was to work for the next two months. He told me the Research Center had been started only a year ago, with three scientists who came out to follow the work that had been begun in 1958 by the Grzimeks. Hans and Uti Klingel were studying the zebra population; two other undergraduates from Oxford and myself were the first assistants to work in the research team.

The scientists lived in an old shooting lodge with thick mud walls. Across a compound a concrete laboratory housed a small scientific library and a herbarium containing all the plants of the Serengeti, carefully prepared by Dr. Greenway.

For the next two months my eyes were assailed by sights utterly strange to my previous experience. Murray Watson lived a life of incomparable freedom. He was studying wildebeest, and spent most of his time on safari following them to plot out month by month the areas covered in their migration. When we were not close on their heels on the ground we counted them by the hundred thousand from the air.

While studying the problem of what controlled their numbers Murray Watson took monthly counts of the ratio of calves to adult females. It was also vital to know how many animals died each year and what it was that killed them. This led to Murray working very closely with Myles Turner, the Serengeti Park Warden, because the greatest predator within the Park system (one which if uncontrolled might very easily exterminate all the game) was still man. In his free time Murray countered this predation by hunting poachers.

Gradually my eyes grew accustomed to searching the distant horizons for pulsating blobs in the heat haze, which might materialize as wildebeest, zebra, eland, kongoni, perhaps lion, hyena, cheetah, or any of the myriad species which inhabit this vast area, but at the moment the most exciting quarry was man. His small upright figure was unmistakable even in the heat distortion. If one such was observed, Murray Watson, as an Honorary Warden, was sanctioned to give instant pursuit, for a man on foot in a National Park could only be a poacher. Everywhere we went we found traces of their work. I learned that to locate the corpses of killed animals it was no good merely looking for circling vultures, for they usually selected the best thermals in which to soar. We had to spot a vulture diving down and to pinpoint the exact position where it disappeared behind the trees, then race over and search, until at last we stumbled on the remains of the prey. All too often there would be a small arrow in the skin blackened with Akocanthera poison. The poachers, on foot, shooting with their primitive weapons, only recovered a fraction of the beasts they killed. Thanks to the antipoaching field force, some control over them now existed; nevertheless they were an ever-present threat.

The biggest poachers' hideouts were in the Northern Extension of the Park where we went to patrol. Acting on information we swept one valley, but found only deserted camps where the ashes were two days old. The next day Myles, Murray and I set off early into country that even Myles had never penetrated before. On the way we burned the grass. The course of our march was marked by columns of smoke. Myles had a theory that regular burning reduced the burden of ticks and other skin parasites which the animals picked up from the grass. In a week's time a green flush would appear on the burned patch and on it the game would concentrate.

I was excited by the thought that we might tangle with poachers. It was the sort of country where they were known to operate, and no one had bothered them there before. Murray went off on his own in a typically individualistic way, and I stuck with Myles hoping to pick up some bushcraft from this wise old Warden. (He was far from old, but he seemed so to me then.)

We reached the hill without seeing any sign of human activity. On one shoulder a huge flattened boulder was poised above a massive slab supported by two smaller ones thus forming a perfect natural shelter with a view in all directions. Here we discovered dried grass and ashes, probably left by Wanderobo elephant hunters who had used the place as a bivouac. These men were true hunter-gatherers, Myles said, who fitted into the environment like any other predator, making little impression on the number of game. They were quite unlike the Wakuria who came in huge gangs and cleaned out an area using miles of snare lines made of steel wire, stolen from the mines, then drying the meat in the sun and later carrying it out and selling it as part of a regular commercial enterprise.

As we sat gazing across miles of wilderness from the top of that rock I had a feeling of great calm and contentment, induced by the unspoiled trackless landscape. Suddenly a strange murmur impinged on my consciousness. I could have sworn I heard voices. I told Myles, but he had not heard anything. Then it came again. This time I convinced him enough for him to send down a Ranger and a porter to investigate an area of forest below us on the far side of the hill. They found a path winding into this patch of forest, but there was no way of telling whether it was a game trail or manmade.

Just as the Rangers were about to disappear from view I heard the voices again, this time quite unmistakably.

"Myles, I'm absolutely sure they are human beings," I said, and raced down the hill to join the two men. We entered the forest beneath the arched canopies of the trees and soon the path broadened to a bush thoroughfare. As the voices became louder and louder the forest began to resemble a charnel house, for everywhere I looked there were the bones of dead animals, some of them split open to remove the marrow.

We now proceeded with the utmost caution. Judging from the voluminous babble there were many men ahead of us. Rounding a corner, we suddenly came upon a thorn *boma* (enclosure) and a neat camp. At least thirty men were lying around under thatch shelters smoking, sleeping or just talking, with their spears, bows and arrows stacked against the surrounding trees. All through the camp large strips of meat were drying on wooden racks and, even outside the *boma,* meat had been laid on the grass, since there was not enough room for it within.

Between us we had one bolt action rifle, a spear, and a Very pistol with three flares, which I was carrying. I felt a little diffident about taking on such odds. But before I could discuss the need for reinforcements with the head Ranger (a splendid man with handlebar moustaches) he signaled me to follow, let off a shot in the air and charged straight into the middle of the camp. Immediately pandemonium broke loose. I followed hard on his heels, and entered a maelstrom of fleeing bodies, jumping over the *boma* in all directions. I selected one poacher and rugger-tackled him around the neck, landing in a heap on top of him and the thorn *boma.*

He shouted "Mimi hapana piga Nyama, Bwana." (I did not shoot the game, Mister.) I told him to be still. Then a flying figure came hurtling over my head.

"Stop," I shouted.

He didn't. So I shot off a flare which described a beautiful arc above the man's head and went on to start a grass fire twenty yards beyond. Although I was dying to try and catch another poacher, instead I pulled this one up on to his feet and marched him back into the camp where the Ranger tied him to a tree with two other captives. Then I dashed off again, but the forest was once more deserted and silent.

Soon Myles arrived, rather annoyed at having missed the attack. By now the bush fire I had started was coming closer to the *boma* and we had to work fast to remove all the snares and stocks of spears, simis, bows and quivers of poisoned arrows which had been abandoned at the first shot. We could not leave them behind for other poachers to use. Murray Watson then turned up and was even more annoyed than Myles at having missed the action, although he had managed to intercept a fourth poacher running away. We had barely time to carry off the last sacks of dried meat when the *boma* went up in a wall of flame.

It was one of the most exciting days I had ever known. I was only half ashamed that hunting fellow man had fulfilled an atavistic urge which satisfied both my territorial and my hunting instincts. But when that evening back at our base camp on the Mara River I saw the poachers tied up, and saw their dull, miserable eyes, and the great weals on their bodies from the scuffles they had had with the Rangers, I felt remorseful, and especially so when Myles told me that they would get a five months' prison sentence each. (Newly independent Tanzania was not sympathetic to those who broke the law or squandered communal wealth.) By then, of course, it was too late to alter their fate and anyway, I told myself, it had all been in the cause of protecting wildlife, so it must be justified. Nor could I entirely blame the Rangers for handling the poachers roughly. A few weeks before, some poachers had caught a Ranger and slashed his arm to the bone. However, a seed of doubt was planted in my mind about whether such a policy as the present one would continue indefinitely to be the most effective way of reducing human predation. It was true that they were a gang hunting illegally for commercial gain, but if they were to be neighbors of the Parks would not our actions totally alienate them?

My experiences during two months in the Serengeti

completely captured my imagination, and thereafter I could think of no career other than joining this élite band of scientists. It seemed incredible that hardly any work on either the behavior or the ecology of the major big game species had at this time been seriously attempted. I resolved that once I had gained a degree in zoology at Oxford, I would select an exciting animal to work on; and since nobody had yet made a field study on lions they seemed an obvious choice. Meantime, I read all I could about radio-tracking techniques, and dreamed of using them on lions.

# 2

# "A Problem at Manyara"

It was not until early in 1965 that I was able to talk to John Owen about my plans. Then during his brief leave I succeeded in badgering him into granting me an interview. I met him in a small well-kept Sussex garden, which was his English territory.

He was vigorously stoking a bonfire with pieces of garden junk, the smoke curling up half-heartedly to feed the autumn smog that threatened to blot out the pale English sun. Turning a little reluctantly from his labors he offered me a chair and called to his wife, Patricia, to make us some tea. His large frame crammed into a small chair, his expressionless blue eyes hiding what he was thinking as he puffed clouds of smoke from his pipe, he listened patiently while I put to him my research program on lions. At the end he said,

"No Iain, I'm sorry, you can't do it. We have someone else coming to study lions."

The someone else turned out to be the American zoologist George Schaller, who was already well-known for his research on the mountain gorillas of the Virunga volcanoes in Ruanda and Uganda. I suggested that perhaps he might want an assistant.

"I'm afraid not, you know how individualistic these scientists are."

"Well surely there must be something I can do?"

"We don't need anyone in the Serengeti right now."
He paused, then, almost as an afterthought, added,

"But we *do* need some research done in Manyara on elephants."

He then went on to describe Lake Manyara, and that thin strip of land along the north-west shore which was the National Park. Although it was one of the smallest Parks in Tanzania there was a high density of animals including lion, leopard, rhino, hippo, and large numbers of elephant and buffalo. Most attractive to the tourists were the tree-climbing lions for which it was famed, and the Park was becoming one of the most popular in East Africa. What concerned John Owen was that recently elephants had started to strip bark, often with lethal effect, off the trees which the lions used as resting places in the heat of the day. Nobody knew what it was that the elephants needed in the bark nor what would happen if they continued this destruction.

Elephant ecology (the relationship of the animal with its environment) was something entirely new to me. I had set my heart on the Serengeti, but, between sips of tea, I listened with growing interest, as John Owen told me what little was known about the elephants of Lake Manyara.

It was not known exactly how many elephants there were but the Warden had told him that during the dry season, from June to September, most of the elephants migrated out of the Park and disappeared into a huge cloud forest which sat on top of the Rift Valley escarpment just outside the Park boundary. John Owen wanted to know what the significance of this alleged migration was and if indeed it really did occur.

He ended his description by saying "If you want to take on this research Iain, you will have to finance yourself, we can't afford to pay you, but we can give you an old Land-Rover and a prefabricated tin hut which you can set up anywhere you like in the Park, provided the tourists can't see you."

To live in a National Park and to follow the elephants on their migration routes sounded a great proposition to me. I accepted gratefully, returned to Oxford, threw myself into my text books to get my degree and set about finding some money for the project.

In the department of zoology on one of the notice boards was a list of opportunities for post-graduates, among them "The Royal Society Leverhulme Scholarship Scheme." Its intention was to provide facilities for young graduates in the environmental sciences, thus enabling them to gain practical experience in tropical countries. The scholarship would pay for the cost of travel and for a certain amount of necessary equipment in addition to £500 for living expenses.

I drafted a research outline on "The Feeding Habits of Elephants and the Way in which they Modify the Vegetation." When it was completed I submitted it to the Royal Society. I left the methods of my proposed study deliberately vague so that I could adapt to local conditions. Much would depend on how close I could get to the elephants. I had no idea whether they would charge on sight or run away as soon as they were aware of me.

In a few weeks' time I was summoned to London. I was ushered into a dark paneled room where some six distinguished-looking men faced me across a highly polished table. One wanted to know if it was dangerous to approach elephants on foot. This I couldn't answer, never having tried to do so, but I said I thought not, provided one moved cautiously. Another wanted to know if I would take a plant press and collect specimens from the forest while I watched the elephants eating. Only one question was tricky: "What, in your opinion, is the use of studying elephants?" I replied that elephants had declined in numbers and range all over Africa for the last two thousand years or more and that even now, within the sanctuaries set aside for their protection, they were possibly still threatened with extinction from overcrowding. Only research could show a way for the proper management of elephant populations.

I never found out who any of these men were, but I was very grateful to them in November when I received a letter informing me that I had been awarded the scholarship for a period of one year. It was worth £1,500 and had been approved as follows:

| | |
|---|---|
| Return air fare to Tanzania | £250 |
| Local travel including aerial survey | £570 |
| Maintenance and living expenses | £500 |
| Scientific equipment | £180 |

I felt as rich as a king, all the more so because by the time I heard this good news I had already spent most of my savings on a ticket to East Africa, where I was devoting my time to learning to fly. (In the event my money ran out before I had completed my course, and it was another three years before I could afford to finish my pilot's training.)

On receiving the letter, I hitched a lift in a friend's plane to the Serengeti from where I could go on to Manyara.

When I arrived at Seronera, Myles Turner was out, but his wife Kay said he would be back soon and invited me to stay with them for the night. I spent the afternoon catching chameleons for her daughter's collection of small animals, which she cherished with devotion. Myles and Murray arrived in the evening after flying together to plot the latest position of the wildebeest migration. It was great to see them again and we soon fell to talking shop.

I heard for the first time about how they had become involved with Manyara's elephants, and had begun a controversy. Apparently they had gone over for two days and counted all the elephants and buffalo they could see from the air within the Manyara Park boundaries. The total had come to 420 elephants and 1,500 buffalo. Making some quick calculations they worked out that the density of elephants was 12 per square mile, which was higher than any ever recorded in Africa. On these grounds they suggested that the Park was probably overpopulated, with the implication that the elephant population might have to be regulated by shooting. They published their views in the *East African Wildlife Journal.*

They ran into opposition. For one thing, John Owen was displeased that they had made their results and opinions public, and for another, the idea of shooting within National Parks was anathema at the time. However they both urged me to keep an open mind and to give periodic elephant census work top priority in my program in order to find out whether the Manyara elephants remained highly concentrated during all the year, or whether what they had witnessed had been a temporary concentration. I chewed all this over and determined not to be influenced by anyone's opinions, but only by the facts as I found them. I believed that if it were possible to make the appropriate records and measurements then the facts would speak for themselves and the right course of management would become obvious.

After a good night's rest, once again punctuated by the roaring of lions, I set off in a tourist's car across the dusty plains towards the Ngorongoro Crater and Manyara.

As we descended the side of the Ngorongoro I caught my first glimpse of the escarpment above Lake Manyara, almost concealed by a smudgy blue haze. Eight miles further and we reached the point where the pot-holed, stony road turned sharply left; we pulled up on the lip of the cliff at the same place from which I had admired the view two years before. It was with a feeling of great excitement that I looked out over the forest stretching towards the south for mile after mile, broken only by glades covered in short grass and rivers which carved their way to the Lake. Observing very carefully I was able to see several herds of elephants, looking at that distance like parties of termites.

After a few minutes we drove on down the steep-sided escarpment. The road here marked the northern boundary of the Park and there were traces of dung where elephants had crossed the road; the bush was

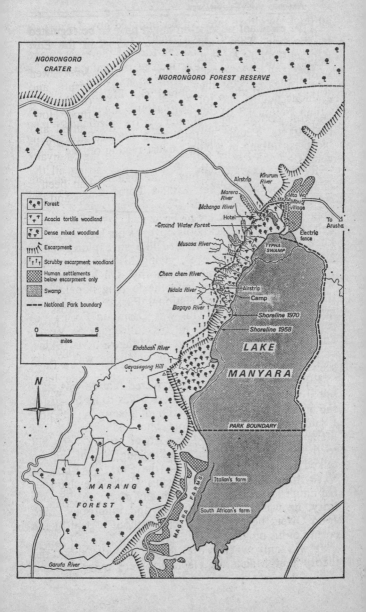

so thick on either side that I wondered how I was ever going to be able to keep track of their movements. Two miles on, we reached the foot of the escarpment, plunged into forest, and arrived at the village of Mto-wa-Mbu; this was as far as I was to go by car.

The packed village throbbed with life. Market stalls full of bananas, tomatoes, custard apples, pawpaw, colorful cotton material and native medicines lined the streets. People were buying and selling, riding bicycles, talking in groups or just resting on the grassy verges.

As I stepped out to buy some bananas an ancient dilapidated Land-Rover with a home-made wooden superstructure drew up. The driver was a white man wearing a dark green bush jacket with a leather belt. Large brown jackboots covered his legs up to the knee. Sturdily built, he looked like an explorer. Dark glasses concealed his eyes, giving his lined face and grey hair a mask of stern authority. On his chest he wore the circular badge with the leaping impala, and the words "Tanganyika National Parks" in gold and green around the rim. This was Desmond Foster Vesey-Fitzgerald, known to all his colleagues as Vesey, and to the Africans as Bwana Mungosi (Mr. Skins, which referred to the boots in which he was always seen).

I introduced myself and discovered that he was staying at the Park Rest House where I was to be based for the first few months until I had built a camp in the Park. I said goodbye to the people who had given me the lift and went in Vesey's Land-Rover up the steep hill to the Rest House. Over a refreshing cup of tea we talked about the elephants in the Park. As soon as Vesey took off his dark glasses his whole face changed. He didn't look in the least stern any more; on the contrary, he was cheerful, friendly and humorous. Like John Owen, he was rarely seen without a pipe in the corner of his mouth.

It was only when Vesey began to talk about the theory that Manyara's elephants were overpopulated that he became aggressive. He asserted that through all these years the National Parks had been trying to protect the animals, and now at last when the numbers had built up to a nice density the cry of overpopulation was raised. He was scornful of Murray's and Myles's two-day research visit, and asked how they could have come to all those conclusions in so short a time? He himself had been working on the Manyara vegetation for years, and saw no signs of destruction by elephant. When I asked him about the damage they had inflicted to the lion's acacia thorn trees, he snorted "Good God man, that's not damage, that's habitat modification."

Vesey went on to explain his pet idea. The elephants, he said, were an essential part of nature's scheme. By opening up rank grass and thick bush they also opened a way for other animals and for more palatable plants which would not otherwise be able to penetrate into these areas. He believed that the best way to manage the Park was to interfere as little as possible with natural cycles.

The two schools of thought were directly contradictory, and neither could be proved right, for lack of evidence. On the one hand, Murray and Miles could not prove that there were too many elephants simply because their destiny was higher than elsewhere in Africa, nor even that their numbers were high all through the year. On the other, Vesey had no figures to show that the elephants were not in the process of wiping out the acacia trees. I now saw that my first year's work would have to include both a study of the numbers of elephants, and the state of acacia trees, particularly in relation to the numbers killed by elephants. But more than anything else, I realized that the intriguing movement of elephants into the Marang Forest might be of the greatest significance.

After a supper lit by hissing gas lamps, I collapsed on to my bed and did not wake until the sun shone the next morning. We then made an early start so that Vesey could show me the entire Park in one day.

The dusty road from the Rest House wound down to the main road. A little further on, a turning led us to the entry gate where a clerk sat in a small booth selling tickets to the tourists. Behind the gate the forest began, and at once we entered the cool shade of tall canopies of trees. Visibility was good enough to see between yellow, black and grey trunks for quite a distance, this because elephants and other animals had eaten most of the undergrowth. Rivulets coruscated between black pock-marked volcanic boulders to flow into ice clear pools, where watercress floated; the pools were fringed by elephant fronds of papyrus that nodded like slaves wafting a pharaoh's fans. Little blue crabs with orange legs eyed us from the rocks before scuttling sideways into the water, and yellow-barked fig trees, *Ficus sycamorus,* which grew along the edges of these watercourses, gave shade.

I learned that one particularly tropical looking tree with broad long green leaves was called *Conopharyngia.* I had only to ask Vesey for a name and he would immediately produce it. According to him the luxuriant forest could not be classified as a rain forest, since Manyara was a relatively arid area with an average rainfall of less than twenty inches. In fact, under such a climatic régime, it was only possible for the forest to grow because it was well-watered by innumerable streams. These issued from springs all along the foot of this part of the Rift wall, but the water originated some thirty miles away from the Ngorongoro Highlands. Rain falling there was prevented from running away too quickly by a thick cloak of mountain forest. It trickled down to the roots and through layers of porous volcanic soil and rock, until it hit an impermeable layer of rock which finally surfaced at the foot of the escarpment within Manyara. Therefore, the Ground Water Forest, as it was named, with all its natural wealth, was dependent on water falling well outside it. If the Ngorongoro Forest were ever to be cut down the Manyara Ground Water Forest might well wither into extinction.

All this I came to know later, but as we bumbled along in Vesey's faded grey Land-Rover the ebullient vigor of the forests with its riotous variations looked in no way fragile, nor as if it were crumbling under pressure from legions of voracious elephants. A few miles south the springs diminished and the forest gave way to more arid *Acacia tortilis* woodland. These beautiful flat-topped thorn trees of the *Mimosaceae* family, with their spreading branches and rough brown bark, to me epitomize Africa. Usually they are found in groves or spaced out with savannah grass which gives a park-like appearance. Now the first portents of elephant destruction were to be seen. Pale ghostly white trunks stripped naked of their protective blanket of rough bark offered a glaring contrast to the surrounding greenery. Above, the foliage was still olive, but doomed to shrivel. The damage was only occasional, but very obvious. Shreds of torn bark hung scrappily from the ring-barked trees, and on the ground nearby a careful search located fibrous balls which the elephants had chewed and then spat out.

The road meandered on, at times coming close to the foot of the Rift wall, and at times running along the Lake shore. From a distance the Lake waters took on the blue color of the sky, or, when ruffled by a breeze, shimmered in the brilliance of the sunshine, but, close to, the colors were dark brown and muddy. Across the Lake it was possible to see a hazy outline which represented the far shore, about ten miles away.

In many places along the bank there were mud flats which Vesey warned me were particularly treacherous for vehicles. After a dry spell the surface cracked and hardened, giving an impression of firmness which camouflaged the liquid mud beneath. It was all too easy to drive along at high speed sending up a cloud of dust, only suddenly to plop through the surface layer and find that all four wheels were hopelessly bogged with the chassis sinking lower and lower into the mire. Yet in many other places these same mud flats were covered in spiky short grass on which large herds of buffalo grazed.

"These alkaline pastures are some of the best in the district," said Vesey.

Half-way down the Park just past a wide sandy river, the Ndala, the escarpment reached almost to the Lake's edge. Then the space between Lake and cliff widened again after another river, slow flowing and clear, the Bagayo, had been crossed. A dry stretch followed showing a change in habitat, as the *Acacia tortilis* gradually gave way to other trees, such as the "desert date" (*Balanites aegyptiaca*).

Next we crossed a plain of long grass devoid of game, and entered thick, sweet-smelling bush. On our right the escarpment once more loomed near, and a huge waterfall cascaded down its side: the Endabash River, which supplied the whole of the southern end of the Park with water. Vesey told me that in dry years this river too ceased to flow. We forded it at a place where a concrete causeway had been built. The thick bush lasted another few miles before we were able to get our next sight of the Lake across brilliant green sedges, where buffaloes were lying in the open.

The track ended nineteen miles as the pelican flies south of the Main Gate, at some hot springs which oozed out of the ground. The local name of this place was Maji Moto, which means hot water in Swahili. Here the escarpment reared straight up from the Lake for a full 3,000 feet. It was capped with a tangled mass of dark green trees which marked the edge of the Marang Forest Reserve, an area of eighty-two square miles. The slopes were very steep, covered in dense vegetation and broken by precipitous slabs of smooth rock and huge boulders, which formed an apparently insuperable barrier to any movement of elephants up to the Forest.

A mile further on the southern boundary of the Park was marked by another waterfall which fell sheer for several hundred feet and then ran as a crystal clear stream through a strip of riverine forest down to the

Lake. A fence, made of three strands of steel hawsers, had been erected here in 1960 by the first Park Warden in a vain attempt to contain the elephants within the Park, and to prevent them from visiting parts of their former range that had been given over to farmers. Now, six years later, the fence stood intact in most places, but where the main elephant path used to run, it was twisted out of shape. The two lower hawsers hung uselessly down to the ground, stretched by the colossal power and weight of elephants determined to get through. From the numerous tracks it was obvious that elephants had no difficulty in passing under the third wire.

On our way back a strong moist wind blew from the south-east, sweeping across the Lake, and piling up against the escarpment formed a layer of cloud. On a mud beach we found two canoes which had been washed up in a storm. They looked sea-worthy and I made a mental note to return as soon as possible and reclaim them before they warped in the fierce sun. I wanted to be able to approach the elephants from the water as well as by land, and one day I hoped I would be able to see them from the air as well.

Then as the slanting evening light began to turn the bushes into pure gold, a group of elephants crossed the road just in front of the car. The long-awaited moment took me by surprise. A silent, orderly column of cows, towering above young of all sizes, filed thirty yards in front of us, their flanks blue-grey in the shadow. Where their heels scuffed the ground there were bursts of incandescent dust. Some ten crossed peacefully and then the younger females scurried over, turning to look sideways at us with heads held high and backs arched. As soon as they were safely across and almost hidden by bushes they wheeled in unison as if at an order. A gust of wind wafted our scent in their direction. Ears flared and a row of trunks performed a snake dance, waving sinuously above the line of their massive heads, sampling our smell and afterwards expelling their breath with a whoosh. Although their faces were relatively immobile, the infinite variety of trunk postures and movements lent the elephants all the expressiveness of a primate's visage. I could no longer see the youngsters apart from glimpses between the legs of large cows which formed a solid wall facing us. We were obviously worrying them. But after a while they became less disturbed, the young ones peeped out, and I was able to examine the whole herd carefully through my binoculars.

That evening, after dinner as we drank coffee, with the moths dancing around the pressure lamp which cast their fleeting shadows on the wall, my ideas began to fall into place. The purpose of the research began to crystallize in my mind. It was no longer just a matter of finding out why elephants ate the bark of thorn trees or where they migrated to outside the Park. Time was now a factor and the controversy between those who wanted to regulate and those who wanted to let everything alone suddenly made my elephant research vitally urgent. The answers I found might solve the question "Should we control elephant numbers by shooting, or should we let nature take its course?" Hundreds of elephants' lives on the one hand and the fate of the whole woodlands on the other, were at stake.

First, I would have to count the number of trees injured and destroyed. But the long-term effect of the elephants on their environment would depend on just how many elephants were eating the plants growing within the restricted area of the Park. Numbers in turn would depend on the birth rate, their movements in and out of the Park and their death rate. There was only one direct way in which I could measure these factors. I could record how many calves were born to a certain number of females per year and I could follow their movements. I could record how many elephants died.

To achieve these observations I would first need

to acquire the ability to recognize large numbers of individual elephants with no more difficulty than an equivalent number of men. This, I realized, would have to be the central method upon which all my research must be based. It would be my first priority for the months that lay ahead and was something which no one had yet attempted. The plan was exciting but of course it would only work if I could encounter the elephants often enough to learn to recognize every one of them by sight.

# 3

# Elephants as Individuals

After Christmas I went out on my own to look at elephants, in a battered old Land-Rover which John Owen had lent me. I wanted to take photographs of them so that I could learn how to recognize them as individuals.

The first I saw was a bull quietly feeding by the side of the road. He was slightly obscured by some low-lying vegetation, but if I could approach him on foot, and vary the angle, I would be in a position to get a clear view. I crept silently out of the car, closing the door gently behind me, a precaution I had learned on anti-poaching patrols in the Serengeti. The wind was perfect, blowing steadily from the elephant to me. With the utmost caution I tiptoed towards an ant-hill half-way towards my destination, taking care not to let my shins scrape against brittle scrub twigs.

Just as I crossed the ant-hill, the elephant was momentarily hidden, and a most terrifying deep growl reverberated in my ears. It was the bull. There seemed to be such implacable hostility in the noise that I was convinced he was after my blood and I fled helter-skelter back to the car. When I turned to look around, the elephant was peacefully munching a palm frond, evidently without a care in the world and totally oblivious of my existence. I felt an idiot. It was the first time that I had heard an elephant rumble. Later I realized that this was simply a contact call by which elephants keep in touch with one another while they are feeding or on the move.

Back safely behind the steering wheel I maneuvered the car noisily off the road until I could get some good pictures. Even the sound of branches breaking and an engine revving did not disturb the good-natured bull. Every time one ear flicked forward I took a shot, then he moved, and I took his tusks from the front, finally he turned and I was able to capture the details of his other ear.

As I finished he drifted into thicker vegetation, and I continued my search for elephants elsewhere, but it appeared that all of them had been driven to seek shade from the blazing mid-morning sun. I decided to try again in the evening. Meanwhile, there were the two dug-out canoes to be collected from the beach where they had been cast ashore, south of the Endabash River near the end of the Park. I drove down the main road thinking of how I would organize elephant-viewing boat trips just off the shore of the Lake.

The canoes hadn't moved from where I had first seen them. I was delighted to find that both had paddles, and even a bailing can and scraps of a fisherman's net. The mud looked hard and had cracked into irregular polygons each with a small coating of salt on the top, so I drove out confidently. Within ten yards of the nearest canoe the car suddenly broke through the hard mud and all four wheels settled down into the mud until the axles were resting on the crust. Vesey had been right after all. Any attempt to drive the car forward or backward only succeeded in digging the wheels yet deeper into the thick, treacly, black substrate which was soon liberally spattered all over the car and myself. The only solution was to jack up each wheel in turn and try to put something solid underneath it. Unfortunately, the "Tanganyika Jack" which I had bought in Arusha couldn't reach the bumper without a block of wood and this I did not have. So I pulled the nearest canoe over, turned it upside down and put the jack on top of its flat bottom. This worked quite well and the back wheels slowly emerged with great sucking noises, until the strain proved to be too much, and with a splintering crash the jack broke through the bottom of the canoe and the Land-Rover once more subsided into the mud. Hot and angry, I gazed at it, trying to think of some other way of getting it out. But there was none. Three times more I jacked it up, before one end of the wrecked canoe held. Then I needed some debris to put under the wheels. Broiled by the relentless blaze and its reflections off the salt, I wandered along the beach to see what I could find. Finally, I came to a heap of bleached bones which had belonged to a buffalo, but which had been scattered far and wide by lions and hyenas. This sight reminded me that here was no suitable spot to spend a night out. Seizing a couple of well chewed scapulas and a massive tibia, I trudged back to the car, and inserted them under the tires. To make doubly sure that it would not bog down again I laid a carpet of thickly matted acacia branches beyond the bones. Then I hopped into the car, started her up, and she popped out of the mud, over the branches and back on to hard ground. I heaved a sigh of relief, wiped the sweat off my face, and then, leaning heavily back on the car, heard a hissing noise. The thorns of the acacia branches had punctured a tire.

Luckily I had a spare. After one more jacking up of the car, I replaced the tire and drove back twenty miles to the Rest House, arriving exhausted and very thirsty. It had been a frustrating day. I decided that for all its small size Manyara was not so tame as I had thought and that I would welcome a bit of assistance from someone who knew the area.

Next morning at eight o'clock I was at the Park HQ where work was beginning. Muhanga, the African Park Warden, listened sympathetically to my request for one of his Park Rangers to show me around and suggested that I should take out one of them every day until I had set up my final camp within the Park, by which time a man would be permanently stationed with me. This arrangement proved a great success. The Rangers were exceedingly sharp-eyed, and I learned from them to peer between tree trunks and catch glimpses of elephants standing in the shadows. Whenever the tiniest portion of their anatomy was sufficiently exposed, I snapped a picture.

One day a young Ranger called Mhoja Burengo came with me. He was exceptionally observant and we located the backs of many elephants above the bushes, but none in the open. I asked if we could go close to them on foot. He only spoke a little English, but answered,

"We can try."

The elephants spent much of the short dry season in the Ground Water Forest at the northern end of the Park. Mhoja suggested that we should go there. I had already learned that there was no greater pleasure than to walk silently down a well-padded elephant trail during the hot month of January. Coolness bathed us as we entered the forest, and we could hear the rustling of small creatures in the shrubbery and the sudden rush of a startled warthog who had seen our legs approaching him.

To find the elephants, we stopped and listened. Elephants are never silent whether resting or feeding. A rumble from a member who is separated from the herd, a squealed protest from a calf shoved forcibly away from whatever his mother is eating, or some youngsters trumpeting in mock fury as their budding tusks clonk against each other; these sounds betray their direction. In the forest the winds are often tricky, particularly at midday, when the air is sucked up in thermals and cold air rushes under the lifting bubble causing eddies in all directions along the ground. Forests are always bumpy to fly over. Equally, stalking elephants under the tree canopy depends on vagrant air currents, which may well give them one's scent, and one is lucky to remain undetected for long.

Mhoja took great care in his observations of the wind; he monitored it by watching the direction of his cigarette smoke. Moving slowly towards a persistent sound of breaking branches, we caught sight of some massive ears flapping gently behind a screen of palm fronds. Creeping up behind ample cover Mhoja found a suitable tree. We climbed it and were surrounded by capacious foliage. I balanced to the end of a thin branch and was rewarded with a clear view of a group of bulls only ten yards away. Delighted, I took many pictures, after which we both slithered down the tree and managed to retreat without the elephants ever becoming aware of our presence.

Mhoja pointed out how white the bulls were. He said that the color of elephants was a sign of where they had been for the past twenty-four hours. Whiteness meant a wallow in the forest, beside tall termite mounds sticking up like rude fingers among the soft greenery. Burnt ochre signified a mud pool in the *Acacia tortilis* woodlands, while a dirty grey characterized the southerly Endabash River and its environs.

The day wore on, and at four in the afternoon Mhoja suggested that we should move to the short grass along the shore at the mouth of the Ndala River. He thought there would be many elephants there at this hour and sure enough, when we reached the mouth of the dry sandy river there were several small groups of cows with their calves and some bulls. We were able to approach into the steady breeze which blew across the lake and sit on the short grass with nothing between us and the herd.

Towering over the others was a bull with a shattered right tusk; three feet of the nerve cavity was exposed. I realized that this must be painful and likely to make him savage. He also had a large rent in his left ear. His appearance was so distinctive that I took eleven pictures of him, as he grazed quietly among the cows. All the bulls mingled peacefully and remained in the open after the cows had departed. Up till then I had secured no resightings of "known" elephants but this bull, whom I named Cyclops, was one so distinctive that I hardly needed the photographs to be sure of his identity should I see him again.

Every day I accumulated more pictures of elephants until I had a pile of undeveloped films—but building up the photofile proved to be more difficult than I had anticipated. Despite their size and relative tranquility, Manyara elephants were surprisingly elusive when it came to taking their pictures.

The elephants spent much of their day in a dark cloak of vegetation, in which as a rule only a few backs were visible or at best a fraction of an ear, or the gleam of a tusk and it was rare to find a nicely defined elephant group with all its members in the open. Even when they were caught like this they would clump together, hiding critical details of the tusks or ears of those standing behind. Anyone who has tried counting elephants in the open knows how difficult it is to obtain an absolute count at the first time round, usually each recount arrives at a different figure.

I had brought a developing tank out from England together with some chemicals, but to get an enlarger and dishes for making prints I had to go to Arusha. An Indian named Malde had opened a photographic shop there which had everything I needed. I bought an enlarger, dishes, chemicals, a paper guillotine and photographic paper. I developed the films and hung them up in a cupboard to dry. By the following evening I was ready to begin printing. The big Rest House had running water that came from one of the springs below the escarpment and I rigged up a dark room in my bedroom. The enlarger worked quite adequately, even though the light flickered a little from the uneven surges of power generated by an erratic dynamo. My main problem was to keep the chemicals cool, and I kept large stocks of cold water in the paraffin refrigerator with which to dilute the concentrated developer.

As the prints came to life in the developing dish I scanned them eagerly.

The first batch were not very good. Too often the elephants' ears were spattered with mud of contrasting shades of grey and black which had the effect of disrupting the silhouette, so that it merged into a variegated background of leaves and bushes. Through binoculars every smallest detail had been plain, but equally clear photographs only resulted when the conditions of light and background were just right, for instance when the elephant was outlined against the sky. The many fragmentary pictures which I had taken were useless. However, the photographs did show one thing —the degree to which individual elephants varied in appearance. I would never have thought there could be such a large number of combinations of tusks and ears. Some elephants' ears had an outline that resembled a rugged Norwegian fjord.

Learning to remember an individual became like a geography lesson, in which the shape of a country's borders had to be memorized. Often an ear would be almost smooth, with only one or two small nicks, but the shape of the nick, whether it had straight or curved sides, its depth and position on the ear, provided useful material. Some nicks looked as if they had resulted from the ear catching on a thorn, others as if they had been deftly cut by a tailor's scissors in neat straight lines. Certain elephants had ears with as many holes along the edge as a Dutch coast line plastered with bomb craters along its dikes. The cause of these holes I never discovered but I suppose it must be due to some internal physiological process, the result of which gave their ears a decaying appearance.

There were also the particularly large rents that came from the center of the ear. Often in young animals these looked recent and some were still bleeding. I later discovered that the cause was the intolerance of older animals, and the instrument the sharp tusks of some old cow who had jabbed the youngster through the ear, either leaving a hole or ripping the ear from the middle outward in a long tear.

In time I found that the details changed slowly, and that ragged ears full of holes changed more rapidly than those with clean straight-edged cuts. Very young animals and a minority of adults had almost completely smooth ears; in such cases I had to record and memorize minute holes, no bigger than a piece of confetti, which would reveal themselves only under a close scrutiny. These tiny holes changed hardly at all. If the ear was clean of mud it was possible to discover a fine network of blood vessels protruding from beneath the thin ear skin and visible as a delicate tracery of ridges. Photographing these could only be done when the light was slanting at the right angle, but if they could be recorded I was sure that they would change very little over the years, whereas over a long period an elephant might obtain sufficient new cuts on his ears and chips off his tusks to become unrecognizable.

Tusks, chips and breaks and broken edges are gradually worn smooth. An elephant's tusks continue to grow all through its life. The rate at which they wear down is illustrated by the calculation made by Dr. Richard Laws that if they did not break during a life-span of sixty years they would reach a length of sixteen feet in the female and twenty feet in the bull. These breakages together with alignment give the tusks great variation. One is generally used as a master tusk and is worn down at a faster rate than the other, and therefore it is usually shorter and more rounded at the point. Very often the master tusk acquires a groove near the tip where the elephant habitually pulls grass over the same place.

One warm evening when I was on the beach I met a large concourse of elephants in the open. Here was a chance to get some frontal close-ups outlined against the sky. They were all standing, some eating the short spiky grass, others drinking from small holes which they had scooped out, the youngsters were chasing each other and engaging in furious mock battles. I saw three one-tusk cows, several with moderate sized tusks and two large and beautiful cows with long curving tusks that swept together in a great gleaming bow. The older of these had sunken hollow cheeks. She stood peacefully, kicking up little morsels of grass with her front toenails, but the other cow cocked up her head, held it slightly on one side, and looked at me intently.

I was about two hundred yards away and clearly the presence of the car was worrying her. None of the other elephants paid any attention, so I took photographs of this panorama of elephants silhouetted like a frieze against the Lake. But as I continued to watch, the larger and more nervous cow began to pace back and forth. Then she stopped, and shook her head rapidly so that her ears flapped like stiff blankets being shaken and dust flew up into the air. Gradually she worked herself up to fresh demonstrations weaving to and fro in front of the group, always looking in my direction. Seeing this a few of the other cows became disturbed and moved in to stand behind her, spreading their ears and twirling their trunks; their calves were by their sides.

I made several counts and came up with the figure of forty. The large cow slowly edged her way in my direction, and the others followed in her wake. Their intentions were plainly aggressive. They reminded me of some massive biblical phalanx with a champion standing out in front of the army. The ground was flat, so knowing that I could leave my escape to the last minute and still be sure of getting away, I decided to test their intentions.

When the great cow came to within forty paces of me she stopped and drew herself up to her full height; her fellow matriarchs fell in behind her. I switched on the engine and she broke into a lumbering charge, her trunk rolled tightly up beneath her tusks like a coiled spring. I let her come to within ten yards, to see if she would stop, but she kept on at full speed so I let out the clutch and raced away keeping just in front of her encouraging her to think she had a chance of getting me. There seemed little doubt that she was in deadly earnest. After some fifty yards she stopped, stood tall again, and emitted a resounding trumpet. Her posture was perfect for an identification picture, and shaking slightly I took it. All forty elephants had closed up behind her in a tight-knit mob.

Despite the strict training I had been given at Oxford not to give human interpretations to animal behavior, it was impossible not to anthropomorphize. This cow looked such a fine warrior queen that I named her Boadicea, after the ancient British chieftainess who, "earnest, rugged and terrible" had defied the invincible oppression of the Romans, fighting for her people to the bitter end.

I returned to the Rest House at dusk, well satisfied with my day's bag of photographs. Vesey had spent the day looking at his vegetation plots, and our two cooks had combined to make a stew of pork sausages and ox-tails.

When I told him of my plan to follow the movements of known individual elephants he suggested that I should make sketches of each one. I pointed out that many elephants looked similar to others and were distinguishable only by minute differences, and that I therefore believed that photography was probably the only method of recording details with sufficient accuracy. Vesey replied that the problem of making notes while taking photographs would inevitably lead to greater muddles, and that even if I did have a few cases of mistaken identity with sketches, the records would at best be approximate.

His research by "progressive approximation" amounted to a philosophy. He scoffed at the desire of young scientists to take accurate quantitative measurements. He believed that in Africa the best way of arriving at the truth was to begin by rejecting extreme hypotheses and to work towards the center by a process of elimination, making approximations that hopefully became progressively more accurate. In many respects it was a realistic way of thought, but as far as the Manyara elephants were concerned I was determined to prove him wrong. I wanted precise observations right from the beginning.

Half-way through dinner Vesey quite casually mentioned that an abandoned elephant calf had wandered into the camp of some VIP guests of the Parks. I nearly shot out of my chair.

"What! You've only just thought of telling me now. If only I'd known I would have brought it in."

I had been hoping that I might have an opportunity to raise a young abandoned elephant, for there is no better way of getting to know any animal species than by living close to one of its members.

The VIP guests were Charles Lindbergh, the first man to fly the Atlantic alone, and his family. John Owen had invited them to visit the National Parks in return for their support for his campaign in America to plead for the cause of African wildlife. I had kept away from his camp imagining that Lindbergh would want to enjoy the wildness of the Park undisturbed by casual visitors and so I had missed the sight of a diminutive elephant calf wandering into his camp while they were putting up their tents. Bewildered, lonely and too young to have learned to fear man, it had walked right up to the nearest human being, who happened to be Lindbergh's daughter, nuzzled up to her, and tried to follow her wherever she went. John Owen, concerned that one of his VIPs might be trampled to death by an anxious elephant mother returning to look for her offspring, ordered some Rangers to drive the calf away. Vesey told me it had last been seen in a clump of bushes not far from the camp.

There was no moon that night, and it would have been pointless to go and look for the calf in such conditions, but next morning at first light I drove down to the camp and found the Lindbergh family heating up their morning coffee. I asked them if they knew where the little elephant was but they could not tell me. I told them that its chances of survival were zero unless it could find its mother, assuming that she was still alive. Lindbergh at once offered to help me look for it in his car and together we drove around the immediate area but found no trace of the calf.

Presently we bumped into a large elephant herd on the main road led by angry looking females who trumpeted nervously and chased us down the road. One old cow lowered her tusks and made a rush at the car. Lindbergh accelerated but kept only just in front of her. For a second it looked as if she would pound her tusks into the rear door of his Land-Rover. Then she lost heart, and decided to halt. I realized that Lindbergh, like me, was curious to find out just how serious the intentions of the charging cow had been and a slow retreat just beyond tusk reach had been the only way to discover this.

We returned to camp and met some Rangers who said they had heard the baby squealing in the night, mixed with the sounds of deep growling. I asked them to show me where, but they were afraid to go into the thick bush so I pushed on ahead in the direction they indicated, with Lindbergh close behind me. Despite the fact that I was much younger than he was, he was ready to follow, because he too wanted to find the baby elephant.

We had only gone a short way when I rounded a bush and suddenly came face to face with a large black-maned lion sitting on the remains of the elephant calf. He crouched down, and glared at us over the top of his prey. His muscles twitched, and then with a bound and a deep-throated *whoof* he catapulted sideways and vanished from view.

"Isn't this one of the most dangerous situations in the African bush?" Lindbergh enquired.

From the books I had read I had to suppose that this was so. In fact, no more than he had I seen a lion face to face on its kill. We beat a discreet retreat, before the lion came back. Although lions were small in number they were important to Manyara and I wanted to study them later. This one's name was Dume Kubwa (the big male) as the Rangers called him. He was the largest of the two fully grown lions that roamed the northern end of the Park. Usually he could be found up a tree lolling on a gently sloping branch, with his full stomach bulging out on either side. The other male lion, who was often with Dume Kubwa, was a rather mangy looking creature with a small reddish mane. Just after the little elephant was killed he was involved in a tremendous fight with a buffalo. I saw him the next day with a deep cut just above his right eye. The wound steadily grew worse and eventually he lost the sight of that eye. The Rangers called him Chongo, which means "one eye" in Swahili.

Dume Kubwa had certainly lost no time in exploiting his opportunity and I wondered whether or not in the past he had eaten baby elephants and how important kills by lions might be in affecting the rate of calf survival. In all the herds I had seen the babies were always protected by an outer screen of large and vigilant cows.

The death of the baby elephant was most depressing. Such opportunities occur very rarely and I would probably never again have the chance of bringing up an elephant calf. However, I did not remain downcast for long and as I drove off, less than two hundred yards from Lindberth's camp, I saw the back of a huge elephant swaying above the bushes which screened him as he headed for the forest. With my camera and a 135 mm lens I slipped out of the car and proceeded on foot to try to intercept him. He seemed in no hurry, but moved steadily towards the distant sound of breaking branches and rumbling. Glimpses of grey skin through the bushes marked his progress. At last he stopped, and tossed plumes of dust in the air. Carefully I worked round in front of him keeping well downwind. There was a distinct elephant path, and finding a good tree I climbed it and waited. Once more bushes crackled and grass swished on the elephant's flanks as he came toward me. He stopped again and I could just make out a tusk, then he swung his head a little and the other tusk came into view. There was no mistaking it. Broken down its length the decaying cavity within was open to view. He resumed his walk and with a clear sight of his torn left ear I knew for certain that this was the old broken tusker first seen at the Ndala River mouth which I had named Cyclops.

He came straight underneath the tree and walked on into the forest without ever noticing me. He was taller than I had estimated and must have stood nearly twelve foot high. I was within easy reach of his trunk, had he stretched it up. He was the first elephant I resighted, and was one I would be able to recognize without a photograph.

In my first two weeks, while adding to my store of elephant pictures, I also searched for a camp. I hoped to find somewhere remote, with fresh drinking water, a river for swimming, a good view, plenty of animals nearby, shade for the hot season and a low intensity of biting insects. I had looked at several possible sites but none fulfilled all these conditions.

One day I went back to the dry mouth of the Ndala River hoping to find some elephants again. I arrived in the midday heat, a little too early for the elephants to come out on the beach, so I decided to explore the white sands of the bone-dry river by following it up as far as the escarpment. Nothing stirred in the scorching silent heat as the Ranger and I walked dazzled by the sand's searing reflections. Then rounding a bend I heard a musical sound and looking towards the escarpment saw a thin silver thread of water cascading down a sheer rocky gorge. A little further on, water plants began to grow and I came to a place where the river sank below the sand. A wide game trail led on between tumbled boulders to a great pool at the foot of the waterfall. Many tracks of lion, rhino and buffalo, but most of all, of elephant, were plainly visible. The water was clear and looked cool. The Ranger went to one of the rock pools and slaked his thirst.

"Maji mzuri sana," he said. (Water very good.)

Overlooking the pool was a raised river bank and to my delight, I saw some flat-topped *Acacia tortilis* trees casting shadows on a level spot ideal for a camp. Under these trees a rhino had his scrape. It was a stretch of truly wild unspoilt Africa and I decided to make my camp there as soon as possible.

Located almost exactly half-way down the Park it would make an ideal center, if it was accessible to vehicles. The Ranger and I walked back through acacia woodland, under an almost continuous canopy of trees. Ten minutes brought us to the nearest track and within twenty minutes we reached the car.

The next day I returned with a friend, Alan Root, the wildlife photographer, and we used his Land-Rover to push a track through the woodland to the waterfall. The Park Warden, Jonathan Muhanga, lent us some members of his road gang to cut down the bushes, and in no time we had a rudimentary motorable path leading to the new site. Alan and I climbed up the waterfall until we reached a small sand bank. "Hell man," he shouted, "what a view."

We were above the level of the trees and the whole northern end of the Park stretched to our left. Straight ahead were the unbroken canopies of hundreds of acacias and beyond them the Lake sparkled. On the other side stood the ribbed mountain Essimingor.

Out of sight of tourists, with elephants all around and a good water supply, the site could not be bettered.

Building the camp and increasing the elephant file proceeded apace. The design of the house was simple. There were to be two large rondavels linked by a thatched veranda. One rondavel I would make into a laboratory and the other into an office, with living space on the veranda in between. I marked out the foundations, and with a collection of laborers, masons and carpenters went to work. The old Land-Rover coughed and wheezed carrying sand and stones up from the river until the exertion proved to be too much for it and one of the rear half shafts broke. Jonathan Muhanga then came to my aid and lent me a lorry to carry the materials, and gradually the heaps of stone and sand grew larger and the walls rose higher every day. I moved out of the Rest House and lived at camp in a large "Manyara"-style tent, so that I could supervise the construction and at the same time begin living in the heart of elephant country.

The Ndala river bed was an ideal place to watch elephants. The big pools that provided water all round the year were strategically placed almost exactly halfway between the game fence at the southern boundary and Mto-wa-Mbu at the northern end. The camp was also near a narrow waist between the Lake and the escarpment which had the effect of channelling all elephants moving north or south toward the most convenient watering spot, right below my camp.

Often I would glance down the river and see a file of elephants deliberately making its way down the banks to drink on the flat sandy edges of the river. This gave me an excellent opportunity to see how many of them I knew. I hoped that after a while the number of unknown elephants I observed in these sightings would tail off nearly to zero. When this stage was reached I would be sure that I knew almost all the elephants living in Manyara.

One very important problem which bothered me was how to estimate the elephants' ages. Unless I could tell approximately how old individuals were I would not be able to get an idea of the rate and success of their breeding. I needed to know, for instance, if a calf was in its first or second year. I wanted to estimate the proportions of the different age groups within the population. If there were a high percentage of young animals it would suggest that the population was in a healthy breeding condition.

At the Ndala pools I saw calves of all sizes and superficially there seemed to be many of them, but this sort of observation meant nothing without knowing how long it took them to grow to such size. Some hunters whom I met passing through the Park told me that elephants lived to a hundred years or more. You only had to look at their wrinkles, they said, to appreciate their age. Beyond this sort of belief little other information existed on how to judge the age of an African elephant in the wild.

Fortunately, just when I began my study at Manyara another scientist, Dr. Richard Laws, well known for his work on whales, had recently switched his attention to the largest terrestrial mammal, the African elephant. He was Director of the Nuffield Unit of Tropical Animal Ecology, based in Uganda, and his main study area was the Murchison Falls National Park (now renamed Kabalega). As an essential prerequisite to any serious ecological study of the species he was already developing a reliable index for ageing elephants.

I asked John Owen's permission to let me take my National Park's Land-Rover to Uganda and after a long drive that took a day and a half I arrived in Kampala. Luckily I dropped in at the Makerere University zoology department on my way through the town, and was fortunate enough to intercept Laws who had come there to give a lecture.

Despite a tight schedule Dr. Laws gave me an hour of his time. I listened intently as he unfolded a remarkable research program which he had already begun to put into action. With all the facts at his fingertips, he talked about the elephant problems of Murchison, overwhelming in their scale compared to those of Manyara. He also clarified the possibility of ageing elephants more or less accurately by a study of their corpses.

The key to estimating an elephant's age was to be found in its peculiar tooth structure and its development. A number of elephants had been shot for research purposes, and together with the remains of dead elephants that had been found, Laws had a collection of 385 lower jaws as material to work on.

Each elephant has six teeth in each side of its upper and lower jaws, making twenty-four in all; these appear and then periodically supersede one another. Of the six never more than two are in use simultaneously. Successive teeth grow forward from the back of the jaw, replacing earlier teeth as they wear down. These older teeth move forward, and then drop out. At birth only the first three teeth are formed. They are easy to distinguish because of their small size, their thinner "wavy" enamel and generally more delicate structure. The first tooth is nearly twice as big as a human's wisdom tooth and is quickly pushed out before the end of the first year. The second molar then comes into wear and lasts until the calf reaches the age of four years, when it is replaced by molar number three. At the other end of the life span molar six can be easily recognized after it has come into wear because no more teeth can be seen erupting behind it, and the bony capsule enclosing the tooth becomes flattened and solid. Molars four and five are more difficult to distinguish and in order to identify them careful measurements were necessary, but when the length and breadth of all the teeth were plotted on graph paper Laws found that the points fell into six well-defined groups, corresponding to the six sets of teeth.

Having identified all the teeth from molar one to molar six he arranged his collection of lower jaws in a series. With thirty different categories he was confident that they truly represented a series of increasing ages, but the absolute ages which he allocated were more or less arbitrary, since there were very few records of known-age animals and most of them referred to captive animals which might or might not be representative of free-living populations.

The best way of guessing the ages for each category was first to establish the potential lifespan, which from captive animals and comparisons with the Indian elephant appeared to be about sixty to seventy years.

Then reasonable guesses could be made as to the time it would take for the teeth to develop from one category to the next.

In this Laws was helped by the existence of seasonal layers of dentine and cement laid down each year on the roots of each tooth. These layers could be examined under a microscope, in a polished cross section, and counted rather like the rings of a tree. This particular technique he had first developed when working on whales, and it had been an effective method of ageing them. In elephants the growth layers were not always so clear but altogether they provided an objective assessment which supported the average ages assigned to each of his thirty age categories.

Since Laws first proposed his tooth-ageing system an elephant called Diksie at the London Zoo, who was known to be twenty-seven years old, had died. According to Laws's index her age would have been twenty-eight, plus or minus one year, a perfectly acceptable degree of accuracy.

The next stage was to relate age, as determined by the teeth, to bodily growth. These measurements were available from the elephants which had been shot. Laws constructed a growth curve which showed what the average shoulder height would be at different ages. The scatter of points was small enough to be able to age an elephant with a reasonable degree of accuracy up to the age of fifteen years provided one was able to estimate its height at the shoulder. He even made a provisional sketch of the heights of young elephants ranged alongside a fully grown adult female whose average height would be 8 ft. 5 in. In contrast a new born baby would stand only 2 ft. 9 in. tall (85 cm), and at one year old it would just be able to fit under its mother's front legs.

I was delighted with this information which I knew would help me greatly in my own research. Laws had killed many elephants to obtain this material, but these facts could be determined in no other way. Now they provided a standard system for zoologists to use so that different populations of elephants could be compared. His system has been used in every subsequent elephant research program in Africa of which I am aware.

Laws also told me much of great ecological interest which made me eager to drive up to the Murchison Falls National Park in the north of Uganda to see the elephants and their effect on the habitat at first hand. When my interview ended my head was whirling with new facts and figures which I only hoped I would be able to remember.

Half a day's drive northward brought me to the Park's boundaries. Entering it, I crossed endless bare plains where once *Terminalia* woodlands had grown. Deceptively green, the grasslands appeared to offer rich bounty to pebble-like herds of elephants flung in clusters across the landscape.

Compared with Manyara there seemed to be very few calves. Was the rank *Hyparrhenia* grass an adequate substitute for the shade and foliage of the *Terminalia* trees I wondered? Here only gaunt and leafless skeletons remained of the once spreading woodlands that had covered most of North Bunyoro. Elephants had systematically chiselled bark round the trunks of the trees, thus severing the life ducts of nutrition to the roots. These hulks, soon to be toppled by decay, would then lie beside their already prone companions and finally all would be destroyed by the fierce fires that swept across the long grass every year. In the face of these two powerful agents, elephants and fire, there seemed no hope that the woodlands could ever return.

As far back as records go, the story of the Uganda elephants was inextricably linked with man. Decimated by the ivory trade, they had a brief respite at the turn of the century when sleeping sickness ravaged the human population. Government action concentrated the unhappy people in areas free of bush and the fatal bite of an infected tsetse fly. Simultaneously, strict new game laws reduced the activities of the old ivory hunters. It was not long, however, before elephants were killed again, this time in protection of crops. As the human population increased and settlement once more crept back into wild uninhabited areas, the elephants' freedom to roam in the ocean of trees and grass left vacant during the sleeping sickness was curtailed. Their movements were reduced, many areas alienated, their migrations severed, so that populations were isolated. In the end Uganda's elephants, once ubiquitous, became huddled into one-twentieth of their former range. Their total numbers steadily declined but did not diminish by the same porportion as their range, with the result that these destructive feeders eliminated, beyond any powers of regeneration, the *Terminalia glaucescens,* the once dominant tree of the North Bunyoro area.

As I drove towards the Nile, which cuts from east to west across the middle of the Park, I thought about the extraordinary response of the elephant population to their shrinking environment, which Laws had described to me.

By examining whether the females he shot were pregnant or not, Laws had come to the conclusion that the breeding rate was depressed, and that although numbers had increased through immigration the population was undergoing a long drawn-out decline. Females were attaining puberty at a much later date. The age structure too, showed an alarming deficit in young animals, which meant that either their mortality was high or very few were being born.

What could be the cause of this decline? Was it the fact that there were no more trees to eat, or was it something intrinsic to overcrowding? Laws himself was undecided but eager to find out whether social causes might have an effect on reproduction. One of the reasons why the question was so vital was that if it could be shown that elephants had the capacity to regulate their own numbers, then it might, theoretically, be possible to avoid cropping.

I crossed over the Nile at Paraa, an ugly township in

the center of the Park which had sprung up around the workshops and tourist lodge.

Further north I went to visit Ian Parker's camp. Here I realized for the first time what cropping elephants for research really meant. When I pitched up at his camp, Parker, with typical East African hospitality, welcomed me in and offered me supper and a bed for the night, although he had never seen or heard of me before. Over hippo steaks he explained his rationale for game preservation. He not only accepted the need for cropping, but also recognized the obligation on the individuals concerned with conservation to face up to the realities of what reduction by cropping meant. It was dirty repugnant work, and therefore not to be shirked by those who professed to be committed to the preservation of elephants. His personal experience extended back to the days when he was employed by the Game Department in Kenya to protect crops from elephants, and later to run the Waliangulu elephant cropping scheme.

Parker decided that private enterprise would be the only way to organize such schemes effectively. He resigned from the Game Department and started his own company, "Wild Life Services," with a group of Kenya-born friends. The concession to crop elephants in the overpopulated Murchison Falls National Park was his first big contract. Under Laws's scientific guidance he secured material for research, while at the same time conducting an efficient and profitable business.

His method of killing came of long experience of elephant reactions to gunfire. The tame herds of the Park were an easy prey. Cautiously approaching a group, he and his hunters would let the elephants become aware of something unusual by deliberately breaking twigs, making metallic clicks, or coughing gently; hearing this the elephants, sensing an alien, unidentified presence, would invariably move in toward one another forming a defensive circle with mothers facing outward and the young and the babies tucked between their legs or stowed safely behind a massive body. The hunters would then close in until they were spread in a semicircle around the tightly bunched elephants, and open fire with semiautomatic rifles of the type used by NATO. The largest cows would be shot first, whereupon the younger members of the group would mill about in hopeless confusion, bereft of leadership but unwilling to abandon their dead leaders. The hunters would swiftly finish off the rest. A group of ten animals usually took no more than thirty seconds to kill. No survivors were ever left and consequently the bad news never spread from one group to the next. The only ones sometimes to be spared were calves between the ages of three and seven; old enough to live without milk from their mothers but young enough to be caught and sold to zoos.

Altogether more than 2,000 elephants were to be killed in this way. The carcasses were utilized with the utmost efficiency. Getting to work immediately on the fallen elephants, Laws and Parker performed speedy postmortems. The ovaries of cows were extracted for examination. From bulls the testes were located and seminal fluid extracted, then sperms were tested for viability by dropping them into a phial containing fluid from the seminal vesicles and watching their reaction under a microscope. If the sperms wriggled violently it meant the bull had been potent. Lower jaws were collected and measurements were taken of the shoulder height and of the body length to find out how these were related to age.

With all this material Laws was able to determine the age at which the male and female elephants reached puberty. In addition the uterus of each cow was looked at to see how many times it had been scarred by the implantation of an embryo: information needed to discover how many calves a cow was likely to have had. Once the ages of all the young were known, Laws could reconstruct with a fair degree of accuracy the probable relationships of individuals within the group.

Little of the carcass was wasted. Meat was sold for local consumption around the Park, the feet were made into umbrella stands, and the entire skin and ears tanned to make an unusual hard-wearing leather. The ivory was the most valuable commodity of all, and found a ready market.

Ian Parker paid the Park authorities £5 an elephant. No one had ever before made a profit from selling elephant products but he was given the opportunity to do so, and it was up to him to succeed if he could. In fact he was highly successful. Out of his company's earnings Parker bought a Cessna 185 and painted it black as night with lurid orange wingtips. It was his hope that the face of conservation could be changed by the application of rational procedures based on thorough research. He believed that emotion should be ruled out when dealing with large populations of animals. Game, in his view, would survive solely as a resource. The only logical action was to utilize it in the most economical way, through tourism, cropping or sport hunting. In areas where the increasing human population came into competition and made the presence of any game undesirable, he advocated eradication programs based on sound utilization practices, i.e. making as much money out of the procedure as possible. When I drove away from his camp the next day on the first leg of the long journey back to Lake Manyara I had much to think about. I profoundly disagreed with Parker's view that sentiment can have no place in the policy of National Parks, since the very reason of their existence is the result of sentiment, whether of an aesthetic nature or plain affection for animals.

I realized, however, that this visit had given me one of the most important keys to my further study. An elephant's age could be estimated if one only knew its shoulder height. All I needed to do now was to find a method of measuring elephants from a distance and thus determining their ages. Knowing the ages of individuals would allow me to calculate the way in which the Manyara population was responding to its environmental change.

The most important fact that I had learned was that the crowded elephants of Murchison had slowed down their birth rate, which in time would reduce their total numbers. Would the Manyara elephants do the same since they appeared to live at an even higher density? If so, what was it that caused the slowing down of breeding? Was it the changing environment with steadily decreasing numbers of trees available for food and shade, or was it the social effect of overcrowding?

Manyara should provide the answers, for despite the record density of elephants there was as yet no shortage of food, water or shade. I would clearly need to investigate the basic social structure of the elephants and then try to see in what ways their density might affect their behavior toward one another.

# 4

# The Indestructible Family

When I returned to Manyara the rains had begun in earnest. Gone were those pleasant mornings with the sun streaming across the breakfast table. Slate grey clouds lowered for more than half the day and the Ndala River ran red and angry. The elephants were around in large numbers, but it did not rain enough to cause them to retreat up into the hills to get away from the sodden woodlands as they had done in other years.

As soon as the walls of my house were up and a roof was complete I moved in, glad to evacuate my dripping tent. The walls were painted white on the inside and geckos soon made their homes in the eaves and hunted flies there. A desk, a table, some chairs and a bed were sufficient furniture.

I organized my patrols to take me to every part of the Park, and day after day increased my score of known elephants, at the same time experimenting with ways of measuring their height so that I could know their ages. One of the first questions I had to answer was what constitutes a stable elephant group. Once I knew this I would be able to study how these basic building blocks of elephant society interacted under the crowded conditions of Manyara, and how social behavior in turn affected numbers. As early as 1961, an American scientist, Irven Buss, had suggested that elephants assembled in family units of closely related cows and their offspring, but no one had yet been able to show that these groups were stable.

The groups I encountered usually had several cows with their young, which might be tightly coordinated, or which might be loosely strung out and overlapping with another group, so that it was impossible to see where one group ended and the next began. The largest groups were of the order of eighty to a hundred elephants, with bulls strung out on the outskirts and cows and young calves tightly clustering in the center, but these large herds never stayed together for more than a few hours before breaking up into many smaller groups.

With these first fragmentary observations I began to wonder if elephants did have any sort of social organization, or if individuals roamed at will and just joined up with whomsoever they met.

Gradually, I discovered the pattern of their movements and the best times and places to watch them. Starting early every morning I would drive along the foot of the escarpment looking up at the steep slopes, where the elephants usually spent their nights feeding on the variety of plant life found there and nowhere else.

With the first rays of sunlight warming their flanks I could usually find some group of elephants rocking their way down the escarpment to gain the shelter of the *Acacia tortilis* woodlands before the sun grew too hot or, if it were cloudy, they might stay until the weather cleared at about midday. One elephant after another would move in and out of view along the green tunnels carved as a network up the slopes. Steepness was no barrier. They tested uncertain corners with their trunks, gently probing for loose ground and slowly transferring weight in a smooth motion from one foothold to the next. The intermittent visibility meant that I had to wait for the elephants to clear the hillside before I could recognize more than a handful of them, but I could sense their group coordination merely by listening to them calling to one another in deep rumbles which were answered up and down the length of the hillside, each little party apparently keeping in touch with the others in this way.

Below, in the woodlands, there were smooth dusty patches under the trees and here the elephants paused and rested when it was hot. They would arrive one by one, each cow bringing her calves with her. It was in one of these dust bowls that I found Boadicea again about a month after I first saw her on the beach. From the uppermost branches of a nearby tree I was able to watch her enjoying a peaceful mid-morning siesta.

Standing on her right was another large cow, with fat convergent tips to her tusks, and two calves at heel; one had a wart on his head and the other had a wart on his trunk. The next largest cow also had convergent tusks but these were thin and sharply pointed; she had a distinctive cut out of her left ear the shape of the Gulf of Suez. Another, whom I named Right Hook, had a tusk that curved sharply inward and there was a small one-tusker female, Virgo. All had been on the beach together, and now I quietly took their pictures for a second time as they stood with eyes half closed and trunks hanging immobile or loosely draped over a tusk. I could only see twenty-two elephants. On the beach there had been forty.

Noises of a second party came from nearby. I crawled down the branches of my tree and found a better perch in the fork of two boughs, underneath the canopy. This was well within the reach of Boadicea's trunk if she cared to take a few paces in my direction, but she was unaware of my presence. From here I could get a good view of all directions.

Standing under a tree, not more than a hundred yards away, was another fine matriarch with long white tusks that curved gracefully inward, longer but very similar in shape to Boadicea's. Her ears had relatively smooth edges, but her temples were sunken. She was the most beautiful elephant I had seen, and I remembered quite clearly that she too had been on

the beach, mixed in with all the others. I named her
Leonora. There was now a distinct unit of her own
round her. I looked at them carefully to compare
them with the pictures I had taken before. Sure enough,
there was the same cow whom I named Slender Tusks
next to her, and close by a barely mature female with a
big V-nick out of her left ear. It took me most of the
morning to count her group of nine, but for once luck
was with me. The wind held steady, blowing from
the south-east across the Lake, and taking my time I
was able to maneuver round Boadicea without disturbing her or any of the other elephants.

Under another tree two hundred yards from Boadicea I discovered a third distinct unit. In it were the
two one-tuskers who had been on the beach. I counted
up this group with growing excitement. The numbers
came out right; there were exactly nine. This made
forty elephants altogether, and included all the distinctive females I had earlier seen together. The only difference was that now they were arranged in three
smaller groups. My puzzle was beginning to work out.
The groups were stable.

The formations I have just described proved to be
typical. At times Boadicea would be in a large herd of
forty, but more often there were three separate smaller
units led respectively by herself, old Leonora, and the
largest of the one-tuskers whom I named Jezebel. Each
smaller unit remained stable in itself, bound to family
ties. These three family units were usually within a
few hundred yards of each other, and I believe that
together they belonged to one large kinship group,
every number being interrelated. (*See family tree
on page 344.*)

During the next few months of 1966 I established
that a similar family unit social organization applied to
all the other cow-calf groups in the Park, of which
there were at least forty-eight. The average size of the
family units was ten elephants, and most of these belonged as well to larger kinship groups. Family units
who were members of a kinship group might split up for

Isabelle's sub-unit

Boadicea's family unit

Jezebel's family unit

Leonora's family unit

Rob O'Moore

Boadicea's kinship group
showing the family units of which it was composed

a few days and go to opposite ends of the Park, but
they would always join later and continue to keep
company.

This discovery came as a great surprise to me, because up to this time, although there had been a hypothesis that the cow-calf groups might be stable family
units, it had never been suggested that larger herds
were anything but aggregations of family units joining
and leaving at random. My observations provided
the first proof of family unit stability and showed that
family ties were far wider and more lasting than had
been thought.

The largest kinship group was Boadicea's, which I observed on 314 separate days in the years 1966 to 1970
—and which numbered nearly fifty before I left. For
the group to reach this size the kinship ties had probably lasted over a hundred years and possibly for much
longer.

Many of the younger cows already had calves, but
they appeared to be continuing to accompany their
old mothers who were themselves still giving birth to
calves.

I had no means of estimating Boadicea's age exactly, for although elephants continue to grow throughout their lives, by the age of thirty they are within ten
centimeters of the height they would reach if they
lived to be sixty. Also some are tall for their age, others
short. Boadicea's tusks were as large as any other female's in the Park and I thought she was probably
between forty-five and fifty years old. She was still
actively reproductive and had a small calf at heel. She
was in excellent physical condition, well-padded on
the back and thighs with rounded contours and had
none of the sunken and angular features associated
with old age.

Individual elephants varied greatly in character. Although Boadicea was the matriarch with the fiercest
threat displays, within the same family unit was the

tamest, gentlest and most curious elephant. This was the small one-tusker Virgo.

The first indication of Virgo's character appeared when one day at about midday I encountered Boadicea's kinship group in the woodlands, near camp. The three family units were under three separate trees, Virgo and her larger companion, Right Hook, standing with about six younger elephants of all sizes. Right Hook started to move and Virgo followed her, bringing up the youngsters. They left the shade, crossed an open piece of grass between bushes, and kept coming towards the mudpool where I was parked. One by one they arrived on the shore, but, just as they seemed to be about to immerse themselves in the inviting muddy liquid, they became aware of the silent car with its tell-tale smell of man. Right Hook merely spread her ears and cautiously sidled away taking the young elephants with her.

Virgo continued to stand next to the pool, irresolutely swinging her trunk and swaying her head from side to side, always keeping an eye on the Land-Rover. Her calf behind her held up his head, weaving his trunk to sample the suspicious smell on the breeze. Virgo seemed to be in conflict about whether to come on and investigate the car or to follow the prudent retreat of the others. Eventually she made up her mind and slowly advanced on the Land-Rover. Her ears were half out, her trunk snaked inquiringly towards the car and then back under her belly in a rhythmic swing.

I was entranced with this close approach. Never before had I been able to see the hairiness around the jaw, nor smell the warm scent of elephant which now wafted over me in concentrated waves. Virgo's steps were deliberate and slow, and brought her to within two elephant paces.

It was a great contrast to Boadicea's impassioned threat charges. Virgo gave the impression of being intensely curious about this metal manifestation which intruded into her world and behaved as if it were itself an animal. I wondered how far her tolerance could be developed, and, if after all the centuries of men killing elephants, she would ever accept my presence on foot. To be able to move around the elephants unrestricted by the car without them minding was an intriguing thought, but I certainly did not expect it would ever be possible.

Although Boadicea was the largest animal, an elephant I named Giselle was close to her in size and looked too big to be descended from some common ancestral matriarch long since dead.

In my first year of study there were six breeding cows in Boadicea's family unit and fourteen immature animals. The younger calves were tightly glued to their mothers' sides. Calves less than a year old could walk clean under their mothers' bellies. Slightly larger calves with tooth-pick tusks also seemed very tightly attached to their mothers, but once they had reached a size that was half as high as an adult it was often difficult for me to see to which female they belonged.

When I began using Laws's rough field method of estimating a calf's age by comparing its height to its mother's shoulder height, the age distribution of the calves gave me a fair idea of the breeding success of the cows. What puzzled me, however, was that although there seemed to be plenty of calves that were one, two or three years old, hardly any calves were born during the first year I spent in the field. This led me to suspect my subjective judgment of calves' ages and I started to search for an accurate method of measuring their shoulder height.

At first I tried a very simple technique. I painted a bamboo black and white at ten centimeter intervals, strapped it to the side of the Land-Rover and went in search of elephants. To measure an elephant's shoulder height I first had to find it in a dead flat place where both the shoulder blade and the foot were clearly visible, and then take its picture. Next I waited for it to move, Mhoja walked up with the pole and placed it in the elephant's footprint, and then I took a second picture to act as a scale for the first. It was a cheap, accurate and easy method, but unfortunately could only be used for single bulls and not for closely packed cows and calves whose footprints became hopelessly intermingled and indistinguishable. I thought about this problem a lot and finally I found the key to it.

One day while in Dar-es-Salaam searching for some old aerial photographs of Lake Manyara at the Ministry of Lands and Surveys, I met a Canadian Forestry Officer who was a specialist in photogrammetry, the science of measuring objects at a distance by photography. He introduced me to the fascinating science of photo-interpretation. Foresters have long used overlapping pictures of trees taken from airplanes, which when laid side by side and viewed through a stereoscope stand out in three-dimensional relief. The Manyara aerial photos viewed this way were astonishingly beautiful. The escarpment rushed up to meet the eye, and the canopy of every single tree stood up like a distinct mushroom. The forester, however, measured tiny parallax differences between images on the enlargements to calculate the height of trees. He too was interested in ageing.

I suddenly realized that by adapting the principal of stereo photography to ground conditions I would be able to measure the heights of elephants. By means of elementary geometry I found that I could get good stereo-prints by manipulating two mirrors and a front-silvered ninety degree prism in front of one camera. I constructed an apparatus with two long arms with a mirror on each, and a prism half-way between, which reflected light into a camera mounted on a T-bar. Through the lens I could now get a double image of any object at which I pointed the apparatus.

The calculation was simple and relied on making two measurements on the photograph, the height and separation of the twin elephant images. I eventually made these measurements on a wonderful machine in the Nuclear Physics Department of Oxford called a "Bubble Chamber Track Analysis Measuring Machine." I never fully understood its real function, but it was able to enlarge my negatives twenty-five times by projecting them on a screen, and with micro-manipulating servo-mechanisms I was able to pinpoint exact coordinates and record them to the nearest two microns on paper tape, which was then fed into a second computer that made the calculations and printed out the elephant's height and age.

The most sophisticated measurements, which were made in my final year, often did no more than confirm the age estimates I had already made in the field, by rule of thumb, comparing the heights of young against old and by recording a hierarchy of size within each family unit.

My final height-measuring apparatus was made of light-weight aluminum and was carried in a foam-filled box in the back of the Land-Rover. Great care was needed to avoid jogging the mirrors which were calibrated carefully before each field trip. The slightest displacement would throw out the accuracy of the calculations. Nevertheless, I was pleased to find in trials that at the ranges at which I used the apparatus it was accurate to within two centimeters.

One useful property was its defensive potential, which would have delighted Archimedes. I discovered this when stalking a bull who caught sight of a glint of silver, tucked up his trunk like the proboscis of a butterfly and charged. The ground was open and totally devoid of cover. There was no question of abandoning the apparatus and fleeing, but at the last minute I tilted the mirror so that white hot sunlight flashed in his eyes. He was so close I had no difficulty in aiming and held the reflection steadily on his mud-caked eye. Quite unable to see what he was doing he ground to a halt, and swung his head to try one eye after the other only to be dazzled in both. Finally, rather bemused he turned back and strode away.

Early on, I learned that threat charges were usually not as much in earnest as they looked. Boadicea had easily the most impressive display, but I got the impression that at times, when I delayed my retreat to the last second, she seemed to hesitate. After some four months in Manyara I decided to call her bluff and remained rooted to the spot when she charged. I was greatly delighted to see her skid to a halt in a cloud of dust just ten paces from the Land-Rover. After this, demonstrations became no more than a nuisance, a hindrance to observation, and it was a short step to almost completely ignoring her. By far the most easily upset in her kinship group, Boadicea often showed her anger and annoyance at my presence. Leonora, on the other hand, would always remain stately and unruffled by even the closest approach of a vehicle. Since Boadicea was so much more aggressive than the others, I made the mistake of thinking that any elephant with a lesser display must be less dangerous.

By mid-1966 I had met almost all the elephants that frequented the more open northern section of the Park and I thought that I had only a few more family units to observe. Consequently, one morning when I caught sight of a new group standing placidly in some long grass I was anxious to record them. A strong wind drowned the sound of my engine and I approached near to them before they knew I was there. Then all of a sudden, just as I switched off the engine, and sited myself on the roof, they swung their four heads round, with ears like hostile radar scanners about to launch a missile. One cow shook her head, and then with no further trumpeting or threat gestures of any kind they charged.

A threat charge was normal elephant behavior, so I sat happily on the roof and waited for them to stop. They didn't. When the first elephant was less than ten yards from the car and still going at full speed I dropped through the roof hatch like a meteorite, and pressed myself flat against the far side of the car. At the last possible instant they stopped, one smashed a dead branch to smithereens with her tusks and, towering above me, let out a strangely savage and piercing trumpet that sounded as if she were using all her breath and emotion to expel it.

I cannot do justice to the effect, but these elephants were certainly quite different from any others I had met. I realized that they were totally hostile and irreconcilable to man. Why they stopped I do not know. I have seen them many times again and I have never known them to stop in a charge since that first occasion.

Now they stood in line for long enough for me to take their pictures. All looked equal in size, with large curving tusks. One had a large, circular wart on her ear. I named them the Torone sisters after a shrill queen of Greek mythology.

When the dry season came at the beginning of June the river lost its red color and fast turned green and then the water became clear. Down the waterfall came snails like little flat spirals. I bathed in the pools every day and washed myself, diving in from the pink gneiss rocks. The pools were a snail's paradise. The water ran gently and ribbons of waterweed provided them with sustenance. One day I felt itchy after a bathe. The itchiness persisted for most of the day and the following night, wearing off near dawn. Too late I realized that the pools were infected with bilharzia, a human parasite carried by the snails.

The pools had been surveyed and pronounced clear of infection, but later this invasion of snails had happened unexpectedly. The critical month was July. Anyone who bathed during or before that month remained healthy, everyone who bathed afterward was infected. Over the following months fifteen people, including John Owen and his daughters, began to suffer from coughs, fevers, general debilitation and lethargy. All had bathed in my pool in the Ndala River. Some of the children nearly died.

Having bathed almost every day for months, I was

severely infected, and suffered from headaches, nausea and vomiting. Work became impossible and I decided that I would have to return to England for a short spell and try to get cured at the Hospital of Tropical Medicine in London.

At the end of October, I noticed one morning that all the acacias were sprouting new leaves. This was strange, since no rain had fallen. The Park was parched and brown, even though skies were overcast and the smell of rain was in the air. The trees seemed to anticipate the coming inundation for each grew a fresh green canopy of new leaves, ready to photosynthesize efficiently as soon as water soaked their roots. I found it amazing that they should have enough reserves of moisture for this growth after five months without a drop of rain.

Just before I left for England a storm broke and a flash flood thundered down the waterfall, scouring the lower reaches of the riverbed and sweeping away all the snails and the weed they relied on. The pools were once more free of bilharzia. In the investigation which followed it was shown that the snails that came down the waterfall had themselves been infected by the Park's baboons who suffered from chronic bilharzia, and had defecated into the water.

One of the last family units I recorded was the Torone group. On this occasion they heard my car from across a swampy patch of ground with tall grass and charged without a moment's hesitation, their heads breasting the stems like battleships in a heavy sea. I retreated fast to a distance, but another party in the Park were not so lucky. Jonathan Muhanga's report for October 1966 contained the following incident:

It is a habit of elephants, during the months of September and October, every year, to eat the roots of some nasty trees. When they have feasted on these nasty roots their behavior is greatly changed. They became very harsh and trumpet unnecessarily.

It was on 13th October that one Pick-up Land-

Rover, full of Tanzania People's Defense Force Officers, came across a herd of elephants which was actually in this great feast.

Immediately, the captain of the herd gave an alarm for danger and the whole group of monsters moved toward the Land-Rover at the same time shaking every tree on the way. Everybody in the Land-Rover was terrified, for their lives were now hanging on a string which could easily be cut by a razor blade. However, the guide, Ndilana Kayange, was aware of the danger, and through his skill, managed to save the lives of these helpless Officers. He directed the driver to dodge the furious elephants by moving from one side to another. But despite all the efforts of saving the lives, one bull elephant overtook the Land-Rover and plunged his tusks on the rear door and broke the glass window, but he never injured any passenger.

The guide almost certainly mistook one of the Torone sisters for a bull, a common error.

After a year of work I realized that I had only begun to scratch the surface of the elephant's social life and ecological problems. I therefore wrote a report to my Professor at Oxford, Niko Tinbergen, with a copy to John Owen, asking if I could continue my study after my treatment for bilharzia.

# 5

# Doomed Woodlands

The red-bricked Hospital of Tropical Medicine at St. Pancras, blackened with London's grime, seemed another world from the unpolluted life-bearing woodlands of Manyara. The only link between the two places was the parasites they had in common, conveyed by sallow, emaciated patients suffering from all manner of infestations. Dr. Walters, who looked after me, conducted seminars at the foot of my bed on bilharzia transmission via baboons. My case was one of the few known to medical science.

One day a letter arrived from John Owen with the good news that I was to be funded by the New York Zoological Society for the rest of my project. He had been over to America and interested them in my research. Moreover I shortly heard from the Professor of Animal Behavior at Oxford, Niko Tinbergen, that he was willing to take me on as a D.Phil. student though I would be working entirely in Africa. Better still, he was coming to East Africa to visit the newly-formed Serengeti Research Institute (SRI) at Seronera, and asked me if he could stay at Manyara. As co-founder of the science of ethology, the biological study of animal behavior, he later shared a Nobel Prize with Konrad Lorenz and Carl von Frisch. He had been a fascinating but distant figure in the department, with whom I had little contact.

Ten days after my return to Manyara he arrived to stay with me and became totally absorbed with elephants. Like so many of the other large mammals of Africa they had not been studied at all from an ethological approach, though some of their behavior demonstrated principles Tinbergen had discovered through observing very different animals in Europe.

For instance, there was "redirected aggression." I remembered his lectures which described gulls facing each other in territorial disputes. Each gull when highly motivated to attack the other would direct vicious pecks at the ground and savagely pull grass stalks as if they were feathers from the rival's head. This was an example of aggression stimulated by the rival gull but redirected at another object.

When Boadicea launched one of her perfected threat charges against us we found she did the same thing. When we remained stationary in the Land-Rover she swept close past us and discharged her aggression on an innocent gardenia bush, with such fury that a shower of leaves fluttered to the ground. This did not daunt Niko in the least, but merely kindled his enthusiasm. He understood and approved of the adventurous side of the work, and was full of perceptive observations.

He told me that redirected aggression was usually elicited by an object that simultaneously evoked fear. This seemed to be true of Boadicea who for all her threat at the same time never dared to press her charges home. In fact it was only because of the usually "redirected" nature of elephant aggression that I was able to study their behavior in the way I did and yet survive. I often wondered what terrible experience Boadicea must have suffered at the hands of man for her to hate and fear us so much.

Another distinct pattern of behavior with practical as well as theoretical interest was the twiddling of the trunk, the swinging of one of the front legs to and fro, and rocking from side to side which I saw when an elephant appeared to be deciding between attack and retreat. These were typical "displacement activities." In elephants they were a great help to me in predicting their behavior. The more marked these activities the less likely the elephant was to charge. Very often the most impressive threat displays emanated from the most frightened elephants which were unlikely to make a serious attack.

Niko was particularly interested in the differences in character between individual elephants where this led to their behavior becoming predictable. As we passed one matriarch named Inkosikaas, with an upswept tusk like a saber, she shook her head in mild annoyance. I stopped the car and told him to watch these elephants, because within about five minutes they would charge. Inkosikaas fiddled with her trunk, then turned to the other cows on either side of her and clashed tusks with them in turn, putting her trunk in their mouths one after the other. This seemed to reassure her and almost exactly five minutes later she delivered a beautifully impressive threat charge. This was her own predictable quirk, unique among the elephants of Manyara: the tendency for delayed action aggressive displays.

We spent many days in the glades of the forest lying on the short cropped grass watching elephants sliding into mud baths and the young playing. Niko kept looking over his shoulder and, when I asked him why, he said that thirty years ago, as a young man he had spent a year in the Arctic living with Eskimos where he had become very conscious of the danger of polar bear attacks. As a result he had developed the habit of scanning his surroundings every few minutes, and now once more in a wild place the habit had returned. We laughed over it, but the principle remained the same whether surrounded by icebergs or trees and thickets, that when man lives in the same habitat as dangerous animals he can never afford to relax.

Under Niko's curiosity was a sense of wonder and a never-ending urge to inquire that I found infectious.

Another visitor deeply interested in animals but with a different emphasis was David Attenborough. He came with a BBC television unit to film the work of scientists at the Serengeti Research Institute, of which I was by now an outlying member. As we drove south to Endabash looking for a tolerant family unit for us to stalk I told him about the woodlands and their inhabitants, and how elephants greatly outnumbered the thirty or so rhino and sixty giraffe that shared the same habitat. It was interesting to speculate on why the rhinos only occurred at relatively low densities. Like elephants they chewed twigs, but they ate a much smaller variety of plants, restricting themselves almost entirely to woody vegetation, while the elephants sampled the majority of the 630 plant species of Manyara, sweeping them into their mouths with their supremely versatile trunk, that could reach up to twenty feet above the ground.

The rhino social groupings were also much smaller and consisted of parties of twos and threes, usually a cow and her calf or perhaps a cow and a bull. The largest number of rhinos I ever saw together at Manyara was six, all lying in one dust bowl. Perhaps their social behavior through the defense of territory restricted their numbers.

Before long we came across a family group of elephants led by a matriarch whom I named Queen Victoria. She allowed us to walk around and film her. Even though she was fully aware of our presence she had become practically immune to the persistent gnat-like human observer who had so frequently dogged her footsteps over the past year.

Returning to camp in the twilight we trundled very close to a large rhino on the side of the road that huffed and puffed. David missed seeing it and since I wanted to show him something special, I stopped the car and reversed. The rhino was much angrier than I expected; he trotted through the bush toward us, and before I knew where he was he suddenly appeared snorting dreadfully and thrust his horn twice with extreme rapidity into my offside rear tire. Then he lifted the whole side of the car like a mad hydraulic jack, until it teetered on the point of balance before crashing back to the ground. After this he left us and as we changed the wheel the second car drew up with the rest of the unit.

"We've been hit by a rhino and he's punctured the tire," I said to the driver, who replied,

"Oh yes, I believe it's all the rage nowadays."

David Attenborough had thought it was a deliberate attempt to introduce some local color, until he had noticed how white my knuckles were, gripping the steering wheel. It was the first time that I had ever seen aggressive threat behavior carried into physical contact, and it should have been a warning.

Although a wide variety of animals lived at Manyara none appeared to benefit more from the combinations of different habitats than the elephants.

They could choose between forest and swamp, nutritious pastures beneath the canopies of shady *Acacia tortilis,* yet richer grass along the alkaline shore, palm trees in the glades and a whole fresh range of delicacies on the slopes of the escarpment. Papery-barked *Combretum,* succulent wild sisal and fibrous baobab, all were found in great abundance. Sausage trees regularly came into fruit in the dry season and *Acacia albida* dropped their strongly smelling orange pods, summoning all the pod gourmets—such as impala, baboons and elephants. Along the shore in places brilliant green sedge grew up to the water's edge, and then gave way to a pool of water plants, kaleidoscopic with birds. At the northern end dense reed mace floated out on its matted roots for several miles. Within the forest, yellow-barked figs spread canopies which touched the neighboring *Trichilia* trees in a continuous shady screen, capturing every speck of direct sunlight.

The abundant water, rich volcanic soil and high temperatures ensured a high primary productivity; the rapid photosynthesis of proteins, carbohydrates and starch. These foodstuffs were fixed in the trees' bulk until death or some animal could rip off a branch and devour the captive energy. If the elephants were not satisfied with all this bounty there was a whole other forest, the Marang, suspended above their heads, more than twice the area of the Park and replete with a new selection of species, provided they could get to it across the farmland. No wonder Vesey, after spending years learning the names of these plants and the complex mosaic of their communities, could not bear to hear talk of elephant overpopulation, simply because elephants were abundant here as nowhere else in Africa. The luxuriance of Manyara, where trees covered more than half the Park, should surely be sufficient for their needs.

Though I had a full program for studying elephants, I came more and more to realize the importance of the trees to the environment and the animals dependent on them. Changes were taking place and nowhere faster than in the *Acacia tortilis* woodlands. In my first year I had numbered, with little metal tags, a sample of 300 trees, running in straight lines through these woodlands. These lines were my transects. By visiting them periodically I intended to measure the precise rate at which elephants damaged and killed trees by bark stripping.

The *Acacia tortilis* were not only important to the elephants which sampled their roots, bark, branches, twigs, leaves and fruits, but rhino and giraffe also fed off them and impala nibbled at the lower branches. The acacia trees were perhaps most firmly associated in the tourists' minds with lions, their bodies sprawling in languid postures of repose along the branches.

The lions had favorite trees, every one named by the guides, after some famous person who had seen lions there, or after its individual looks. So there was Mti wa Haile Selassie, Mti wa Julius Nyerere, Mti wa

Nasser, as well as Mti wa Majani Mingi (the tree of much leaf), Mti wa Giza (the tree of darkness) and Mti wa Muhanga, the tree into which the Park Warden had inadvertently backed his car. Like all lions, the Manyara tree-climbing lions looked peaceful and sleepy most of the time, but I knew another side of their character and always kept a good lookout when walking the transect.

The Manyara lions had very little fear or respect for human beings, and although at the time man-eating had not yet started, they had been known to chase villagers on bicycles down the main public road and one lion had actually swiped a man on the backside as he pedalled frantically for his life. He escaped with a few scratches and a story to tell. Later others were less lucky.

These were rangy lions, with scraggy manes, torn ears and flanks, scarred by thorn bushes and buffalo horns. Stephen Makacha, a Park guide, and George Schaller, working together, found that 62% of the lion's prey were buffalo. Consequently they had to fight nearly every time they killed, which they did most weeks, and their looks were not improved by these encounters. They could not be compared to the magnificence of the Seronera lions which lived off less pugnacious prey, or to the Ngorongoro lions which Hans Kruuk usually found feasting off hyena kills.

The Chem-Chem and Mahali-pa-Nyati prides of lionesses lived in the northern half of the Park. With overlapping ranges, they were mutually hostile and took good care to avoid each other, but the two males, Dume Kubwa, with the black mane, and one-eyed Chongo, shared both prides of lionesses equally between them. They would not tolerate any other males, however, and drove away one of the male cubs, Satima, when he reached the age of one and a half years.

I developed a healthy respect for these tough specialized killers. The days when their ancestors had been hunted by the Masai with spears had long since been forgotten. Twice I came inadvertently face to face with their blazing eyes at three paces' distance. Each time, fortunately, I had not crossed the critical distance, and they bounded away uttering deep *whoofs;* but the third time in the river below the camp the lion had second thoughts and turned and crouched behind a boulder, with muscles twitching and tail flicking. I stood still and put out my arms to make myself look bigger as he growled, then I slowly backed away leaving him in possession of the river pools.

If I ever needed advice in my work I could now have stimulating discussion with my official supervisor Hugh Lamprey and the other scientists who lived at Seronera, 130 miles away by road. Hugh, a pioneer in the study of big game ecology, was director of the Serengeti Institute which had succeeded the Serengeti Research Project. He was happy to return to research after heading the Mweka College of Wildlife Management for training young Africans to become Park Game Wardens.

In February 1967 Hugh asked me to give a talk to the scientists. Murray Watson had departed to write up his wildebeest work at Cambridge University, but there were already several others, including George Schaller, working on the lions, and Hans Kruuk from Oxford who had recently discovered that hyenas actually hunt for themselves and that lions often take their kills away from them. Hans renamed the king of the beasts the "King of the Scavengers." Apart from the scientists, John Owen and the Wardens Myles Turner and Sandy Field attended the research meetings when they could.

All in all they were an extremely able group of wildlife experts and I felt my project would benefit from their ideas. As the only full-time elephant biologist at that time in the Tanzania Parks, I was to tell them what my research problems and priorities were and what little I had been able to discover in one year, and then a discussion of my results would lead on to general management problems posed by elephants in the Serengeti, which were suddenly causing great alarm.

I explained the Manyara problem of elephants and trees, and questioned whether the Park was large enough for elephants to live in balance with their environment, adding that it was too early yet to come to any hard and fast conclusions. So far, I told them, I knew 130 elephants whom I could recognize by sight and showed them a map which plotted the sightings of Victoria's family unit over a month's period. This unit had stayed well within the Park during that time, and I was not yet in a position to assess the importance of outside areas such as the Marang Forest. I was able to confirm that these groups of females and young were stable, at least over the one-year period during which I had watched them, and that they were not led by old bulls as had been suggested in most of the traditional hunting literature. I went on to say that I intended to find out how their density, which might be ten elephants per square mile, affected their social relationships and breeding success. So far I had only one year of birth data during which only six calves were born to the ninety-eight cows entered in my family unit notebook. This, if representative, was equivalent to each cow producing a calf only once every sixteen years: an average which looked like the beginning of a population decline. Was the density adversely affecting the elephants' breeding rate? I would have to investigate every subtlety of social interaction to find out, but one year's data by itself meant little.

Then I told of how many *Acacia tortilis* had been knocked down or stripped of their bark in the different parts of the Park. I was able to relate that contrary to what had been said about the Tsavo National Park in Kenya, the elephants did not eat bark in the dry season but attacked trees in the rains; perhaps because at this time the sap flowed. The damage was serious. In the worst hit areas 35% of the trees were dead and more than half of these had obviously been killed by elephants. There were few young trees to replace the casualties; I said that I had found that seedlings could not germinate under an adult tree which in some unknown way suppressed the growth.

Hans Kruuk asked why it was that the Manyara elephant population, which from past records appeared to have remained at much the same density, had only just now started to destroy the trees. I answered that I thought that the damage was caused by the effects of immigration and overcrowding, but that damage had probably been steady for a good many years. If the elephants destroyed a fixed number of trees every year the effects would probably not be noticeable until many of the trees had been thinned out, after which the steady rate of destruction would suddenly become more striking.

Once again I couldn't give any figures on the extent of the regeneration or the rate of tree growth. I felt rather embarrassed at how little of the fundamental botanical information I had been able to produce, and how many questions remained to be answered. Luckily everyone realized that building up an identification file on any animal is a painfully slow process and they appreciated my difficulties. But it was only as the meeting progressed and it appeared that nobody else knew much about elephants' effects on habitats that I began to feel a little better.

The discussion progressed to the Serengeti elephants. They had only recently become a problem and Myles Turner had delved into their history which he now summarized for us. He had collected records of hunters and explorers in the previous fifty years but none of these mentioned elephants in the Serengeti. It was later to be shown that yet earlier records of elephants did exist but at this meeting we all accepted that elephants had not lived in the Serengeti area until very recently. The influx of elephants over the previous decade had been recorded in Myles's diary. Numbers had increased dramatically until the first total aerial counts that were made revealed about 2,200. The population increase had stopped at that period and for the last four years their numbers had remained steady.

It was believed that 700 of these elephants had come from the Maswa district and 1,500 from the Mara area of Kenya, driven south across the Mara River into Tanzania and the Serengeti by the rigorous elephant "control" practiced by the Kenya Game Department, in which 600 elephants had been shot in thirty years.

This invasion of elephants might have been welcomed as an increase in the diversity of the Park's animal population, both for the enjoyment of visitors and as an interesting example of an animal invasion for the scientists to study, but with the elephants came their disturbing ability to transform their landscape, so instead of receiving a welcome their very existence was questioned.

The immediate reason for this guarded response to the arrival of the elephants was that groups of bulls had moved along the Seronera River and pushed over numerous yellow-barked fever trees, *Acacia xanthophloea*. Seronera's unique attraction was the ease with which tourists could see leopards in their natural state; it was about the only place in East Africa where leopards were often visible without first putting out a bait. But now the elephants were knocking down the very trees in which the leopards spent their days reclining.

Hugh Lamprey organized a tree count and discovered that 27% of the fever trees had been destroyed within the space of two years. This finding, if it could justifiably be extended into the future, signaled an acute crisis. Not only might leopards become unfindable, but if the Seronera destruction rate of trees applied to the rest of the 2,000 square miles of woodland in the Park there would be no trees left in eight years, and what would happen to Serengeti's plains' game when they were deprived of the shade that they all so tightly clustered under in the dry season?

A debate now took place. "We must consider that elephant are not a part of the Serengeti ecosystem, but have become superimposed upon it," remarked Hugh Lamprey, the chairman of the meeting, "there is none of the undergrowth and bushy vegetation usually associated with elephant habitat."

He went on to say that the situation might now be so serious that there might not even be time to wait for a research project to run its course, before acting to control the situation. (Out of the meeting he told me that if elephants were considered undesirable they should be eradicated.)

John Owen countered this view by saying that he thought that management should be conservatively applied with the minimum of human interference, particularly at this early stage, and that perhaps the presence of elephants in the Serengeti might be part of a long-term cycle. The idea of cycles in which numbers of animals and plants oscillate is a well-known concept in temperate climate ecology, but at that time it was a new idea when applied to elephants. If the cyclical concept were true it would undermine the idea that there was anything sacrosanct about the current levels of animals and plants, or the idea that the management aim "to preserve the variety of plant and animal life in approximately the numbers existing at present" had any natural basis.

The rate at which young trees were replacing the adults destroyed was obviously a key factor, but this was another subject which research had totally neglected. It was decided that a forester should be recruited to join the staff as soon as possible.

This meeting was the first time that the SRI members discussed their advisory function in relation to management policy. John Owen wished to establish the principle that the Park would be run on scientific lines and that the function of the SRI was to give suitable advice based directly on research.

The scientists all felt that the research organization should not advise on policy, but should only suggest management techniques and practices once a policy had been decided upon by the National Parks. They preferred to restrict their role to predictions of trends under whatever management option was chosen. This was an example of scientists not wanting to abandon their tidy objective world where all that mattered was facts and how they could be interpreted as trends, or paths of causation, or interacting systems. Scientifically there was no objective reason either for or against the shooting of the elephants that were doing the damage.

Here was an issue that could only be decided in relation to aesthetic, economic or political considerations. In ecological terms the Seronera tree damage was insignificant. The very desire to preserve animals was a subjective statement of faith in the animal's intrinsic worth. It was a feeling possessed by most of the scientists there, who regarded the wildebeest migration with the same awe that others feel for the Mona Lisa, but they would not admit this sentiment into their arguments because it could not be backed up by facts; the right and wrong of aesthetics being imponderables not open to scientific analysis. At the end of the meeting there was a consensus of opinion on only one fact, that there was an urgent need for research before taking any hasty action.

Next day before driving back to Manyara, I took a walk with Vesey through one of the Serengeti woodlands. He had stated fairly emphatically at the meeting that if there were any imbalances between woodlands and elephants they were caused by man and his injudicious use of fire and not by elephants. As we walked we could see small thorny trees sprouting everywhere from the ground. We examined the stems of one and dug up the roots. The root was well-developed, but the stem was charred and looked as if it had been burnt back to the roots by the grass fires which scorched the whole of the Serengeti every year. So the regeneration potential was massive after all. Poachers and honey hunters would always light fires but if the effects could be reduced either by early burning, which only ignites avenues through the half-dry grass thus making firebreaks, or by complete fire protection, these young trees would perhaps in time be able to replace the adults destroyed by elephants.

But even if fire could be controlled, how long would it take for the young trees to grow up? A search of the scientific literature in the SRI library did not produce any further information. These trees were mainly scrubby commiphora or acacia species that grew on poor agricultural land, and none of them had the least economic value as timber. Consequently no one had thought them worth a study before the era of National Parks and elephant problems.

Everyone had agreed that Manyara, with its perennial springs and high primary productivity was exceptional in the number of elephants it could support. The Lake and escarpment acting as natural firebreaks also allowed plant species vulnerable to fire to proliferate.

I realized that the botanical side of the elephant question was as relevant as the elephants themselves. The growth rate of *Acacia tortilis* would be of paramount importance to me. Once I had measured the growth rate I would be able to estimate the ages of the mature stands the elephants were knocking down and I could work out how long it would take a comparable stand to grow up. If it turned out to be a fast growing species then the damage could be viewed lightly, but if the decimated groves proved to be several hundred years old, then their total destruction in a few decades must be viewed as a drastic process. I realized that here again I would need several years to get representative information, for rainfall varies extremely from year to year in East Africa, and with rainfall so varies tree growth.

Back at Manyara, highly stimulated by the fundamental discussions on elephant problems, I immersed myself once again in the incredible detail needed to answer any of the important questions. I fitted some trees with steel bands taken from packing cases, fastened around the trunks with a metal spring so that as the tree grew I could measure the increase in girth.

Then I turned once again to the problem of elephant movements and the significance of the Marang Forest Reserve. This thick, varied forest could be a vital refuge and food supply particularly in hard years, provided the elephants could get there. I was at that time still very puzzled by the movements of the southern elephants. To the south of the Park, under the Rift wall and under the Marang Forest were a series of European-owned farms that ran along the Lake shore. Formerly part of the elephants' range, it was possible that they might still infiltrate through the farms and up easy slopes to the Forest. A safari to this area involved a hundred mile journey by road right round the Lake, for the Park roads ended at Maji Moto and swamps made the last half-mile impassable to motor vehicles.

On one farm a South African lived, curiously unbothered by the arrival of independence and a black government. He carried on planting his crops and left a corridor along the Lake shore for the long established passage of elephants. North of him was an Italian, the Park's nearest neighbor, who with little capital had spent ten years cutting down bush which grew up almost as fast as it was removed. He was trying to farm in the face of continuous elephant, buffalo and antelope pressure on every crop he grew. All of this was delicious new food for them. He bemoaned the fact that on average he lost nearly 50% of his maize every year. For him it was war with the elephants. Their persistent presence on his farm would spell his ruin. He shot tens of elephants at a time, but at night more would come back. He swore to me that he had shot fifty the previous year, "But still they come, one herd here, another there."

One elephant from the Park who probably ended her life in his crops was the saber-tusked matriarch Inkosikaas, who had charged Niko Tinbergen. She was a great wanderer and one day I found her right down at the southern end of the Park next to Maji Moto, the hot springs. The next day she vanished and I never saw her again. She was probably shot in the maize, standing out while her family made its escape. Like that she would have made an easy target. Her family unit returned, led by an extremely nervous cow called Aethra, who tamed down over the years, but who never to my knowledge returned to the southern boundary of the Park.

It was obvious to me that, however slowly and painfully for him, the Italian was getting the better of the elephants. His fields stretched unbroken for more than a mile's distance from the escarpment to the Lake. No corridor was left for the elephants, so they had no way of avoiding his crops. In time it seemed inevitable that he or his successor would drive the last elephants forever from their former range. Already the other farmers between them had shot some 300–500 elephants, and most of the rest were assumed to have fled to the Park or up into the Marang Forest.

One ironic twist was that the trees benefited from this mass destruction and exodus of the elephants. In abandoned sisal fields and wherever the land was uncultivated, the *Acacia tortilis* proliferated in dense stands thicker than any in the Park. I looked at them longingly, thinking how delicious they would be for my elephants.

If the Italian's land was to present an insurpassable barrier, I wondered how the elephants were going to travel between the Marang Forest and the Park. The slopes from his land up to the Forest were gentle and gave easy access, but from the Park they were steep, rocky, precipitous and covered in dense trees. I explored the base of this escarpment with Mhoja, pushing through tangled thorns and spiky wild sisal, but we could find few tracks of animals and each time we ended up at the foot of an insurmountable cliff. There was, however, one other possible route at the northern point of the common Park–Forest Reserve boundary. It was near the Endabash waterfall, underneath an emi-

nence marked on the map as Geyasagong Hill. I could
see tracks winding up the hill from below but I had
never been on foot to see if elephants could travel all
the way without passing outside the Park into the area
of expanding human settlement.

My mother was staying with me at the time and
since she was a keen birdwatcher and a strong hill
walker I planned a day's excursion to this area. While
she looked for new species of escarpment birds, I
would be able to explore the potential elephant route to
the Marang Forest. Mhoja was away on leave, so we
took another Ranger called Kiprono, who carried a
.470 Rigby rifle to protect us all.

We parked the car in a grassy riverside glade below the Endabash waterfall and waded across the shallow waters. Narrow tunnels led through thick undergrowth up the opposite bank. The path wound along
flat ground between two deep-cut erosion gullies, then
entered thickets of a scrubby plant *Ocimum suave*
that smelt of sage and closed above our heads so that
we had to stoop. Looking ahead we could see for perhaps five yards, but to either side no more than arm's
length. Some fresh rhino droppings lying dispersed on
dust, which had recently been scraped by rhino's
hooves, reminded us that we were not alone.

It was a relief, 400 yards further on, to reach the
safety of the escarpment, after that tense walk not
knowing what we might meet. At least here, on the
steep slopes, we would be able to run faster up or down
hill than any of the larger animals of the Park. We
climbed up interlocking elephant trails until the hill
rounded out in gentle slopes and pleasant parkland
where *Terminalia* trees stood in a meadow of brilliant flowers. Looking back, Kiprono spotted a couple
of rhinos browsing in the thickets near our path. We
were fortunate to have missed them, but so far most
of the rhinos I had met on foot had been very willing
to run away.

The elephant trails faded out in the grass, all except
one which we followed. Over another rise I found the

answer to my day's work. The elephant path zig-zagged up the hill almost to the summit of Geyasagong Hill and then disappeared into the tree line of the Forest Reserve. It was carefully graded, as are all elephant paths, and looked an easy climb, but right next to it, within less than twenty yards, was the framework of a new Mbulu house. The expanding agriculturalists had already arrived just where the path passed outside the protection of the Park. There could be only one outcome if the elephants and men came into conflict. This route was destined to be cut.

We trudged on up to the point where the path entered the forest, and found a boulder where we sat and ate our sandwiches, the damp and dark woodland forest with lichen draped trees on the one side and a view over the upper Endabash valley, all territory outside the Park, on the other. New huts were springing up wherever there was any ground with a slope gentle enough to allow agriculture.

Trees had been cut down wherever I looked, and goats and cattle scoured the grass. The result was that gully erosion was beginning to take hold. Without trees to break the force of the tropical downpours the soil was flayed off the surface of the earth and washed away in streams. Water retention was also poorer since in a brief shower there would be no branches and leaves from which the rain could drip and slowly soak into the ground long after it had stopped falling. The erosion was becoming so bad that the rivers in the Park were filling up with silt from these settlements above the scarp.

This area was uninhabited seventy years ago. In the days of the caravans elephants had been reported as plentiful in these highlands by the geographer Farler, who interviewed traders returning to the coast in the 1880s. I later saw copies of old German maps made by explorers who criss-crossed this area when it was a tribal no-man's-land between the warring Masai and Wambulu at the turn of the century, and nowhere were there any settlements to be found. Even the thriving

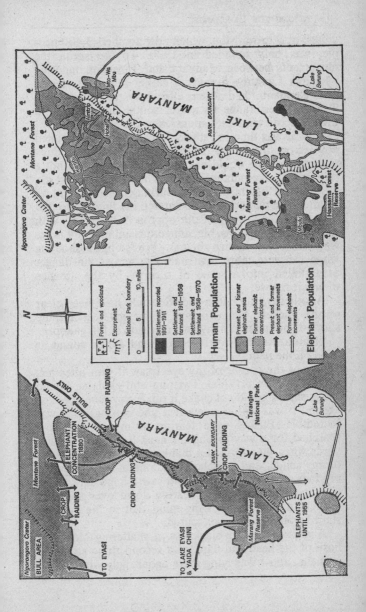

**Human Population**

- Forest and woodland
- Escarpment
- National Park boundary
- 0   5   10 miles
- Settlement recorded 1891–1911
- Settlement and farmland 1911–1958
- Settlement and farmland 1958–1970

**Elephant Population**

- Present and former elephant areas
- Former elephant concentrations
- Present and former elephant movements
- Former elephant movements

village of Mto-wa-Mbu, which now numbers 3,400 people, was only founded in 1920. To the south the movements between Manyara and Tarangire reported by Hugh Lamprey five years earlier had now ceased, and elephants had been effectively alienated from 70% of their range to north, south, and west, with the Lake barring their expansion to the east.

Now it was time to return. Starting back, we looked down from the lip of the escarpment upon the thick undergrowth we would have to cross. There was not a sign of life. Presumably the two rhinos had moved on. Just in case they might still be lurking in the vicinity we shouted and whooped as we entered the thickets so that they would be warned of our approach. Normally, with hardly any exceptions, big, dangerous animals will make way for noisy human beings. We stopped shouting when we were more than half-way across the danger area, lulled into a sense of security by the absence of any response.

Another twenty paces and we would have been clear of the thickets, when, almost below my feet a rhino snorted and burst into my field of vision at full gallop.

"Rhino, run for it," I shouted and darted round its head off the path.

Out of the corner of my eye I saw it turn after me, and I ran for my life. Twisting and dodging round the bushes, I could not shake it off. Every time I looked around it was within a few feet and closing in. It was incredible. Bushes were tearing at my clothes as I searched for a way through, I must have covered fifty yards when they formed a blank wall. A strap snapped on my sandal and I pitched headlong at high speed on my face. As I fell I twisted and saw a huge dark shape with its long sharp horn bearing down over me. The thought flashed through my mind that in the next instant I would be killed or spared.

A split second of blackness, a shattering blow, the flash of the head and flank of a second rhino streaking past me, and I was lying there agonizingly winded, but deliriously happy to be alive. Luckily, I had been tossed, or kicked, to one side avoiding a second trampling. I knew that the rhinos had merely been seeing me off and there was no chance that they would return to finish the job. The first rhino must have been a female, mother to the second.

Gasping for breath, I lay waiting for the winding to wear off, euphorically gazing into the blue sky. It was like the rugger matches we had been forced to play at school. The only difference was that the pain did not wear off. I rolled on to my stomach and found that I was still clutching a folded map. Pushing my hands on the ground I raised my body on all fours, but the pain was intense. It was impossible to stand up, my back muscles would not respond. I subsided again and shouted for help.

In the distance came an answering hail; a minute later my mother and Kiprono materialized, hot and disheveled. They had run back along the path, and Kiprono had even let off his gun in the air in the hope of scaring away the rhinos. I told them that the rhino had got me and I thought I had slipped a disc. A few years before, my brother had fallen 1,500 feet down a mountain in the Alps, from Switzerland into Italy, after being electrocuted by a high tension cable which he had inadvertently touched with his ski stick and he had slipped a disc, so it was by way of being a family tradition.

After wiggling my toes to test that my spinal cord was still functioning, I asked my mother and Kiprono to put their shoulders under my arms and raise me to my feet. They had to support my dead weight, because, although I could move my legs in a semblance of walking, I found it impossible to support my trunk. We moved very slowly, and after ten paces I had to beg to be put down. Several times I tried to walk but I could only stand the pain at the most for a minute at a time. Eventually I asked them to put me under a tree, and to go and try and bring the Land-Rover to where I was, even though I knew it was very difficult country to cross and my mother had never driven a Land-Rover before.

As the flies buzzed around my sweaty face, I heard the engine start up in the distance. It changed tone, and I imagined they must be fording the river. I fervently hoped that my mother had remembered to pull the little red lever which would put the car into low-ratio four-wheel drive. The soft sands of the Endabash River had bogged down many a car for hopeless hours. Then it changed pitch again and I knew they were across and climbing the steep bank, breaking through the overhanging branches. Then the roar of the laboring engine changed to a fatal high-pitched whine. That was a bad noise that meant one or more of the wheels were in the air. This went on for about five minutes until I shouted at the top of my lungs.

They heard me, abandoned the car, and came back to the spot where I was resting. Once more they put their arms under my shoulders and we struggled by stages back to the car. My mother had done very well to get so far up the steep narrow elephant tracks leading from the river, but the car was now mounted on a small hummock with all four wheels suspended in the air. I lay by its side and told Kiprono how to set the jack to unstick it.

Eventually we turned the car around, and replaced the wheels on firm ground. I lay across the front seat, and we jolted agonizingly back down to the Endabash River. The journey to camp has mercifully been blotted out of my memory. I can only recall that the pain was very bad. At the end I was grateful to be able to roll into a camp bed and consume a third of a bottle of whisky. A fine Scottish glow seeped back through my limbs and I began to feel a bit better.

The district nurse was called from Mto-wa-Mbu, a pleasant man who assured me that nothing was very wrong. A doctor was located in a tourist party and asked to render first aid, but he was enjoying his holiday and refused to interrupt his schedule. Jonathan Muhanga, the Park Warden, arrived and offered to drive us to the hospital in Arusha eighty miles away. We gratefully accepted.

Night had fallen by the time we started. Half-way to Arusha one of the front wheels of the car fell off. It listed to one side and we gazed up at the incredibly beautiful sky and sang Scottish songs to pass the time. The pain had been completely muted by the whisky.

By chance John Owen had received news that I had been gutted by a rhino and had immediately taken his Land-Rover and driven to Mto-wa-Mbu. We must have passed him in the night. When he reached the village they told him that we had already gone to Arusha. Some said that the rhino's horn had gone in one inch, some said nearly a foot, and some said it had gone right through. When he caught up with us he was relieved to find that I had merely been trampled.

We transferred to his Land-Rover and said good-bye and thank-you to Muhunga, leaving him disconsolately trying to fix on his wheel with broken nuts. Thirteen hours after the accident we rolled into the Mount Meru Hospital, Arusha, and that night I slept well under morphia.

# 6

# Birth

After I left hospital I spent some weeks lying flat on my
back on the floor of John Owen's Arusha house. It
was an opportunity to improve my Swahili and I laid
my hands on a phrase book written for pioneers in the
1920s. Soon I had no trouble in reproducing such
phrases as "Split the skull and give the brains to the
cook," "Hang up the carcass so they will have to
jump to get it," and "Make way for the Master," but
I could find little that could conceivably be of use.
Luckily the education officer, Hugh Russell, at the time
also convalescing from a bad motor smash, was able
to give me lessons and under tutelage my Swahili rapidly improved.

A bone specialist, Garth Williams, flew down from
Nairobi to inspect me and immediately released me
from the plaster encasement in which the Arusha doc-
tors had wrapped me from chest to rump. He told me
that the enforced walk back to the Land-Rover, by
exercising the damaged tissues immediately after the
initial shock, had probably taken weeks off my convalescence. Otherwise, he said, I would have seized up
for months. I was really cured, however, by Elly
Boyce, a physiotherapist in Nairobi who gradually
massaged life back into my ruptured muscles.

As soon as I was fit I returned to Manyara and

checked up on all the family units to see which cows had given birth and which animals had disappeared. It was important not to be away for long if I was to make the essential observations relevant to the question of numbers.

After the rhino incident I was more wary of the south of the Park and I temporarily shelved my study of elephant movements there. Luckily Mhoja returned to stay permanently at Ndala. He was as alert as anyone I ever met in the bush and always forewarned me of rhinos.

He became my companion and instructor for the next three years, and a very great friend. He was exceptional in his attitude to animals and to bush life. Most of the other Rangers enjoyed nothing better than the chance to go to Mto-wa-Mbu and visit the bars and indulge in a social life, but Mhoja was happy to stay in the bush and enjoyed himself most when we went out together on patrol. He had a good knowledge of the tribal names of the plants, and learned English and Latin names with equal facility. Mhoja and I used to go out and collect any plant we were unsure of and bring it back to Vesey's reference collection of pressed plants for identification. He became an expert and while I was writing up my notes for the day he would pore over these fragments of dried-up plants. The time came when I could ask Mhoja the name of any plant and he would be almost sure to know it; he would also show me which wild fruits growing in the forest were good to eat. He was able to imitate the calls of the birds and was a superb mimic of human beings too. Once a visiting Russian agriculturalist came to my camp and we had to talk through an interpreter. Within minutes Mhoja had picked up the sound of the Russian speech and later was able to give a creditable imitation of Russian sounding expostulations. Without him life would have been more difficult, dangerous and lonely in those first years, and far less amusing.

So far I had recorded few births and therefore I

wondered if overcrowding had slowed down the birth rate. Then in 1968 the dearth of baby elephants in the first two years was followed by an avalanche. Practically every cow that could gave birth. At the same time the rains fell in a continual downpour that broke all records and carried right on through the dry season so that no month passed without rain. With every river in flood the Lake level rose, steadily covering the mud-flats, creeping into woodlands and eventually submerging several miles of the main road. Some trees, which I estimated to be seventy-five years old, were flooded. The wide swamps were suddenly immersed in deep water and drowned. Nobody could remember any year like it. Below the Marang Forest whole sections of the mountainous escarpment came away bodily. Cottage-sized boulders rolled and slid with the mud for a thousand feet sheer. Where greenery had thickly clad the slopes were raw fan-shaped smears, with a few trees flung headlong down the scarp.

The Endabash River flooded and swept away a brand new concrete bridge less than a year old. Vesey had advised against its construction and had predicted that a freak rainstorm would sooner or later wash it away. The southern end of the Park became sodden and impassable to all vehicles.

In the heavy dampness the elephants climbed the escarpment and stayed up in the hills, but when the rain stopped, however briefly, they returned. Then everywhere family units were seen with their half-shut-eyed new-born calves as they stumbled through the slippery woods and forests.

Elephant births in the wild have seldom been observed. The gestation period is twenty-two months, but there are few signs that tell when a cow elephant is pregnant. Most other gravid mammals become huge, like Manyara lionesses whose bellies almost scraped the ground at this time. In contrast, pregnant elephants show almost no visible swelling, and if they do it is more likely to be caused by intestinal gases rather than a foetus. In Asia the birth of a calf to a domestic elephant may surprise even the Indian mahout or Burmese oozie who lives with her.

The breasts of a young African elephant, pregnant for the first time, swell up from her flat chest in preparation for lactation, but older cows may lactate from one birth to the next and the size of their breasts cannot be used as a clue. I never actually witnessed the moment of birth although I came close to it on three occasions. As such observations are rare, I have drawn fairly fully from my field notes to describe the first hours of life.

The first time was when I encountered the family of the matriarch Deino in a clearing in the South Endabash Scrub. She was a fairly wild elephant and needed to be approached with caution to avoid scaring her. One of this group, a young female of fourteen years, had just given birth. Under her belly stood a very small calf which was still smeared in wet blood. Blood also covered the mother's hind legs and trunk, and was daubed on the trunks of two large females of this group, suggesting that they might have picked up the afterbirth or somehow assisted in the delivery. The calf was red brown and hairy. Its membranous ears fitted perfectly like leaves around the heart of a cabbage. Its body was thin and crumpled compared to the bulging stomachs of older calves. The mother stood exhausted, unwilling to move, but the older cows began to shake their heads and trumpet. Knowing their nervous behavior, I did not wish to disturb them further lest the calf should come to harm, so, after a few minutes, I left.

Another time I was able to get much closer to a young cow named Tusked Ear who had just given birth. She was one of those juveniles that become pregnant at an early age; she must have been still under thirteen years. At some stage in her life her left ear had been severely ripped by a bad-tempered elder. Her matriarch, a one-tusker named Aphrodite, lived in the Ground Water Forest near the Park entrance gate, and seldom came out of it. They were not driven to seek cover because of a nervous disposition, but they seemed to restrict themselves voluntarily to this small but rich segment of the Park. Part of their range included either side of the escarpment road going from the village up to the hotel, on the way to Ngorongoro, and it was here on the Park Boundaries that Tusked Ear bore a male calf at about midday.

I happened to be passing just at this time and saw the bloody afterbirth freshly deposited in the middle of the road with a cluster of six elephants on the verge standing around a tiny calf. He was smaller than average for a new-born, which is often the case when the mother is still a growing adolescent (genetic factors presumably being modified by the internal environment). The matriarch was a little way off browsing as if nothing had happened that concerned her. Within the group around the baby were a full grown cow, Electra, her two calves of five-and-a-half and a year, a nine-year-old female and Tusked Ear herself. The young mother looked exhausted. Her head dropped and her legs sagged as if she could hardly stand. She had no energy left for her baby and seemed withdrawn and somnolent. The only attention he received was from the nine-year-old female, who let her trunk wander over his face fondling every smallest part.

The calf tried to suck with its mouth, unsuccessfully, once or twice from his mother and then tottered over to the large cow Electra. What followed amazed me. Electra paid absolutely no attention until he was right under her stomach and then suddenly kicked him with a hind leg three times, sending him sprawling. The new-born calf bowled over in the dust, picked himself up and staggered back toward his mother.

The nine-year-old, who had been following his movements intently, opened her forelegs and pulling the baby under her belly, straddled him protectively. This action moved Tusked Ear enough for her to extend her trunk weakly and touch the baby on his forehead. He swayed gently under the female calf for a few minutes and then tried once again to approach Electra.

He was sent flying with another kick. The female calf stood over him and rubbed his back.

Several cars passed by, or stopped so that the tourists packed inside could take pictures, and chat and shout to each other.

A noisy tipper truck clattered down the road showering the elephants with dust and alarming the female calf so that she pushed the new-born male to his feet with her forefoot.

Tusked Ear kicked up dust a little distractedly but the others continued browsing undisturbed. They were used to cars here. Electra's one-year-old was allowed to suck from her, and the rejected new-born tried to suck from his protective nine-year-old friend. Shortly afterward Electra began to move off downhill, summoned by a rumble from Aphrodite. The female calf started to follow but the new-born who went with her collapsed after a few paces and she would not leave him. Tusked Ear growled and Electra turned around and came back. Painfully slowly they made their way down the steep rocky hill, with the new-born calf collapsing every few paces and the whole group standing for long periods before moving on.

When I saw this calf again after several weeks he was thriving well, and had filled out, losing his crumpled bag appearance, but since his matriarch chose to live in the sheltering forest and seldom came out, I could not follow his progress in detail.

I never saw such intolerance again as Electra had shown to the baby, although reading through the literature on elephants I found that such behavior was not as rare as I had thought. It seemed that elephants were strangely unpredictable in this respect. One of the Tanzania Park Wardens once saw a cow pick up a two-month calf in its trunk, hurl it down and trample it to death. However, as a rule, the cow elephant's behavior towards very young calves is a byword for tolerance and gentleness, with every member of the family unit taking part in caring for them.

This sort of aggression, leading to the death of an elephant, could be one of the factors capable of controlling elephant numbers, if it could be shown to increase with density. I needed to record information from as many family units as possible, but at the same time I wanted to study in detail the development of a calf from birth and the way it interacted with its society and environment.

The opportunity occurred in the Boadicea kinship group. Boadicea's own family unit was ruled out for study, because of her hysterical but empty threat charges, which only succeeded in stirring up all the otherwise placid members of her family, but Leonora and Jezebel's associated families were both suitable for behavior studies and tied to Boadicea's family by kinship. One morning I found Leonora's family following Boadicea's down to the river to drink. As usual Slender Tusks was with the old matriarch. Her looks and behavior were perfectly normal and I took a few routine notes and went on my way.

It wasn't until evening that I saw Leonora's family again. To my great delight Slender Tusks had with her a tiny blue-brown calf, covered in red wavy hair; it had not been there in the morning. The calf peered out at the unknown world from under her belly. His head had the elongated squashed look of new-born elephants with a short trunk, and his two ears which resembled maps of Africa hugged the contours of his body in a perfect fit. His toenails, five on each forefoot and four on each hind foot, looked as if they had just been scrubbed. He was a male with clearly visible sex organs. No blood was visible on the calf or the mother, so I knew that the birth must have taken place before a shower of rain which had fallen seven hours previously.

The calf still appeared to be very unsteady on his feet. His legs were weak and he placed the round soft pads gingerly as if they hurt when he walked. With eyes half shut, embedded in deep wrinkles, he moved his trunk up and down exploring for a place to suck. Eventually he found a teat between his mother's fore-legs and made hesitant attempts to suck, but every so often the effort was too much and he fell down. Each time Slender Tusks nudged him gently upright with her forefoot and trunk.

The calf then wobbled over to his elder sister who was about four-and-a-half years, and she turned to-wards him and extended her trunk. The calf nuzzled under her right foreleg as if searching for a nipple; evidently he was too young to know how to identify his true mother but he showed a strong desire to find a suitable object to satisfy his sucking instinct. His sister was sympathetic and spread her forelegs and tried to straddle him.

The calf promptly collapsed, regained his feet and wobbled back to Slender Tusks, who paid little atten-tion to him as he explored her underbody with his trunk held rigidly out in front of him. She walked on and he immediately collapsed. She turned round, ex-tended her trunk and growled; Leonora and the others answered. The calf then stood still with his eyes closed; swaying gently for about ten minutes.

At this moment the family unit was widely dispersed. Leonora was a hundred paces ahead with her two calves, the other two young cows with their calves were slightly nearer. Slender Tusks was only accom-panied by her own daughter who seemed fascinated by the new-born, and could not leave him alone. The mother's behavior appeared to be quite unaffected by our presence for she walked past the Land-Rover with her two calves at ten paces' distance.

The calf raised his head again and sucked for fifteen seconds, paused with head down for twenty seconds, then up again for forty seconds, until his mother pulled away. His older sister tried to push in to share in the flow of milk. Slender Tusks growled and shoved her away with a forefoot. A giraffe passed by and Slender Tusks shook her head, warning it to keep away from her baby. Shortly afterward it became too dark to see any more and I left.

The next day I located the family soon after dawn. They had moved under one mile in the night. I watched them for fifteen minutes in dense vegetation, before they became disturbed, during which time I was able to measure their shoulder heights by the pole method. Slender Tusks had a height of 8 ft., the elder sibling 5 ft. 3 in. and the new-born 2 ft. 9 in. equivalent to ages of thirty, four-and-a-half years and zero years. The new-born would have scaled about 260 lb. Though still rather unsteady at times he was noticeably firmer on his feet. He fell down twice near to his mother, was helped up once, but the second time he recovered by himself without assistance.

The family normally walked about three miles a day; I made a special effort to find them every day, searching by car and on foot and ignoring other groups until I saw them. I had decided to study this calf because he was in one of the family units I knew best.

In the first few weeks of his life he rarely strayed more than a few steps from his mother's side. After two days he had found his legs and kept up with the family's easy continuous amble in search of food. Their route took them into swamps, forests and up the steep-sided escarpment along hazardous paths. When wallowing, his mother and the others took great care not to tread on him, and whenever the going became rough Slender Tusks would reach down with her trunk and push or pull him over the obstacles. By the end of three months he had visited almost every corner of his kinship group's range.

I named him N'Dume ("male" in Swahili), because he was a real little male. To begin with he was nourished exclusively by his mother's milk. Whenever she and his elder sister stopped he would nuzzle under their bellies, particularly between the front and hind legs. It took him about three days to learn that the proper place to suck was between his mother's front legs.

Her breasts hung down amazingly human in shape and size but he had to stretch to reach them. When sucking, his pink mouth with its triangular hairy lower lip was firmly fastened on the teat, and his trunk lay limply to one side or was held back in an S-bend above his head. Slender Tusks occasionally touched his forehead with the tip of her trunk as if to feel who it was that sucked her breast. Like all new-born calves he sucked little but often, probably consuming two-and-a-half gallons of milk a day. At other times his trunk hung down straight, or was brandished like an uncoordinated, whippy, rubber hosepipe. Sometimes he just sat down and put the tip in his mouth and sucked it like a child sucking its thumb. Perhaps it served the same function of reassurance. Slender Tusks continued to suckle her older calf and sometimes both mouths were simultaneously fastened to a nipple each. N'Dume soon learned that he could also get a free drink from his grandmother, Leonora, who was gentle and tolerant of all the calves.

Weaning was a very gradual process. Already by the end of the first month N'Dume was biting at grass and pulling out clumps with his mouth, not knowing how to use his trunk, but although some of this material may have been swallowed, the activity seemed to be essentially exploratory. Within the family unit calves continued to suck for as long as they were allowed and long after they had switched to a predominantly vegetarian diet. One of the female calves, Leonora's eldest immature daughter, named Two Holes, was still sucking at the age of nine. When she thrust and tugged to get at the nipple, her eight-inch long tusks poked the old matriarch in her breasts until often she pulled away or detached Two Holes with a shove of her trunk or tusks. Slender Tusks would not let Two Holes anywhere near her.

From the moment of birth N'Dume became an important member of the family. He was very playful, often aggressively attacking his elder brothers and sisters, ramming them with the front of his mouth where the tusks would appear later. They put up with him in a good-natured way and he enjoyed a blissful period of being allowed to do whatever he wished with no discipline.

Throughout the first year of his life, I noticed that Slender Tusks was keenly aware of the movements of her calf. Any attempt by the baby to run further than fifteen to twenty yards away usually caused her to go and retrieve him. Much of the time they were in actual physical contact, spending long periods with N'Dume leaning on his mother. There were few minutes which passed without some form of tactile contact, whether it was the rubbing of flanks, a touch of the trunk, or a bout of suckling.

At five months he became very bumptious, shoving against his elders and climbing on top of them when they lay down in the middle of the day to go to sleep. He seemed to be activated by a never-ending supply of energy that made him chase falling leaves or scatter the egrets that came to catch insects around the elephants' feet. Often he ran about at random pretending to charge furiously at some imaginary object, trumpeting in treble. One evening I saw him on the shore tearing around the outskirts of his family when suddenly the ground gave way under him. He had cracked through a thin crust of mud into thick glutinous mire. The more he tried to pull out his legs the deeper he sank. He rolled and struggled but remained firmly embedded. He gave a terrified squeal which immediately brought Slender Tusks and Leonora, rumbling with concern, over to the edge of the mud flat. He was just beyond trunk reach and Slender Tusks gingerly waded out, her feet ploughing black treacly furrows. Fortunately she found firm ground under the surface layer. First she tried pulling him with her trunk, but when this failed, she moved around him and placed her tusks under his belly and shoved. Leonora stood watching, not yet committing herself to action. With N'Dume struggling and Slender Tusks pushing with all her might he gradually floundered back to firm ground covered from head to tail with a sticky black coating. I don't think he ever forgot that lesson. It was an experience which might save his life later on.

By six months he lost his baby looks. The red hair fell out and was replaced by stiff black bristles. His body grew fatter and he assumed the elephant proportions which change very little with age; only the tusks were missing. His skin was the color of mud, the shade depending on which wallow he had last visited, except when rain drummed hard on his back and he became a dull bluish gray. His ears turned back slightly at the top, so that they no longer fitted snugly against the side of his neck. His penis became surrounded by loosed wrinkled skin until it was difficult to distinguish his sex at first glimpse.

His male character, on the other hand, developed very obviously and before his first year was out he was mounting other calves in infantile sex play, becoming sufficiently excited for his male organ to regain temporarily its former prominence. Never did I see a female calf mount a male this way. It was the earliest fundamental difference in behavior between the two sexes, occurring some thirteen years before any possibility of true sexual consummation.

At one year old N'Dume stood 3 ft. 9 in., one-third taller than his birth height. For the first time I noticed traces of the oily pungent musth secretion in his cheek. It did not wet his cheek permanently but appeared intermittently. It is never found in calves in their first year but can be seen with increasing frequency as they grow older. Whatever its mysterious function it does not seem to be necessary to the very young.

As N'Dume grew he became more dexterous in his movements and more playful. Also his relationship with his mother underwent some subtle changes. He began to wander at ever increasing distances from her. In part this was due to the natural growth of his independence, while simultaneously his mother became increasingly indifferent to the moment to moment activities of her calf. Where before she would have come rushing to his side if he were knocked over by a large boisterous calf, now she let him fight his own battles. From intensive mothering the relationship changed and N'Dume had to keep up or get left behind.

One hot afternoon when the family were drowsing through their siesta, he lay down on a bed of cool earth at the foot of an acacia tree surrounded by a ring of trunks and legs. He was soon fast asleep. Leonora usually rested for an hour or so before moving to the next patch of shade, but today for some reason she was restless and soon ambled off with Slender Tusks close by her side. The other youngsters scrambled to their feet, but N'Dume slumbered on and was soon left all alone except for Leonora's eldest immature daughter, Two Holes, who stood over him. She rumbled but he did not awaken. Then she tickled his tummy with her forefoot and trunk and he leapt to his feet, realizing that his mother had gone. Were it not for Two Holes he would have been left behind; or perhaps Slender Tusks knew that Two Holes would look after him. Two Holes had developed a special maternal interest for the young calf and was almost always near him. If she had any chance of doing so, she would straddle him rumbling with what appeared to be pleasure.

Then there was the time when he fell sick, and I found him moaning continually, as if he were in great pain. This was in the evening at feeding time, and while the rest of the family stuffed grass into their mouths he kept walking around and around in circles, opening his mouth to groan but not to eat. Only Two Holes seemed concerned, and between taking mouthfuls of rich fodder walked up to him and placed a reassuring trunk on his forehead. During about a week N'Dume grew quite thin. Then the moaning stopped but still he didn't eat very well. Eventually his appetite returned, but I never found out what had been wrong with him. Since I could only have examined him by postmortem I was very happy to remain in ignorance.

Slender Tusks' apparent indifference did not mean

that she would not have helped him had he been in serious trouble. She merely seemed to know that so long as he was somewhere in the confines of the family unit, he was safe. Should he need her he could call for help, and then she would have rallied instantly to his defense. In fact, when they met hyenas in the river bed below camp she trumpeted furiously and she, Leonora and the others bunched instantly, restraining their calves, and pulling them inward with their trunks. Finally Slender Tusks made a sortie, and while the others guarded the calves, she chased off the potential predators.

She was already an experienced mother by the time she had N'Dume, for she had three older calves still following her. Younger mothers, in particular those with their first born, are far more solicitous and run after their calves to a much greater degree. Like inexperienced human mothers, they have not learned to take the raising of children as a semiautomatic repetitive routine and are still fascinated with the experience of maternity.

Boadicea, as an elephant mother, appeared to be overanxious and too busy watching out for imagined dangers that might threaten the security of her kinship group. Even the sound of a car was enough to stop her feeding, and she seldom suckled her new-born calf. Consequently, it did not survive its first year, but, if anything, this was an example of death caused by too many tourists rather than too many elephants.

Differences between calves are also very marked. Some are very independent, and from their first few weeks set out intrepidly to explore their environment, others remain glued to their mother's side. Some are high-spirited and playful, others are listless. One exceptional calf in another family unit spent most of its first year away from its mother by the side of the matriarch Sphinx, who was pregnant and already flowing with milk. Her own calf was born three months after the other calf had adopted her and the two became like twins, playing, sucking, running and sleeping together, all under Sphinx's careful eye. The abandoned mother in this case had to come to the matriarch's side if she wanted her own calf to pay her any attention.

Like all young elephants N'Dume's brain at birth was only 35% of the weight it would reach when he was fully grown. Most other mammals are born with a brain nearer the adult weight. An elephant's brain grows slowly, and because of this period of prolonged immaturity during which learning plays a crucial role, its eventual development is all the greater. The same is true of human beings where the lengthening of child-hood and the delaying of the age of puberty are factors associated with the evolution of intelligence.

All the time N'Dume was growing he was learning. His movements were experimental and often comic, he adopted dozens of postures that adults seldom use, and only later did he learn to coordinate his motor patterns. Slowly he learned to sprawl on his tummy, roll on his back, drag his hind legs like a wounded buck, and sit up like a dog with his ears hanging down.

His trunk caused him great problems. Even drinking with it was a mystery and during the first year he knelt at the river's edge, holding the tip of his trunk out of the water and drank with his mouth, as do all very young calves. Gradually, fiddling with his trunk in the water and sucking the tip, by trial and error he learned how to suck up water, hold it in his trunk as he raised it, and then pour it down his throat. Many times he got sand up his trunk where it seemed to irritate him so that he shook the tip and wiggled it in knots. He learned to hang, swing and twirl his trunk, and slowly exploring every possibility became more adept in its uses.

An elephant's trunk is a most versatile instrument. Derived from a combination of upper lip and nose it possesses thousands of muscles, each of which needs the appropriate orders from the central nervous system to function. No wonder it took N'Dume a long time to master its intricate possibilities. When it itched inside he could roll it under a forefoot; at its tip were tiny little hairs which were probably useful for feeling the shape, texture and temperature of things or perhaps in locating the precise bearing of a scent on the wind.

Slender Tusks used her trunk with great precision, often in combination with her feet or her tusks. She could use it as a scoop for removing sand which she had loosened with her toes, when digging for water, or she could pluck grass by holding it in place while her toes cut across the stems in a sweep. If the roots came up full of dirt she beat them against her shins until they were clean. When stripping a tree her trunk would be used to grab the shreds of bark and exert a steady pull while the tusks pushed, levered and chiseled. If one of her eyes needed massaging she would rub it in a sinuous rolling motion, and her trunk also anointed her back with mud and dusted it with sand.

On one occasion I saw another elephant pick up a twig in his trunk and scratch his leg with it, an example of yet another animal that uses tools. All these activities did not appear early in N'Dume's behavioral repertoire, many were only learned with the passage of time. Sometimes it looked as if he were watching Slender Tusks and deliberately imitating her motions, though I could not prove this. Occasionally he put his trunk up into her mouth and sampled what she was eating, pulling some of it out and then chewing and swallowing it. This is probably the way in which calves learn what to eat. The same action develops into a greeting gesture which elephants use when approaching a superior. A first-year calf may greet a fully grown bull this way should it temporarily wander into his family.

N'Dume also learned fear. When he was very young he once rushed right up to my Land-Rover and threatened it with his little ears wide apart, head raised and piggy eyes squinting aggressively. He was not in the least afraid until he noticed he was alone. Slender Tusks, watching his performance some twenty paces back, twirled her trunk anxiously. Then suddenly he lost heart and rushed back to his mother's side, with his tail in the air, squealing. He never again approached.

At other times Slender Tusks seemed to moderate his fear, by touching him with her trunk in what appeared to be a gesture of reassurance until he calmed down. Two Holes was also protective, and once when a tourist car swept around a corner and startled N'Dume into a panic-stricken run that took him away from his family, Two Holes raced after him, headed him off and pushed him back in the right direction with her trunk under his chin, the tip in his mouth.

At two years the pearly tips of his milk tusks appeared briefly before dropping out to reveal the permanent tusks hard behind them. This moment varies greatly from one calf to another and unfortunately cannot be used as an ageing criterion. Naturally, like all young things he was eager to try out a new-found capacity and now participated, rather ineffectively, in the general scraping of ivory against bark when the family next stripped an *Acacia tortilis* tree. He also butted his elder brothers, sisters and cousins, and the new sharp point gave him a serious weapon and an ability to inflict pain, but at the same time a social inhibition seemed to grow against the all-out use of these weapons.

His social education was an important part of his survival equipment. Quick reactions to the reactions of others in a moment of danger or the knowledge of how to behave in a competitive situation with another elephant all needed to be learned.

These social encounters usually begin with two little elephants wrapping their trunks around each other in an embrace followed by a pushing match, although often the calves are of such uneven ages that the result is a foregone conclusion. But rather than shoving the smaller one roughly the bigger will use the minimum force necessary to achieve his object. The younger the calf the gentler is the procedure.

As the months passed N'Dume came to know his little world and all the elephants that lived in it. His kinship group pursued its never-ending cycle quartering the home range, up to the forest to eat fallen figs, then down to Endabash for the delicious vegetation of the swamps that survived the dry season and afterwards back to the acacia woodlands in time for the annual pod crop. The matriarchs, Boadicea, Leonora and Jezebel, each with their separate brood, followed each other, usually keeping station a few hundred yards apart, but often intermingling when they came together at the river or on the beach in the evenings.

This was a time of great excitement for the calves, and they would race around in large play groups, hopelessly mixed up so that I could no longer distinguish to which family each calf belonged. In their rough and tumble play they resembled puppies and took on all sorts of elaborate three, four, or five-cornered combinations. If the level of aggression ever threatened to get out of hand there was usually a nearby mother or adolescent female who would sidle effortlessly into their midst and single out her calf to be eased away.

N'Dume knew his own family intimately, and was soon familiar with every one of the members of the Boadicea kinship group; he had in addition a passing acquaintance with the roughly five hundred other elephants that shared parts of his home range, and whom his family unit met from time to time.

The blissful period of tolerance passed and as N'Dume grew older he encountered occasional hostility not only from his peers, but from Slender Tusks herself. It was at the water-holes that they came into conflict. Certain springs were highly favored by the elephants, probably for their mineral content, and at these there was often space for only one elephant to drink at a time. Also in the dry season when the Ndala River percolated beneath the sand the elephants could only obtain water from a limited number of holes which they scooped out with their trunks.

N'Dume didn't seem to be able to accept the idea that Slender Tusks was not digging the water-holes exclusively for his own personal use. He would insist on pushing in on her while she tried to siphon water up her trunk in a controlled flow, slowly enough not to suck up quantities of sand.

The trouble was that in his clumsiness he would inevitably crumble the edge of the sandy hole so that Slender Tusks had to dig it all over again. She was very skillful at keeping him out with the minimum effort. I once watched her shove him away with her trunk eighteen times in five minutes. He would grumble his protest in a sort of squall, and she would rumble at him to keep away. Slender Tusks also used her feet to thwart N'Dume's attempts to gain the hole. He would lean against the foot and try to get around it, and when that failed just collapse in a heap with his trunk still creeping like a hopeful caterpillar along the ground towards water. When Slender Tusks raised her head he sometimes found a chance to insinuate his long nose just enough to get a sip before he was once more shoved out.

Slender Tusks' rather selfish behavior was typical of all mother-calf relationships. If there was competition for something to eat the mother would almost always take the desired food, by force if she were in a position to do so. With water it was the same—altruism was restricted to mutual defense and did not extend to the sharing of food and water. Older calves were often treated more roughly, although the tolerance of cows showed great variation, as with suckling. I have sometimes seen older calves forcibly removed from a water-hole with a vigorous prod of the tusks so that blood was drawn and they bellowed with pain.

Calves over five years old usually do not attempt to push into a large female's water-hole, so they do not get jabbed out. On several occasions I observed an older calf waiting for more than an hour before it could get a drink. When they have quenched their thirst the older cows walk away leaving the calves maybe only a few minutes in which to gulp down some water before rejoining their family. Also it is not uncommon for another family unit, which has been waiting for the first to finish, to arrive and push away the waiting calves before they have had the chance to drink at all.

I was only able to follow N'Dume's development for two and a half years from his birth in March 1968 to the day I left in September 1970. He was then full of health and energy but still very dependent on his mother and family. I did see both him and his family again in March 1973 as I describe in my postscript.

The older calves that I studied showed that for at least the first ten years of their life elephants continue to be nurtured by the love and protection of their family. Even when the next sibling is born, the older calf still receives plenty of affection from his mother which goes on until adolescence and in some cases long beyond.

The calves continue to play and fight, improving in skill all the time. They learn to use a slope to their advantage, so that each can press down more effectively on his opponent. Occasionally, the play becomes serious and loses its harmless nature; then their movements become rapid and jerky with the weight of the body behind each thrust, but this is a rare occurrence and normally their encounters are characterized by gentleness, and the vanquished merely receives a slight prod in his flank as he turns away. However, should an obstacle such as a fallen tree come between the two contestants during their play fight then they will suddenly threaten with redoubled fury, each knowing that in fact it cannot get to grips with the other. Their behavior is rather like that of dogs barking at each other through a fence.

Play-fighting must be of functional significance to an elephant; probably it teaches an animal its exact strength relative to the others that inhabit the same area. In this way, through friendly contests in which animals do not get hurt, a hierarchy originates in which each individual knows its place. The experience gained in the techniques of maneuvering and thrusting may also help an individual to win if it does get into a serious fight. In later life when competitive situations occur over water or food, the dispute is usually settled by a mere threat display which may be no more than the extension of the ears or the wave of a trunk in the direction of the opponent. Serious fighting is extremely rare. Threat in elephants, as in so many species, appears to protect an animal from actually being attacked.

As adolescence approaches, at about the age of eleven to thirteen years, bull calves indulge in vigorous play-fighting, interspersed with bouts of mounting each other and the female calves. This is the last burst of activity before they become totally independent and leave the family units for ever. Their story I discovered fully when I started radio-tracking.

Female calves at puberty become increasingly reluctant to fight with their brothers and male cousins, and become more and more maternal to the younger calves. Two Holes showed this tendency and if she played it was only with calves that were much younger than herself. Sometimes she would roll over on her side next to N'Dume and the other young calves, holding out her trunk as if soliciting them to come and crawl over her. When they approached she would fence them off for a while before allowing them to clamber up her rounded sides, often to slip from the top in a mass of sprawling limbs and flailing trunks. At times if fights between small calves began to get serious she would intervene by putting her trunk between the combatants until the intensity of their aggression subsided.

Mothers sometimes resented the attitude of these teenage "nannies." This was particularly the case in younger mothers with their first calf, but the "nannies" were undoubtedly useful, as when Two Holes woke up the sleeping N'Dume and prevented him from being left behind. Simultaneously, she was probably gaining valuable experience for the time when she herself would become a mother.

There was nothing in the treatment of N'Dume to suggest that older elephants were hostile or neglectful of him because of the population density. On the contrary he was almost invariably treated with kindness and tolerance. If social causes were to limit the population then it was not through maltreatment of young calves. In the older age groups, however, aggression was more readily seen. The effect of this later became clear during the period that I tracked Boadicea's kinship group intensively.

From 1966 to 1967 thirty-four calves were born to my special sample of ninety-eight cows. Only eight had been born the year before. It became apparent that the birth rate fluctuated wildly, and only long-term information would be valid for statistics. Eventually, I came to the same conclusion Richard Laws had reached in Uganda, that the better the rains the more cows would conceive. This explained some of the unevenness which I detected in the age structure. The size of the population would also depend on the number of deaths. I intended to balance the death rate against the birth rate at the end of my study to see exactly what was happening to elephant numbers at Manyara.

In the meanwhile I also wanted to know how movements affected the elephant density. For this I needed some method of following elephants in the thick and dangerous Endabash thickets, which led to potential routes that wound up out of the Park to the Marang Forest. Radio-tracking equipment might be the answer.

Dr. Richard Laws had immobilized a couple of cows and placed radio-collars around their necks, but the collars had not been strong enough and had fallen off, one a day later, the other after eleven days. Further experiment would clearly be necessary.

# 7

## Radio-Elephants

After my encounter near Endabash Waterfall with the rhino, I avoided foot patrols in the southern area for here the type of vegetation made observation both dangerous and unsatisfactory. The result was that while by now I knew a great deal about the elephants in the north and their range, I couldn't even identify all the elephants in the Endabash region.

This was because the strange, fierce southern elephants who lived there scarcely ever came out of the tangled bush, and when visiting elephants from the north entered it they simply disappeared.

When one day I confessed to Hugh Lamprey that I didn't know all the elephants in the Park he replied, "Well Iain, you had better get to know them. You have chosen your method and you had better make it work."

After this, however much I disliked the idea, there was going to be no alternative to penetrating the thickets and meeting the Endabash elephants on their own ground. I did force myself to walk back to the exact spot where I had met the rhinos, this time with Mhoja and the big gun, but there was a group of Endabash elephants in possession, who set up a loud commotion as soon as our scent was carried to them on the breeze, and when we tried to work our way around them, we bumped into another rhino. Luckily he crashed off in the opposite direction, probably because that was the way he happened to be pointing at the time.

Down some of the trails it was possible to force a passage with the Land-Rover until it brought one to the river where they had come to drink. Here I waited for thirsty elephants to come, but often the wind changed; I was then upwind and nothing would induce an Endabash elephant to come anywhere near the water because of the smell of the car or of man. On other days I simply chose the wrong spot for that day's drinking.

It was therefore with a feeling of relief that one day I encountered Queen Victoria who had come down to this area attracted by the sweet ripe *Balanites aegyptica* fruits, known as desert dates, that were then in full fruit. I had a friend, Katie Newlin, a member of the American Peace Corps, staying for the weekend. She was delighted to see elephants at such close quarters. The whole family was following a bull who went from one tree to another, putting his trunk up each and shaking it until the fruit tumbled down in a shower. Victoria's family would then rush up and join in the feast which the bull tolerated in a good-natured way. Only the elephants' backs were visible above the bush as my stripped-down Land-Rover edged toward them. Mary, the other large old cow in this family, standing in a small clearing, barely looked up from her food, but she shook her head in mild irritation when a thicket splintered as I drove over it. I was glad to see them as they had been missing for over a month.

Mhoja, standing in the back, spotted another group, composed of strangers, which he could see through the foliage. I drove toward them crushing branches in the way. In front of me a young female with a small calf whom I could not recognize, ran off in alarm, behind a gardenia bush. Seconds later a huge, bow-tusked female came headlong around the gardenia and without uttering a sound, nor pausing in her stride, plunged her tusks up to the gums into the body of my Land-

Rover. Mhoja, and a temporary laborer Simeon, who had remained standing in the back just behind the cab, saw the tusks appear beneath their feet and with the huge shape looming over them, jumped out of the car and vanished into the bush.

The first shock threw the car half around. The elephant pulled her tusks out and thrust them in again.

"Don't get out of the car," I shouted to Katie. She lay down on the floor.

Now more elephants with babies in the forefront burst out of the bush on the right and joined in the attack. A three-year-old calf butted the mudguard and then stood back bewildered. Fortunately, because of our relative sizes, only three elephants could concentrate on the Land-Rover at one time, but it was enough. It felt half-way between being a rugger ball in a scrum, and a dinghy overtaken by three contradictory tidal waves. The car teetered on the point of balance but just missed overturning. Tusks were thrust in and withdrawn with great vigor. Loud and continuous trumpeting rent the air, together with that fatal sound of tearing metal. However, I was not thinking just then of what John Owen would say about my new Park's Land-Rover, because an enormous brown eye embedded in gnarled skin with long eyelashes materialized through the upper door. This belonged to a cow who was using the weight of her head to force down the roof of the cab. The cab cracked and gave, but then held firm, while her tusks ripped sideways across the door. I could have touched the eye with my fingers. To my relief it disappeared without apparently perceiving that it had been looking at the undamaged brain of this metal animal. I could imagine her picking off our heads just like bananas off a bunch.

A huge latecomer with as much zeal as the rest put together now came into contact with the front. One wing folded up like paper and a tusk went through the radiator. She stabbed again and wrenched her embedded tusks upwards like a demented fork lift. Then digging her tusks in again she charged, and the Land-

Rover was carried backwards at high speed for thirty-five yards until it squashed up against an ant heap surmounted by a small tree.

They left us now at rest, adorning the ant heap, and retired thirty yards where they formed a tight circle and after a few excited trumpets and growls, dissolved into the bush, with streaks of green paint on their tusks.

My Peace Corps friend picked herself up and dusted her blouse. She was a little shaken, but unharmed, and accepted the situation with sang-froid. My first awful thought was what had happened to Mhoja. The only responses to my shouts and whistles was sullen rumblings. The car looked a write-off, but I pressed the starter and to my amazement it worked. One tire was punctured, a tusk had passed clean through it, and twisted metal scraped against one of the front wheels. However, it was possible to lever the metal away and we limped off on the flat tire to begin our morbid search. Elephants were all around but their destructive rage appeared to be sated.

At the first point of impact we stopped. There was no bloody smear on the ground here nor even a chip of ivory. I stood on the Land-Rover and shouted again. A faint mocking echo came back from the woodlands, or was it a shout? I drove on deeper into the bush and tried again. This time there was a definite answer. Eventually, after about a mile, Mhoja's green uniform materialized out of the twilight.

We were both relieved to see each other, and in the relaxation of tension, doubled up with laughter. Mhoja described how he had dodged between the legs of the oncoming elephants and around bushes and had to run after Simeon, trying to stop him. Simeon's one thought was to get to the escarpment and climb up it and out of this horrible place with so many wild animals and it took Mhoja a mile to catch him. They were starting on their way back to see what had become of us when they heard my shout.

In the excitement of this attack I had been so engrossed with the elephant activities that I had not even looked at their features in any great detail.

"Who were they?" Mhoja asked.

It was dreadful to admit it, but I did not know. I could only make a pretty good guess. Only once before had I seen an attack that started with no threat display in total silence, and that had come from four equally large cows. It must have been the Torone sisters. The silence of the attack was uncanny. The lack of hesitation contrasted strongly with the normal threat behavior of the Lake Manyara elephants. However, it is a theory of ethologists that threat displays evolve from behavior that originates in conflict situations. In the case of elephants, swinging the forefoot, throwing dirt over the head or at the object of aggression, twiddling the trunk and tossing the head, are examples of such behavior. It is easy to see how they develop into threat displays.

A possible explanation of the presumed Torone leader's direct, silent and unhesitating attack is that she felt no internal conflict. Alternatively, it is possible that when she first swung around the gardenia tree she was going too fast to stop, and only encountered me visually after the critical distance had been crossed within which an animal fights for its life to destroy what it considers to be an aggressor. Lion tamers know about this distance and come close enough to lions to elicit ferocious snarls and growls, always taking care not to cross the threshold where defense switches in a flash to outright attack. I was interested also to see that they had used their advantage of weight to lean on and try to crush their adversary. We escaped lightly that time. The Land-Rover was not seriously damaged and after some panel beating, the patching of a number of round holes, and the installation of a new radiator, the car was almost as good as new. I thought of armor-plating the door, through which the tusks had narrowly missed me, but in the end it was too much trouble.

After the rhino incident in Endabash and the Torone's attack on my car I continued to search for safe ways of plotting elephant movements. First, I tried a tracking experiment.

The bed of the Ndala River was a smooth sandy stretch from the base of the waterfall to the river mouth on the Lake shore. Tracks of animals that crossed north or south showed up clearly. Mhoja and I went down on several mornings in succession and counted how many elephants had crossed in each direction. When they had passed in single file we took great care to sort out how many footmarks of different diameters we could score. Some elephants would wander up the river in a zig-zag which looked as if many more had crossed in both directions than was actually the case. However, it was interesting incidental information and I divided the river up into four sections on the map.

Mhoja walked down early every morning, scrutinizing the patterns in the sand and came back with his report of what animals had passed in the previous twenty-four hours. If Manyara had contained few elephants it was a method that would have worked well, but with 450 elephants passing backward and forward across this half-way mark, and sometimes the same elephants making the journey several times in one day, the wealth of tracks became impossible to separate or interpret reliably. In any case the experiment came to an abrupt end.

One morning I watched Mhoja hopping over the rocks with his nonchalant, long-legged gait, his gun across both shoulders behind his neck, until he disappeared behind the first bend. Five minutes later I heard a booming report of the heavy .470 Rigby, and then silence. I leapt into the car and drove by the track down to the Ndala bridge, and there on one side of the bridge stood an angry lioness twitching her tail and staring at Mhoja, who leaned against a pillar on the other side, smoking a cigarette and keeping her covered with his gun. I drove up beside him and he jumped into the car.

He told me that he had just reached the edge of the bridge and put his gun down to light his cigarette when he glanced up and saw a lioness charging him at high speed about fifteen paces away. He grabbed the gun and with great restraint loosed off a shot from the hip into the ground just in front of the lioness less than two paces away. It stopped her alive in her tracks, but she was still furiously demonstrating when I arrived.

Once Mhoja was concealed in the Land-Rover she loped back into the bush where we could make out other lionesses and the corpse of a buffalo which they had killed during the night. Chongo, the one-eyed lion, was there, looking rather thin and eating ravenously. His big companion Dume Kubwa had vanished, probably shot by hunters when he wandered out of the Park. Chongo had to defend his territory against strange males who appeared for the first time, but then Satima returned fully grown and they teamed up together. In the meantime the two prides of lionesses still did most of the hunting.

After the narrow escapes we had already survived I decided we could take no more risks and rather than sending Mhoja out alone every day, it would be better to abandon the tracking experiment.

Soon after these rather alarming experiences my chance came to follow the elephant movements in what I hoped would be a safer way.

Over in the Serengeti, George Schaller and Hans Kruuk were in contact with an American electronics expert called Howard Baldwin, whom they had engaged to make radio transmitters suitable for tracking lions and hyenas. When I heard one day that he had arrived in the Serengeti I went straight over to meet him and asked him if he could spare one of his radios for an elephant.

Howard Baldwin is a man fired by wild enthusiasms to do unusual things and he needed no persuasion. He thought he could adapt the lion equipment to withstand the rigors of elephant life, so long as we could first catch our elephant.

Fortunately, there was a vet in East Africa who had spent the previous ten years or so perfecting methods of immobilizing elephants. His name was Toni Harthoorn. He was already associated with George Schaller's project, advising on the dosage rates of tranquilizing drugs, and he too immediately consented to come.

Toni arrived early one morning with his attractive dark-haired wife Sue. They were a most entertaining couple. I took them on an introductory tour to meet Boadicea, always an acid test for my visitors, and after the initial impact of one of her shock threat charges the Harthoorns habituated rapidly, and settled down to enjoy the subtle interactions of mothers and infants, ignoring the occasional demonstrations of matriarchs.

Howard, who had arrived the night before, remained in camp all day tuning the elephant radios and receivers, testing walkie-talkies, and delving into a large trunkful of wonderful American tools which he applied to his equipment making scores of last-minute adjustments.

We had three guns suitable for projecting the flying syringe, which would automatically inject its contents on impact with an elephant. Toni had brought a powder-charged gun that could be fired from a distance, and a gas-powered pistol for extremely short ranges. A Capchur gun operated by compressed carbon dioxide would take care of the intermediate ranges.

It was agreed that I would do the driving, Toni the shooting and Howard, his wife and Sue, would stay in a second Land-Rover, ready to be called up on the walkie-talkie as soon as the elephant was down.

A fruitless morning introduced my guests to the Lake shore alive with pelicans and wading birds, to the escarpment fragrant with crushed sage brush under our wheels, to the forest shaded in solemn green, and to the woodlands where Satima, Chongo and their lionesses lay gorged above the remains of yet another buffalo, but nowhere did we catch sight of tusk or hide of an elephant.

It was not until afternoon we sighted some bulls and cow-calf family units near the Ndala River mouth. They must have been hiding near camp in the one corner of the woodlands where we had not looked. I selected a well-known peaceable bull named Chisel Tusks as our target. He was mature and independent, and I thought it unlikely that any other elephant would come to his aid. I wanted our first transistorized elephant to be a success, which seemed more likely to be the case with a docile character, after which I hoped to move on to more ambitious targets like the Torone sisters. We had decided to avoid cows and calves until we had gained some experience, since they were more likely to defend each other.

Thirty yards distant Toni fired at Chisel Tusks through the window. The dart flew through the air and embedded itself in the bull's rump, clearly visible there as a sliver of silver with a red tuft at the end. Chisel Tusks jerked forward and rushed in the direction of some bushes, where he disappeared. There was no hope of following by car so we went on foot. Many elephants were around and we moved cautiously between them.

I rediscovered the excitement of hunting. We had our prey to follow until he dropped, and he had to be kept in sight. Nothing must be allowed to disturb him, the wind must be tested and other elephants remain unalarmed. Soon our quarry slowed to a gentle amble and then stopped under a tree. We waited for the drug to take effect. Twenty-seven minutes after darting, Chisel Tusks swayed from side to side. His eyes closed, he hung his head and his hindquarters started to droop. Then he awoke with a jerk and started to walk once more. I asked Toni to go back to the car and take a track which would head him off. In the meanwhile I followed alone creeping from one tree to the next, always seeking to keep him in view. He teamed up with another bull and all the while his movements became more lively. After one and a half hours from the striking of the dart he seemed to be fully recovered and I left him.

There was not enough daylight left to repeat the action so we postponed operations to the next day.

That evening we discussed the question of increasing the dose. Toni was against endangering an elephant's life, even though we might have a quicker success. I felt the same. The margin between an ineffective dose and a lethal one might be narrow. I remember that years before in the Serengeti a wildebeest had been accidentally killed with an overdose of succinyl choline chloride, a widely used but dangerous narcotic. Yet the drug we were using, M99, had been successfully employed in the South African National Parks a few years previously to immobilize thirty-one elephants, with only one fatality.

There followed six days of frustration. Toni had perfected the technique of darting with a reliable powder-charged gun that could be fired at a distance. Unfortunately the trees and bush at Manyara were so thick that elephants usually only became visible at ranges so short that the gun might well drive the dart right into the body. The only time we did try a long distance shot the report was so loud and sharp that all the elephants within earshot stampeded. One young animal tripped and drove its foot-long tusks into the ground letting out a pained bellow. Meanwhile our selected bull started forward and crashed into a tree. It picked itself up and limped away. Luckily the damage was not serious and next day it was fine, but I loathed the unnecessary disturbance and wondered if I was not getting a bad reputation with the elephants.

We fell back on the old Capchur gun, but after years of service with a former Warden it now leaked badly, and the compressed gas escaped inaudibly. The result was that one day when Toni pressed the trigger with a bull in his sights it misfired. Instead of an explosive "phut" there was a sibilant hiss. We couldn't see where the dart had gone, but there was no time to look for it because the bull had remained stationary, an ideal target.

While Toni loaded a new dart, I put some fresh gas powerlets into the gun. Toni took a second shot. There was a muffled crack and suddenly it looked as if Toni had fixed a bayonet, for there was the tip of the first dart poking out of the top of the barrel.

Howard came to the rescue with his technical expertise. He dug both darts out and back at camp dismantled the Capchur gun and inserted extemporary gas seals until it was completely gas-tight.

Yet we were still dogged by failure. One dart bounced off after a perfect shot. Another time the needle snapped on contact; Howard solved this problem too, by manufacturing new reinforced needles which did not break. In yet another case we lodged a dart ideally in the muscle of the shoulder, but the elephant showed no ill effects for two hours. He eventually rubbed the dart off on a tree and when we picked it up we found that the detonator, which was supposed to fire on impact and drive the drug solution into the animal, had not gone off. Another bull became very drowsy and eventually collapsed only to rise again and walk off, something which Toni had never seen before.

When it appeared that Manyara's elephants were more resistant to the drug M99 than any elephants he had previously encountered, Toni gradually increased the dose rate.

We were a determined and compatible team; had we not been we would never have persisted in our tedious succession of failures. When our drug supply was exhausted I drove to Serengeti to beg some more from Hugh Lamprey, who gave it generously from his own stock. It was a rare commodity at that time, but Hugh was keen that this radio-tracking should succeed. It was my responsibility to select the elephant and to keep it in sight after the dart had gone home.

This was extremely important because if the animal should subside on its belly it might easily die, since the pressure of its guts against the diaphragm might prevent it from breathing. There was also a risk of it overheating if we were not able to pour water over its ears. These act as an extremely efficient cooling organ, as later experiments were to show.

We shot and followed almost entirely from the car. Toni was averse to foot work after the experience of another keen elephant immobilizer, Ted Goss, a Warden of the Meru National Park in Kenya. Ted Goss had done some immobilizations with Toni and then later on his own. Unfortunately his study was interrupted when he approached a bull which he thought was standing in a dreamlike trance of immobility. The bull was still awake enough to chase him and when he tripped, to seize him with its trunk and trample him —shattering his thigh before he could crawl to safety. Up till that day Toni and others had always approached bulls when they were still standing.

At the end of a long and disappointing day during which we had not managed to get a proper shot at a bull we encountered the matriarch Victoria and her family in open *Acacia tortilis* woodland. None of the animals was really suitable for immobilization but, hoping for the best, I chose a male calf of eight years, the son of the huge and beautiful old cow Mary. With luck I thought she would be more concerned with her younger calves, and might abandon him to be radiotagged by us.

Victoria's was a cohesive, highly integrated family unit with five mature females and their calves, numbering sixteen in all. I knew them well, and it would have been very interesting to follow them.

Behind these came Florence and her family of eleven who were members of the same kinship group. At the same time the three family units of the Boadicea kinship group were walking in parallel a mere 150 paces to one side; forty elephants in close formation. The two kinship groups met and consorted very frequently, and I saw them together on over fifty separate days, so they must have known each other well. Yet statistical tests showed that they were not together more often than might be attributed to chance, so I had no reason to suppose they were closely related.

The relative position, degree of intermingling and numbers of each family unit are sketched below.

The dart struck the calf in the loose skin below the armpit, apparently hitting an insensitive spot, as he neither checked his stride nor made a noise. One adult cow in his family unit, Kali Ears, swung her head towards the "phut" of the Capchur gun, but continued to walk slowly at the same pace and in the same direction as before.

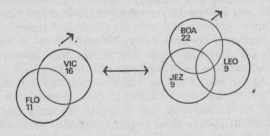

For exactly twelve minutes the calf walked on normally, until suddenly he keeled over flat on his side. Immediately Mary, who was nearest to him, swung around and trumpeted. She rushed forward to investigate, extending her trunk in his direction, her ears flapping forward. All the other cows converged until they surrounded the calf, with their ears out and heads down, trumpeting and growling. Anna, a female from the Florence family unit looked in our direction but appeared to decide that we were not connected with the fuss, since she made no demonstration. Loud trumpeting and growling continued.

Boadicea, Leonora and Jezebel and their family units charged over on a broad front to join Victoria and Florence around the fallen calf. I tried to head them off but only succeeded in stirring them up to a coordinated demonstration. They stampeded on the ground, threw up dust, screamed and smashed bushes. I could see Kali Ears and Mary trying to lift the calf while Victoria, the matriarch, paced back and forth between us and them. The calf never lost consciousness and his trunk moved up toward these great mothers each time they tried to lever him into a standing position.

They would not leave him alone. Their movements were violent and they jerked him upward so that he fell back with a crash each time. I was afraid they might hurt him. Each of the three cows made an attempt in turn and together. They leaned their bodies together at acute angles and formed a solid wall between us and the calf. The three families of the Boadicea kinship group were completely integrated in this phalanx of sixty-seven united elephants.

The young milled around, backed into each other and charged into space in a vacuum release of aggressive drive, all the while trumpeting, groaning, bellowing and growling in an indescribable and continuous confusion of noises, some of them remarkably human. I tried half-heartedly to drive them off, but Toni was very much against any attempt, and I had no idea how elephants would react in such a novel situation. We therefore withdrew to watch from a distance. A pall of dust had been thrown up in the air through which came the now intermittent sounds of turmoil.

To our astonishment, three-quarters of an hour after the collapse of the calf, the parental family unit, Victoria's, including the mother Mary, and the members of Florence's family unit wandered away, leaving the unrelated BOA-LEO-JEZ kinship group guarding the calf. This they did in exactly the same way as his own group, other big cows trying to raise him, one after another. Forty-five minutes later Victoria and Mary reappeared with their family and resumed their attempts to lift the calf. Gradually, with their help, he began to raise his forequarters; but every so often collapsed. Disturbed dust throwing and trumpeting continued at a reduced level.

Finally much to our relief the calf rose to his feet and stayed up. All the females of the five family units mixed once more in a huge conglomeration curious to find out how he had fared. Many came up and touched him with their trunks. It was now almost dark, and with the knowledge that we had made a bad mistake, and narrowly avoided killing an elephant, we left them two hours after the calf first went down.

The Harthoorns had already postponed their departure twice, and now Howard was due to leave. Immediate success was needed or the whole exercise would be wasted.

On the last possible day we set out from the camp a good deal less optimistic than on the first morning. However, just north of the Ndala River, we soon located a loose assemblage of several family units, including the huge cross tusker, Sarah, and some independent bulls.

We drove up to an outlier and put a dart well in his flank, where it hung as if it had gone off. He was known as M4/3, a number which through repetition acquired its own familiarity and significance, so that I never properly renamed him. He ran back into the middle of the cows and calves but they continued grazing, browsing and walking and presently he began to lag.

A young cow called Eleanor (not to be confused with her namesake, the famous orphan of Tsavo whose story is told by Daphne Scheldrick) seemed to sense there was something wrong with him, approached, and felt his face and ears with her trunk, then resting her tusks on his forehead pushed him gently backwards. It looked like a gesture of reassurance to a sick animal. Her two calves also touched him with their trunks. The young bull had stopped and now swayed from side to side, picking up grass and throwing it away. From time to time he touched the dart in his shoulder with his trunk. Meanwhile Eleanor left him to catch up with Sarah, her matriarch, who had wandered on with the other family units.

M4/3's hind legs now began to buckle, but all the time he was putting up a determined fight against the effect of the drug. As it seemed to be taking too long for him to go down, Toni shot another dart at him. It bounced straight back. He put in another, and then when that did not work, another, so that he had a cluster of darts in a three-inch group in his left shoulder, with red, yellow and blue tail feathers.

It was more than an hour since the first dart had gone in, when Toni put in one final dart into his left rump and he started to lurch backwards in decreasing circles. It was unbelievable to see him leaning back at such an angle without going down, but still he swayed and resisted.

At this point Toni abandoned caution, and leaping out of the car grabbed the elephant by the tail and tried to pull him down backward but, however unstable the young bull looked, his mass was so great as to make Toni's efforts negligible. At last in his own time he subsided but still remained conscious, his trunk twirling defensively in our direction as we closed in with collar and instruments.

I immediately doused him with water on the back of his ears and along his flanks. Howard had already clambered on his neck to insert a temperature probe under the skin, which had a wire running to its own transmitter in a pad that had to be tied with thread to his head. Sue handed instruments to Howard who was sitting just above the reach of the young bull's trunk, which searched inquiringly backward, while Toni took blood samples. Meanwhile Mhoja and I now tried to get the collar, which had the major transmitter attached to it, under the elephant's neck, at the same time avoiding his flailing trunk.

Howard took some time putting in his last stitches. The pad and the probe would need all the attachment they could get if they were to withstand even a few hours of elephant life. The elephant's eyes slowly closed and his breathing grew stertorous. He was lying on his belly which was dangerous. He looked pretty bad now, his breathing was only just observable.

"Quick, get the rope," yelled Toni. "Put it round his tusk and tie it to the Land-Rover, then pull him on his side."

I hooked him up as quickly as possible and by rocking the Land-Rover back and forth we heaved his ponderous bulk over.

Immediately he gave a deep sigh and a few rapid breaths, after which his breathing steadied and remained deep. Now that he was more heavily anaesthetized his trunk was still. I managed to push the end of the collar under his neck through the dust, using the full length of my arm, far enough for Mhoja to pull the end from under his chin.

The radio capsule we adjusted to sit on his neck. A counter weight had to be fastened to keep it upright. Howard joined the two ends of the collar together with wire, epoxy resin and rivets. The holes for the wire had to be drilled in situ, because the exact length of collar could not be calculated beforehand.

With the collar and pad both firmly attached there was just time to take a few measurements of body length and height, hoof circumference, tusk length and width, and shoulder height. His height from the sole of his foot to the tip of his shoulder-blade corresponded to an age of 20–25 years according to Dick Law's growth curve. For our future reference, when next measuring a collar, the tape tight round his neck measured exactly six feet.

Sue now handed Toni a full syringe containing the antidote to M99, a drug in the same morphia series labelled M285. This drug had a much milder effect than M99, but was injected at a much higher concentration and displaced the M99, allowing the animal to recover. Toni cleaned an area of skin behind one of the bull's ears and gave an intravenous injection. We all returned to the car and within a few minutes the bull's ears started to flap.

With a jerk of his head he heaved himself back on to his belly and slowly stood up. His struggle and the drug had altogether exhausted him and he stood quietly in the shade of a tree. His overall temperature must have been very high despite my efforts at cooling him with water, for he now did something which I had never seen before. He put his trunk deep inside his throat and sucked out some water which he then splashed on the back of his ears and shoulders.

I had read accounts of this behavior. One nineteenth-century hunter, Gordon Cumming, wrote a vivid description of a bull, who after being pursued on horseback for several miles, regurgitated water from his stomach and sprayed himself. This remarkable capability was also seen by Hugh Lamprey when he chased a bull for some miles in a Land-Rover away from the Seronera fever trees which he had been pushing over. Later during the 1971 drought in Tsavo a very small calf was photographed doing the same thing after he had stood for many hours in the sun beside his mother who had died in the drought. Luckily the calf was rescued by David Sheldrick, the Warden, and today Sobo lives happily in their orphan herd.

M4/3 walked slowly from the shade into the sun and back into some more shade where he stopped. He "fingered" his collar, but rather to our surprise made no attempt to get rid of it. Howard recorded his subcutaneous temperature as a pulsed signal which had to be decoded. It decreased from about 100°F to 96°F.

As the twilight faded the massed families who had been with him in the morning reappeared and surrounded him. Many elephants in succession came up to touch his new acquisitions, the collar and temperature pad, intensely curious and eager to investigate the objects and spots where we had touched him that smelt of man. None of them tried to pull anything off.

We were all tired. Toni and Sue were going off next day so for that first night we left M4/3 unobserved. At camp we had a celebration and farewell party. The Harthoorns not only do not eat meat they do not drink alcohol either, but all the same the spirit of the evening was gay.

They left the next day. Sadly the temperature transmitter was already defunct but Howard and his wife stayed one more night, during which we followed M4/3 without cease. It was a dark and rainy night and hippos came out at dusk near our elephant on the shore. He kept company with three others of varying sizes. There was no moon and clouds obscured the stars. Most of the night the best we could record were the occasional sounds when the elephants broke some branches and later in the small hours we heard distinct snores.

The chink chink chink of the elephant transmitter became engraved in our brains; the only noise that went on non-stop. It had an unearthly quality, pure and electronic. As we sat in the Land-Rover cab, lighting our notes with a torch masked with a red filter, which we hoped would be invisible to elephants, we could have been tracking spaceships through the galaxy. The sound had nothing to do with elephants and the red glow cast by the torch gave the whole episode an atmosphere of science fiction.

When the long night ended in a drizzly cold dawn, M4/3 was busy pulling a tender green *Salvadora persica* bush to pieces. The others were close; they had moved less than half a mile in the night.

Howard could postpone his departure no longer. We returned to camp, where he made some last-minute adjustments to the receivers and mounts for the antenna, now fitted to my Land-Rover, and, after breakfast, left for his next assignment, which was back in the Serengeti with lions and hyenas.

I now had seventeen wonderful days and nights when I kept on the tail of the young bull as he wandered up hills and into forest, along the densely forested gorges that sliced into the escarpment, and down again to the Lake front. While plotting his movements on the map, I recorded what he ate, what he drank and above all with whom he associated, for bull social organization was still very much a mystery for me and I was curious to see if he had any special friendships. At times, after hours of watching, I would race back to camp to refuel with water, petrol and tins of food.

The first night out alone in my own Land-Rover, I was devoured by mosquitoes which flew straight in through the open windows. The next night I carried a net. It was dark and after listening to the monotonous chink chink for two hours, involuntarily I fell asleep.

I awoke with a start at midnight with the feeling I was not alone. Moonlight was pouring down on my face and a noise like the repeated hitting of a cricket ball with a bat was coming nearer to the car. I looked up and silhouetted against half the stars in heaven were M4/3 and another enormous bull that I had never seen before, their trunks entwined. They pushed and prodded, parrying each other's thrusts with their tusks. Each time the ivories hit came the sound which had awoken me. They gleamed and flashed in the moonlight while the two giants struggled in mock fury.

Nothing else stirred, only the sound of the night wind as it blew very slowly down from the hill and the two black forms surging back and forth, rustling the bushes.

At dawn, once more slumbering, I was woken by a noise exactly like a short burst of machine-gun fire in the distance. I sat up shivering, for it had been a cold night with heavy dew and I was wearing light clothing. The sky was once more overcast and my elephant was nowhere in sight. The distant machine-gun rattled again and at the same time a little bird shot dramatically up in the air. I looked through binoculars as he did it once more and saw that he was rapidly beating his wings and that the noise came from him. It was a flappet lark advertising his territory.

M4/3 kept new company every day. Altogether he met twelve bulls, both larger and smaller than himself, and associated temporarily with four different family units. The longest he kept with one other bull was five days, but at other times he was alone, though never for a whole day. In other words he enjoyed a loose shifting association with whomsoever he met or pleased to join for an hour or more. There is little doubt that throughout his calfhood and in his spell as an independent bull he must have met all the inhabitants of his world time and time again.

As the days and nights passed the transmitter gradually weakened, until finally I had to be within 300–400 yards before picking up the signal. Howard had incorporated locally-made batteries which were failing fast. The collar quickly took on the color of mud and became so inconspicuous that not a single tourist remarked on it. Then the polystyrene foam capsule which housed the transmitter became frayed, as protective tape around it peeled away, and the temperature pad ripped off, although the sutures with little strips of material remained firmly attached to his head.

When the signal finally expired I located him visually for two more days, which gave a record of twenty-two days of continuous movement. All in all it was a successful experiment.

In November Howard came back briefly with another collar. This time, benefiting from former experiences, we first serviced and thoroughly tested the Capchur gun. We also used a heftier dose of drug.

It immobilized with no trouble another bull called Sphinx's young male. He went down eight minutes after the dart went in. A family nearby pushed their tusks against him so violently that we did not know whether they were trying to help or to attack him. At any rate they made no attempt to defend him from us. When we came up, he was marked with five cuts made by tusks along his back. We fitted the collar rapidly and had him back on his feet within less than twenty-five minutes. This time we did not try to fix a temperature probe. The young bull stood shakily on his feet and remained dopey for several hours afterwards.

I came to the conclusion that a large dose which puts an elephant down fast is safer than several smaller cumulative doses spread out over a number of hours, always with the risk of losing sight of the animal. I also came to believe in the importance of minimum disturbance whilst darting, which was later well borne out in practice. If an elephant were unaware of anything unusual, he would react to the dart as if he had been stung, running a few paces before slowing to a walk, which made it much easier to keep him in sight, and put less strain on his system.

Unfortunately there were still some bugs in the radio system and this second transmitter only had a life of three days. In that time I plotted the detailed movements of a mass of seventeen family units that roamed round the Ndala area in a temporary feeding assemblage, followed by this young bull. Independent though he was he still seemed to like the company of other youngsters around him and the presence of adult elephants not too far away. He often touched his cuts which seemed to discomfort him. Once he picked a "handful" of grass and carefully wiped the cuts with it, afterwards putting the grass in his mouth and eating it.

I also followed him at night and watched him through an American army starlight intensifier, which after use in Vietnam had recently been taken off the secret list. I could understand why, it was much less efficient than a pair of ordinary binocular night glasses.

With collars on M4/3 and Sphinx's young male I had successfully applied the technique of immobilization. The important questions of population movements could only be solved by radio-tracking cow-calf groups,

but the difficulty was to tackle or circumvent the matriarchal defensive-circle, which, I supposed, would
inevitably form every time a family member became
stricken with the drug. Since elephants were so variable
in their behavior I hoped it might be just a matter of
choosing the right individual in the right circumstances
from the right family unit.

There was also a possibility of much easier radio-
tracking if this could be done from an airplane. Howard had made some experiments in his old Piper Cruiser before it was crashed during one of the Serengeti
elephant counts, and found that the efficiency and
range of reception was greatly increased with elevation.
The receiver's H-shaped Yagi antenna could be
strapped to the wing struts quite simply. Here was one
way of getting at the Marang Forest elephants, which
could never be followed for any length of time on foot.
I came round to the idea that an airplane was essential to round off my study. It would also allow me to
keep a regular check on the numbers of elephants in
the Park over every month of the year.

# 8

# Eyes in the Air

I needed a plane of my own. The total perspectives of flying would be invaluable. When Hugh Lamprey, or the Serengeti Wardens, Myles Turner and Sandy Field, came over in the Super-Cub to help me count the elephants, I had been enthralled by the masses of elephants suddenly visible, the sensations of freedom and the views. I knew however that John Owen could not provide me with an airplane. He had taken me on as a low-cost student who was to work on foot or in a Land-Rover, not as an expensive high-flier.

Fortunately my father had left me some shares and with the Stock Market booming in 1968, I sold them and raised enough money to finish my pilot's training and to buy a cheap plane. In November of that year I divided my home leave between visiting the London Hospital of Tropical Medicine for a second bilharzia "cure," the first having failed, and the Oxford Flying School at Kidlington, where I learned to fly a nose-wheel Cherokee 140. However, I still needed to placate John Owen, who often said that "planes tempt young men to take their eyes off the ground." I argued that a plane was necessary to get to know the total range of the elephants outside the Park and also that I could cover the country in minutes by plane whereas on foot I would take days. Finally I said that, with superb visibility, I could pick out the secret reaches of the Endabash thickets and that a plane would make radio tracking more effective.

Hugh Lamprey, as my supervisor, backed me up and to my delight John Owen agreed to my request, and even earmarked a small portion of my grant, which was administered from his office, to pay for some of the running expenses.

In January 1969 I found the ideal machine at Wilson, the airfield for small planes near Nairobi. It was an eighteen-year-old Piper Pacer, with a 150 horse power engine, costing £1,650. Once the windows were modified so that I could remove them at will, the visibility for elephant counting was excellent.

Now I had to learn tail-wheel flying, which was tricky because the center of gravity was behind the two large front wheels and tended to make the aircraft swing violently when the brakes were applied on landing. If unchecked the swing developed quickly into a ground loop, the aircraft spinning out of control in a horizontal plane until it tipped over and its wing tips smashed into the ground. The Pacer had a reputation for being difficult to control.

When I was ready I flew down to Manyara solo. The strip there, which is poised on top of the escarpment cliff near the hotel, was displaying its usual crosswind and I crawled in on "finals" like a crab, before straightening the plane on the rudder a second before touching down.

Over the days and weeks that followed I gradually became confident of being able to land without ground looping. Up in the air the plane flew sweetly; it was immediately responsive to the controls, and very "forgiving" of any mistakes; it was difficult to stall her even in practice, which was just as well since I would be flying low and slow on most of the counts. Nevertheless I took great care to master the art of taking off and landing. The airfield at Manyara was over a thousand yards long, but I wanted to learn the exact capabilities and limitations of my plane and to graduate to all kinds of bush strips, which were often short, bumpy and narrow.

I remembered vividly an experience of two years before on the last day of the annual Serengeti elephant count. Hugh Lamprey and I were observers in Howard Baldwin's old Piper Cruiser, piloted by Bill Holz. We had come far south of the Serengeti boundary to an immense salt lake named Eyasi. An elephant population was rumored to live along the jagged escarpment that rose 2,000 ft. or more from the flat shores and it was possible that they roamed to and from Serengeti. There was also the intriguing speculation that Manyara elephants might come here via the Marang Forest and that the two populations might mix or even wander on into each other's ranges.

We flew a wide pattern, over valleys, deep gorges lined with trees and broken rocky hillsides. Half-way through the morning, having seen no elephants, we stopped for a cup of coffee at an old hunter's strip, near a village named Makao. It was 600 yards long and we sideslipped down and landed gently. When the moment came for takeoff the Cruiser took a long time to gather speed. The machine was slow in rising from the ground owing to the fact that the grass of the strip was more than a foot high. Then the speed picked up a bit and we began to jump like a kangaroo, bounding up in the air and then back down again. All of a sudden trees loomed dead ahead and we left the end of the runway.

Bill diverted the machine toward a gap. We must have developed a speed of nearly fifty miles an hour, and just as the plane was about to quit the ground there was a violent shock and we were thrown sideways. The machine continued at speed until a stump arrested the fuselage and the plane tipped over driving the port wing into the ground. We sat for a second while little cascades of aviation fuel poured out of the ruptured wing tanks before making our escape.

On inspection we found the detached port undercarriage where it had first struck a concealed stump some thirty yards from the end of the strip. With both wings fractured, the fuselage bent and the undercarriage ripped off, the plane was irreparably damaged.

Bill Holz was an experienced pilot but had never met with long grass before. It was one more variable like altitude, wind speed and direction, time of the day and weight of the passengers, which had to be juggled mentally before taking off. I hoped to make enough experiments on the long Manyara airfield, where there was plenty of room for error, before coming to any decisions that demanded a narrow margin.

Flying gave me a heady sense of freedom, and for the first months became an obsessive pursuit; indeed I found it as absorbing an activity as watching elephants. I came to know every square yard of the Park from the air. Hanging in space on an up-current, diving in a roar close above the waters of the Lake, or cruising in the still air above the clouds were equally delightful. The unlimited horizons gave me the feeling of personal control over destiny: below was the whole earth to explore, in any chosen direction. I could roam at will across the landscape peering into nooks and crannies in the hills, or over high unscaled crags hanging above sweeping bluffs that hid them from the ground. The fact that I could combine it with my work gave my pleasure the added dimension of respectability.

From the air I could now see how much the Lake had risen during the 1968 floods. It was twenty-six miles long and ten miles at its widest, a shallow expanse with no outlet, which filled and sank with the seasons. In some years it dried up altogether. The water was too saline for crocodiles, but a few hippos lived in the swamps at the northern end and along the rivers of the Ground Water Forest. Now the swamp had been submerged and all the reeds had drowned, except for those which had broken away in huge islands and floated around the Lake. The prevailing wind from the south-east eventually blew them up again on new high shores, and for some months green shoots poked up from the mass of rotting floating vegetation. But their success was short-lived, for the elephants developed a great appetite for these islands, and waded out to devour them. This habitat had been 10% of the Park area, and its loss was a serious blow to elephants and hippos. Such changes show how important long-term variations are to plant and animal numbers.

Wide belts of *Acacia tortilis* were also submerged by the Lake and their gaunt skeletons, lapped by water, lined the shore. All the alkaline pastures were gone, and the buffalo and elephant were pinched as never before between the rising Lake and the advancing Wambulu settlement. Along the Endabash cliffs the scars of the 1968 landslides were almost fully healed and young pale green plants covered the red earth that had been stripped bare.

In the short dry season of January and February 1969, the Lake receded slightly and outlying pools became isolated and dried up. Saddle bills, yellow bill storks, sacred ibis and the strange-looking hammerkops concentrated on the helpless fish trapped in the shallows, probing with open beaks or, in the case of the hammerkop, scratching like hens, and gulping down several fish in the space of minutes. Sandpipers probed for smaller mud-dwelling life.

Having given permission for me to fly, John Owen became anxious for my safety. I suppose he had already enough burdens without adding further to them and my reputation at its mildest was that I was "an accident-prone young man," and at its worst "a goddamn reckless fool." I stoutly maintained that I never took risks; however, reputations tend to stick.

My mother, with infinite trust, came out to stay a second time and happily her visit passed without incident, but while shopping in Arusha one day she met John Owen who had looked after her and reassured her two years before, while I had been in hospital recovering from the rhino accident. This time he fixed her with a steely glare.

"It's very dangerous for Iain to have an airplane, you know," he warned. "We only let our pilots fly in game counts after they have 200 hours of experience, and at Manyara there's an added hazard from vultures."

This was hardly reassuring for someone who viewed my flying with great trepidation, enhanced by a family history of fatal aerial mishaps. However, my mother concealed her feelings, and I did not hit a vulture.

But chance plays strange tricks. Two weeks later it was John Owen who struck a stork which he had failed to notice while flying in a straight line. Luckily he retained control of the plane by applying extreme rudder to compensate for the distortion caused by the impact. He never mentioned the Manyara vultures again.

Large birds are one of those integral hazards for bush pilots in East Africa and may cause fatal accidents, as in the case of Michael Grzimek. It is very difficult to concentrate on circling, so that your observer can count easily, and at the same time keep an eye on every bird in the sky. Even Hugh Lamprey, one of the best pilots with whom I have flown, hit two vultures in the space of two days during one of the Serengeti elephant counts.

Manyara was not ideal country for counting elephants. In places the forest canopy was continuous and to calculate how many elephants were concealed underneath was a matter of guesswork.

In my early counts I recorded a total of about 230 elephants and could not understand how it was that the numbers had fallen so much since 420 were counted by Murray Watson and Myles Turner in 1965. However, my eye became attuned to the slightest hint of an elephant's shape and my scores increased. This is a common phenomenon amongst elephant counters. With practice the observers become more efficient, and then may gain a false impression of a dramatic population increase, when in fact the elephants have been there all along. It was only after a year's continual flying and observing that my totals increased to around the 420 figure; then I realized, shamefacedly, what a bad observer I had been.

Even final results are usually minimum estimates. Nobody ever overcounts elephants. This has been confirmed many times in the Serengeti when photographs have been taken as a check on counting by eye. Visual estimates even in open country are usually around 40% low, according to Mike Norton Griffiths who was the scientist later to collate ten years of combined research data.

Many factors affect the numbers seen; for instance on hot days more elephants move under the trees for shade, also some elephants hearing the noise of the airplane become nervous and rush for cover, while others pay no attention and remain visible. I found that a soft light with moderate shadows was better than direct sunlight for counting animals under the trees. The condition of the foliage also affected visibility, and when leaves withered and fell in the dry season more areas became countable.

At Manyara I was able to make empirical checks on the accuracy of my counts. When I found a group of elephants in a small block of territory with well-defined boundaries I would circle and count them until I reached a consistent figure, then I would hasten to meet them on the ground before they had moved out of the block. Knowing the exact numbers in each family unit all I had to do was to identify which units were present and add up the total, including whatever bulls I could see hanging around. In fairly open country I was sometimes dead accurate, but in bushy areas I might be as much as 80% low. On average I needed to increase my air counts by 27% to reach the ground estimate.

The original supposition that Manyara had the densest overall population of any park in Africa was confirmed. There were well over ten elephants per square mile in each season of the year, and taking into account the tendency to underestimate it was more likely that there were 13–14 per square mile. I concluded that total numbers fluctuated between 400 and 500 at any one time, though the total number of elephants that used the Park on and off during my study was about 600.

Within the Park, elephants dominated the large-mammal biomass, a term summing the weight of animals upon the land. Nearly 49% of the large-mammal biomass were elephants. Buffaloes made up 42% leaving a mere 9% for others such as hippos, zebra, giraffe, rhinoceros, all the antelope, baboons and the predators. There were inexplicably more elephants living down in the Endabash thickets than in the northern half of the Park. Perhaps some were "refugees" driven up from the south of the Lake during intensive extermination campaigns in the late 1950s, when the European farmers sought to rid their lands of crop raiders. I could well imagine the Torone sisters fitting into this category. On the other hand numbers in the south may also have been swelled by elephants coming down from the Marang Forest to eat salt along the Lake shore, a substance mainly absent from the highly leached cloud forest.

From the air the Marang Forest presented mile after mile of closed canopy, broken in a few places by swampy glades. I once saw a herd of a hundred elephants in such a glade, but could find no way of estimating the total population that dwelt there. On the ground, from indirect traces of broken vegetation, tracks and elephant droppings, it appeared that the elephants were not nearly so dense as in the Park. I began to suspect that the Marang Forest and the Southern Farms in the past had been an integral part of the elephant's range and without them the Park would have much less capacity to absorb the gross ecological changes that were taking place.

The problem of whether the Park could continue to support such a high elephant density remained constantly in my mind, but I could not begin to answer how important these external areas still were to the elephants until Howard Baldwin returned with some more radio collars.

In March my plane was due for a fifty-hour check so I flew it up to Nairobi and that evening I went to a party on the outskirts. City people were packed in a smoky room chattering to each other over cocktails. In this throng was a girl with long, dark hair, and slanting, almost oriental eyes, that flickered wickedly upon one person after another. On her sunburned forehead silver and golden specks of some curious metallic composition gleamed. Wearing a loose African robe which clung to her lithe figure, she danced with demonic energy, radiating an entirely un-Anglo-Saxon warmth and gaiety, and hanging pieces of silver clashed as she moved. Before the evening was out I worked my way through her many admirers and beguiled her with tales of noble elephants, lions in trees, hair's-breadth escapes, and I know not what else, all set on the shores of a far-off enchanted Lake called Manyara. She listened, warmly sympathetic, never giving away that she had already been there.

Oria Rocco, as she was called, came from an Italian-French family who lived on the shores of Lake Naivasha. She was Kenya born and bred and belonged to that city scene no more than I did. Impulsively she agreed that she would love to see Manyara, and we made an indefinite plan for the future.

Up in the air next day, on my way back to the elephants, my memory was imprinted with those restless, incendiary, brown eyes.

Not long after I returned to Manyara, Howard materialized unexpectedly with a plentiful supply of new electronic devices. This time each transmitter was sealed in a capsule of fiberglass that had been premolded to fit an animal's neck comfortably. There were several for lions and two for elephants. Each capsule contained a spiral antenna no bigger than two matchboxes laid side by side. Howard assured me that, protected by the fiberglass and layers of dental acrylic, there was nothing an elephant could do to destroy the unit's efficiency, and they had been tested in Arizona and gave a range of thirty miles. The batteries were long lasting, of American manufacture, and should be serviceable for six months.

The day after Howard arrived I went to Nairobi to collect Toni Harthoorn, who, tall as he was, could only just fit into the plane by bending into the shape of an S, with his knees pushed against the dashboard. Toni was to provide the surgical expertise for a new and more ambitious scheme of charting internal temperatures. The intention was to investigate the role of the African elephant's ear in cooling the blood. I was mainly interested in plotting movement, but the two projects could be combined.

Howard had designed two small implantable transmitters with thermistor probes that could be inserted into an artery and a vein. A third heat-sensing transmitter was to be attached externally to the collar to give readings of the ambient temperature. Each thermistor had a resistance to the current passing through it which was related in a precise mathematical way to the temperature. The information was encoded by modulating the pulse rate of radio frequency energy.

On the first morning we quickly found a suitable young bull. With no second thoughts, he was given a strong dose of M99, 1 milligram per 1,000 lb., and, as hoped for, he soon collapsed in a clearing. Unfortunately the bull's head rested firmly against a fallen log, which made attachment of the main collar difficult. It contained the relay transmitter that would pick up, amplify and broadcast the coded pulse signals from the internal transmitters. However, the operation went as planned and after two hours Toni and Howard had between them cleaned and penetrated the surface layers, exposed the large blood vessels, inserted the probes, and closed up the wounds again. I had eventually managed to fasten the collar, though loosely.

The bull was soon back on his feet. When he stood up, streaked with blood from the surgery, we christened him Bloody Ear. I should add that the operation was in no way cruel. It is impossible for an immobilized animal to feel pain, since it is heavily sedated with that best of pain killers, morphia.

The apparatus with which the bull was now saddled was far more sophisticated than anything we had tried before. The signals from the sensors were retransmitted up to thirty miles away by the main relay station in the collar, on a time-sharing basis. In effect we were able to record the blood temperature inside the artery going into the ear and the venous temperature of blood coming out. The results were extremely interesting. While the venous temperature remained fairly steady between 95.7 and 96.4 the arterial temperature zoomed up and down, and was usually no less than 5.4°F above the venous temperature.

One night Bloody Ear suddenly took to the hills. He was lost to sight, but his progress up the escarpment could be marked as we followed in the Land-Rover, by sounds of heavy breathing and the usual breaking of long-suffering vegetation. The arterial pulses changed frequency, and when decoded indicated a dramatic leap, in the space of a quarter of an hour, to a temperature of 112.6°F, which we could scarcely believe. Even the Grant's gazelle when it heats up throughout a sunny day only reaches a temperature of 107°F, as discovered in the physiological experiments of Richard Taylor, and this is partly because they do not pant or sweat in order to reduce their water loss. Marathon runners in hot weather attain 105.8°F, and the highest human temperature ever recorded was 112°F, in a very sick woman who was lucky to recover. No healthy mammal to my knowledge ever reaches as high a temperature as we were recording for the arterial blood of Bloody Ear.

Meanwhile his venous temperature remained steady, and I can only assume that he must have speeded up flapping his ears to achieve greater convectional cooling. The drop between the blood going in and out of the ear was 16.9°F, a remarkable rate of cooling. This was the greatest difference we recorded, and unfortunately we were never able to duplicate this experiment on another elephant nor switch the probes. The result remains as an interesting preliminary finding, which ought to be repeated.

All the evidence points to temperature regulation as the major function of the African elephant's ears. Elephants do sweat, but with their huge bulk they have solved the problem of heat dissipation with the surface area of their enormous ears. Spraying water behind the ears and flapping them in still air or simply spreading them when there is wind increases heat loss. In the hottest time of the day the elephant does nothing but stands in the shade. If an elephant overheats, like any other mammal he will die, but as we had seen, if hard pressed he can use the emergency expedient of drawing water from his gullet and wetting the ears with it, although this seems only to be done in extremis.

Unfortunately time was not on our side. Howard began to worry for the safety of his precious equipment, the more so because the collar with its relay station, which had been loose when I fastened it, now threatened to snag on a stump and drop off altogether. We would soon have to recover it.

At the same time I was deciding on which new elephant to select for the long-term radio tracking.

With the few collars that Howard could supply (he gave them all free) I was faced with a difficult choice. At one end of the pole lay the exceptionally tame groups that lived mainly in the north, and at the other the wild and totally mysterious groups that confined themselves to the south and wandered I knew not where. It may seem that the wild southerners were therefore the obvious choice, but I had two good reasons for choosing a northern group. In the first place, behavior in the darting operation would be more predictable. In the second, well though I knew them, they too disappeared from human ken from time to time, and I was very curious to see just how far they wandered into the Endabash bush, and whether or not it led them out of the Park.

Since Boadicea's was the best known group I decided it was she that I must follow, so that there would be as few mysteries left about her life as modern science could allow.

The key to tracking a cow-calf group, I realized, was to select a member who was held in generally low esteem by the other members of the group and whom they, hopefully, would not defend when it came to the crucial moment. Boadicea's own family unit had just such an individual.

He was called Robert after my assistant. At nineteen they were the same age. The elephant Robert was unusually old still to be attached to a family unit. I had watched his progress for three years. At first just another calf, he had now filled out and had the contours of a bull, a fine pair of tusks and a well-developed body. Unfailingly he could be found in the near vicinity of Boadicea's family, usually trailing them at several hundred yards' distance.

Like all young bulls he was fond of testing his strength and frightfulness against various moving objects of his environment—of these I was one. When he found me as usual near the family I was often subjected to high-spirited charges. If I did not move he ended these demonstrations with elaborate head-shaking, weaving and swaying from side to side. He was an excellent marker for the group, but I hoped I would be able to find him isolated and get him down before the others had noticed what had happened.

Apart from plotting Boadicea's full range, I would try to find out what social forces held such a large group together and what effects the bonds or separations were likely to have on the size of an elephant population. I was also interested to see what would happen to this young bull now that he had reached the critical age of puberty and was about to take the fateful step to full independence. I already had many observations of other young bulls, but to follow one night and day would test the hypotheses I was beginning to develop. Then after some months I would take the collar off him and put it finally on one of the truly wild and challenging Endabash "baddies."

Before I began this operation I had to return Toni Harthoorn to the University in Nairobi and his work there. Furthermore I had decided to try and persuade Oria to come down and take part in the next operation. I dropped Toni at Wilson airfield in Nairobi and immediately took off again heading for Oria's home on the shores of Lake Naivasha.

# II

## Oria Douglas-Hamilton

# 9

# Elephant World

Against a small green hill, overlooking Lake Naivasha in Kenya, stands my family home, a strange sort of castle painted dark pink with wooden slatted roofs bleached pale by the sun. It is on a 3,000-acre farm, most of it hills covered with rocks and grey-yellow scrub. All the year round we grow vegetables and cattle food on a strip of land along the water's edge.

Early in 1969 while I was running our farm I took a couple of weeks off to work for an advertising company who had asked me to organize their safari and to find them the best locations, where they could film commercials. We moved all over Kenya, never spending more than three days in any one place.

One evening at a farewell party for our film unit and other advertising people, men with tired alcoholic faces talking about new ways of flogging things, each of which they praised as instant magic perfection, suddenly a stranger entered the room. Obviously he did not belong to this milieu. Dressed in an ill-fitting tweed jacket and grey trousers, which I afterwards learned were borrowed for the occasion, he seemed rather shy. I was acting as hostess and went up to him and asked him what he did. "I do elephants," he said. He was a visitor from the bush. For him it was a rare event to be at a party, to see girls, have good food and drink, and to be able to talk to people. After telling me all about his elephants, it did not take long for him to say "I've just bought an airplane and I can fly you to Manyara if you want to see them." He left me instructions on how to send him a message over Tanzania National Park's radio. It sounded exciting but I had to get back to the farm as soon as I could. It was the middle of our exporting season and one of our busiest times of the year. I went home.

Sunday morning at the farm in Naivasha was always special. Silence surrounded our house which stood between tall yellow fever trees from which pairs of black and white fish eagles called to each other with forlorn cries. The only other sounds came from the thick-leaved fig trees which were alive with starling chatter, and from the dusty tall cypress trees where the doves were making their liquid call. No noise of tractors broke the peace.

Inside the house the servants moved like barefooted ghosts preparing for the day's events. On the veranda, overlooking the lawn, the long oval table was laid with an old blue and white Florentine tablecloth, wine-red glasses, and gay ceramic plates. I had invited some friends for lunch and Moses, our cook, had decided on a cold buffet. At about midday cars arrived leaving a trail of white on the drive, and our first guests tumbled out, stretching and shaking the dust off their clothes.

As lunch began the house echoed with talk in Italian, French and English. All of a sudden, a tremendous roar swept down from the sky and reverberated over the top of the roof. The noise slowly faded into the distance. We rushed on to the lawn, and gazed skywards watching a small red and white plane silhouetted against huge rain clouds. It turned and headed towards us flying fast and low. "Oh God," I thought, "this must be Iain and he is going to hit something!" The plane shot past making some of the guests duck as if they were being attacked. All heads turned to follow the aircraft as it disappeared towards the hills. A hand over my eyes to shield them from the glare, I noticed it was circling around our cattle *bomas,* and it looked as if the pilot were trying to land.

I rushed down the drive, jumped on to my yellow Benelli motorbike and raced along the red murram road waving an arm and hoping that Iain would understand that I was trying to tell him not to land. Instead he swooped down, touched the ground, and flew off again. Then I saw him come in more slowly, hop over the telephone wires and drop in to the *boma.* Knowing the place was full of holes covered over with long grass I was transfixed with fear as I sat on my bike, my hands over my face peeping between my fingers. The plane came running down the field and stopped in front of me on the other side of the fence. I was greatly relieved not to be standing among scattered bits of airplane, fighting the flames. Instead out jumped a young man, dressed in green, with no shoes on his feet. His face had a big grin on it as he pointed at me and told me how pale I was.

"You're crazy, you don't understand, this place is full of stones and thorns and enormous holes," I shouted.

"What are you worrying about?" he said laughing at me. "I told you this plane can land anywhere, and don't you tell me you didn't enjoy that arrival."

"It was fantastic." I jumped off my bike and threw my arms around him.

"We are going to dart elephants tomorrow," he said, "And I would like you to take some pictures for me. Can you be ready to leave in a couple of hours?"

I was still shaking and had no idea how this could be arranged. "I don't know, I can't tell you right now. We have guests for lunch," I answered quickly. "Come and have some food first." Iain got on the back of my bike, kicked the starter for me and we sped home.

It had begun to drizzle, rain drops stung my face and my blouse was soaking. We ran up the big curved stairway and into the house. I introduced Iain to my parents and to the others. His arrival had caused a great commotion. It was an unforgettable event at Naivasha. Even old Moses, the cook, came to shake hands and welcome him to the farm.

"Tell me young man, do you always fly like that?" asked an elderly gentleman who had just arrived from Europe and was unused to the kind of life we lead in Africa.

"Only sometimes," Iain answered. "I was hoping to be invited and just wanted to see what I was going to have for lunch before landing." Soon his plate was heaped so full, that my father remarked with a laugh, *"Salute,* haven't you been eating lately?"

My mother, sitting at the other end of the table, told Iain her favorite story of how she flew for the first time in 1910 with her brother in the Paris Air Show where the Wright brothers and Blériot demonstrated their machines. Dressed in long flowing skirts and a big hat, she had to sit on a little ledge between her brother's feet as he hoped to bring the nose down with some extra weight.

"Did you also fly?" Iain asked my father.

"Yes, but a long time ago. I flew Spads above the Italian Dolomites in the 1914 War."

Iain then told my father about his work with elephants and how tomorrow he hoped to take a small apparatus out of the ear vein of a bull, with which he had been able to measure the bull's temperature.

"Can you spare me Oria for a few days?" Iain asked. "I need some help in this operation."

"Well, you had better make some kind of a strip in the cow *boma* first or you won't be able to take off," my father replied. "I don't want to have any accidents here."

My parents, Mario and Giselle Rocco, came out to Africa in 1928 to hunt elephants in the Belgian Congo (now known as Zaire). They walked for over a year, moving camp whenever they felt the urge to explore another part of the country. Then, due to the imminent arrival of my brother, Dorian, their journey ended in Kenya.

Soon after, they bought the farm where my sister Mirella and I were born.

For a brief period, they found gold not far from Naivasha where we sifted through the sand in search of nuggets. Then my mother spent her days sculpting, and my father bred and raced Irish horses. I was put in the saddle aged four, and taught to ride like a cavalry officer.

Our knowledge of elephants came from exciting tales of hunting, or by reading our favorite books, by our cousin Jean de Brunhoff, who created the king of elephants, "Babar." But we children believed the elephant was king of all animals. If ever we met one on the road, we would look at him with great respect from a safe distance for he might charge and turn our car over with as little effort as we used to turn a page in a book.

One evening in 1940, we listened to the words my parents dreaded: Mussolini declaring war. The police arrived and surrounded our farm and took my Italian father away, as an "enemy alien." But my mother was an "ally," being French, and she was allowed to stay. The gold mine was confiscated, the horses were sold, and the race track dug up; pigs took their place as we struggled to remain self-supporting. We three children were sent away from school, as we were half "enemy alien," so we stayed at home and ran wild. We spent our time hunting in the back hills where scores of buffalo, eland and zebra roamed. My mother soon found it impossible to control us and asked a young Masai *moran* (warrior) to look after us. His name was Reson; he taught us all he knew about the bush and he is still with us now in charge of 500 cattle.

Eventually we were sent to an American Missionary School, the only one which would have us, and then the war ended and my father returned white-haired, temporarily shattered after four years in a South African prison camp. The stupid enmities which we children had experienced faded completely away, and I was sent to another school from which I was expelled for gross indiscipline and leading a revolt among the other girls for better food and living conditions.

After that little episode my mother thought I needed to be civilized. I was sent to finishing schools in Paris and Rome to go through the drill of becoming a well-educated girl. It was a dreadfully boring period, until I joined the existentialist underworld on the left bank of Paris where I spent my days dressed in black, listening to Sartre and Cocteau in the cafés, but longing to return to Kenya to the sun and the land of many adventures.

All my life I have been driven by a burning restlessness to search for new experiences. I traveled, and learned to speak five languages and tried many professions but each time I began to succeed the charm suddenly vanished and I moved on. Inspired by Africa's colors and its people I designed textiles and clothes for high fashion, then turned to photography and filming to try and catch the beauty and feeling which I loved so much.

No one was working on the Sunday that Iain arrived, so all the people on the farm came to look at the plane. She was marked 5Y-KIX, pronounced "Kicks." A hundred men, women and children, all dressed in their best clothes, stood around talking and laughing. The *boma* was only 450 paces from fence to fence, but the slope ran downhill into the wind and Iain assured me it was long enough. Volunteers came along to pick up stones, fill in holes and cut down the thorn bushes which, by some sort of magic, the plane had missed on landing. By evening we had a good strip. Iain decided to test it. He ordered me in, strapped me up, taxied to the high fence line, wheeled around and revved up the engine, at the same time pulling a lever that operated the flaps. We lifted effortlessly into the air while below the people waved and clapped as we flew around them, and over the house and farm, then to the hills and back to the strip. Our landing was as soft as a butterfly's kiss—perhaps a rather passionate butterfly.

We tied the plane to two big stones as a precaution against the savage gusts which sometimes blew across the lake at that time of the year, and were easily capable of turning a plane on its back.

Iain stayed the night and at dawn we filled Kix with fruit, vegetables, and as much cream, butter, meat and wine as could be fitted in. I also packed my cameras and lenses. As the sun rose, the heavily laden aircraft took off into the cold dense morning air and we headed south across the lake.

It was a beautiful clear African day, and we could see the whole Rift Valley cutting down through Kenya. As soon as we were over the mountains that surround Lake Naivasha, we dropped to a couple of hundred feet above the plains. Long lines of cattle and sheep were going out to graze, trailing dust behind them that was swept across the empty land. Here and there was a winding river-bed or Masai *manyatta* (village), otherwise this vast area was uninhabited. The rainy season was about to break. Massive clouds drifted above us, their shadows moving over the landscape. I had never flown so low before and I gazed spellbound at the beauty of Africa.

We flew over Lake Natron. Iain had taken one of the windows off as it was very hot, and at once a strong smell of sulphur filled the air. Natron is a soda lake, and has a crust of pink and mauve and brown salt interspersed with blood-red pools. A few flamingoes live on it, but there was not a sign of human life anywhere. The lake was glassy calm and the active volcano Ol'Donyo Lengai seemed to float on it at the southern end.

As we skimmed over this desolation memories sprang into my mind, frightening memories of family flying accidents: when my father was sent to the front in the 1914 war he had only had fourteen hours flying experience, and was shot down by the Austrians. Unexpectedly, he survived, but the Austrian squadron leader was so sure he was dead that he flew over the smashed plane and dropped a wreath. Then Iain had told me how his father had died when his Mosquito Reconnaissance plane burst into flames in a forced landing after returning from a long mission over Germany in 1944, and how his uncle had recently crashed and been killed in a forest in the Cameroons, in West Africa. Perhaps aware of my anxieties, Iain had assured me that little modern planes such as Kix were much safer than their predecessors.

"Even if we have engine failure, we can easily land on the lake-shore," he shouted.

Through the haze we saw the flat sheet of water that was Lake Manyara. We first buzzed the camp so that someone should come to pick us up. Below us was a thick evergreen forest, which in places dwindled into patchy acacia woodlands. Elephants were everywhere. Suddenly I saw a little house and two trees pinned against the base of the escarpment near a river. A man was waving at us but there was no car.

We flew on over the Park and then saw a car on its way to the strip, so we turned up and came in to land, heading straight for the top of the precipice where the airfield began. We touched down. I was very grateful to be standing on the ground. As we were unloading, a small open Land-Rover, with "Manyara Elephant Research" painted on the door, pulled up and out jumped Iain's assistant, Robert. He was about nineteen, good looking and well built. Dressed only in shorts, with a knife hanging from his belt, no shoes and a mass of long tangled black hair, he looked like a jungle boy.

I asked Robert where he came from; he told me he had been an assistant at the Research Institute in the Serengeti, but had been sent to Manyara because his hair was too long. I thought it funny that today long-haired men weren't tolerated for I remembered reading that in the 1790s a man could be disinherited if his hair was cut short.

Iain immediately wanted to know if all the darting equipment was ready and if Howard was in contact with Bloody Ear. Robert told us that the bull had been sighted near the Ndala River earlier on and was being closely watched by Howard and Mhoja. Howard was expecting us at about 2 p.m.

As we drove down the escarpment we could see that many of the elephants we had spotted from the air were still in the same places. Entering the Park, Iain selected one group and drove straight up to it, edged in beside the elephants and switched off the engine. We must have been less than twenty yards away from them. The elephants hardly moved. Only the young ones turned inward with their backs toward us, the big cows just looked at us, their heads still, trunks down and ears perked up. Then suddenly one great beast emerged, her head held high and her ears stretched out to such an extent that they looked like wings. Her tusks pointing at us, she advanced four terrifying steps, loomed up beside us, shook her head from side to side, slapped her ears against each other with a loud clap, kicked up the dust with one of her forefeet, crossed them and stopped. I nearly died of fright.

Then she let out a shrilling trumpet, flipped her trunk forwards, kicked up more dust, turned and ambled off in that amusing baggy-pants trot so characteristic of elephants; finally she pushed herself back into the group, causing a lot of commotion. There were more trumpets and growlings and rumbling noises and then she stood side-on to us, with her head held high, fixing us with a piercing eye.

Turning to Ian I asked him, as coolly as I could, "Isn't that a little dangerous?" He just smiled, signaled to me to keep quiet, and started taking down notes and observing the other elephants who were standing under the trees.

"Don't worry about Boadicea," he whispered, "she's an extremely nervous elephant, but she's only bluffing. I wanted you to meet her because she is the most important lady in this Park, the grand Matriarch of the largest family."

I had never been so close to elephants before and was very surprised to learn about the dominance of the cows in the elephant family. I had believed till then that big fierce bulls were the leaders.

There must have been another twenty or thirty elephants around us. Iain pointed to a young bull eating quietly on his own. "That's the fellow we want to put a radio collar on tomorrow, if we can. He's called Robert after my assistant." Boadicea shook her head at us a couple of times, and very quietly Iain eased out of the bush back on to a bumpy road. We passed zebras and looked for lions, crossed dry river beds and sand drifts, drove through saffron-shiny impalas, and finally turned toward the hills on a narrow track that led to the camp.

I heard the noise of a waterfall and saw a river flowing beneath us. I met Mhoja, and Mshaka, Iain's cook; together with Robert they unloaded the car, while Iain took me round his camp.

His house was perched at the edge of an embankment, under two wide umbrella trees. It was made of stone, with a semi-thatched roof. Two rondavels about thirty feet from each other were joined together by a rectangular room. There was another little house nearby which was half a kitchen and half a bathroom. Thick bush surrounded these buildings, except for a small clearing around the house, which was the lawn. Going up toward the waterfall, following a squiggly path through the dense vegetation, we came to another rondavel, also made of stone, with a thatched pointed roof, and big windows covered with mosquito netting. A large wild gardenia tree grew on one side. This was my room. Still further up, next to the waterfall, was the last house. This one had the most beautiful view of all. Two trees, an *Acacia tortilis* and a *Terminalia,* were clinging on to the sheer rock, bending over the cliff with their roots sticking out. The water was rushing down into a large pool and the wind blew spray over us. I sat down on a rock where blue agama lizards with bright orange heads kept popping up and looking at me. There was no need to talk, not even to say "how beautiful." Why say something so obvious?

When we returned to the main house, I was introduced to the two mongooses Pilipili and Ndogo (meaning "pepper" and "small" in Swahili). They really only liked Iain and vice versa. They kept biting my toes and drew blood, scuttling underneath the table while Mshaka brought us lunch. It was a typical everyday bachelor meal. Tinned meat, boiled potatoes and tinned vegetables, but with a big bowl of fresh fruit salad and cream from our farm.

Iain fed scraps to his chickens which came running when called. They were tough African chickens, who had a hard life avoiding hawks, genet cats and the other small fierce predators that lived near by.

Lunch was hurried and immediately afterward we went to look for Howard and Bloody Ear. We found Howard in his Land-Rover under an acacia tree, towards the Ndala River bridge. He had an aerial strapped to the door of his car, earphones over his head and a little black box on his knee. Howard pointed towards the woodlands, signalling that the elephant was quite near. He was checking his notes which were now complete and seemed pleased with the results.

We all got out, whispering to one another. Howard quickly showed me the recordings of his experiments. On the face of the box were needles from which he worked out temperatures at one minute intervals and plotted them on a graph. Indicating a point where the graph had shot up sharply a few hours before, Howard explained: "This is the exact moment when Bloody Ear came out of the forest and suddenly caught sight of the car." Although the elephant had not seemed to be in the least disturbed, his emotions had registered on this graph as a sharp increase of the temperature. It was extraordinary to think how little I knew about the elephants.

When Howard was ready Iain picked up the aerial

and the earphones and signaled me to follow him through the very thick bush of the woodlands. I could hear through the earphones the pip-pip of the radio transmitter. Holding the aerial high and turning it from side to side, we were able to track the invisible experiment through the dense vegetation. Iain sprinted up a tree, and after a while spotted Bloody Ear moving away. Then a dart was prepared with the tranquilizer and loaded in the gun, and off went Iain, Howard and Mhoja in front of me, Stupidly, I had on a pair of loose sandals, the only shoes I ever wore on the farm. I managed to keep up quite well, but my sandals constantly slipped off and my feet were scratched to pieces. I had not realized that elephant research would mean walking on foot, as no one ever did this in a Park. I didn't dare utter a squeal in case Iain thought that I was a nuisance, but he must have sensed that something was wrong as he sent Mhoja back to walk next to me, which was most reassuring.

Suddenly there was the sharp clap of the dart gun, and then some thrashing in the bushes, but nothing was to be seen. "He's hit him, and now you have to run," Mhoja said taking my cameras from my neck, holding them in one hand, his gun in the other, and leaping forward. I followed through the undergrowth, hands and arms pushing branches away from my face. It was impossible to see anything beyond the ten foot high green twigged wall, so it was without any warning that we came face to face with the elephant who was sitting on his haunches like a dog. It was an amazing sight. His eyes were blinking, and his ears flapped once or twice. He was breathing very slowly and deeply at about ten second intervals. He raised his trunk to sniff us, then rested it on a tusk. It slid off slowly and hit the ground with a thump. Iain told me he was completely conscious, could hear us, smell us and see us, but couldn't move.

Robert and the Land-Rover arrived, summoned by the "walkie-talkie"; Iain took a four-gallon can of water from it, clambered up the elephant's back as if it were a rock and poured water over his head and shoulders. Meantime Howard sliced the stitches behind the elephant's ear, cut into the vein, and pulled out a small cylinder—this was the thermistor. Then he performed the same operation on an artery. Blood was spurting all over the place and samples of it were collected. After this the incision was quickly stitched up. Meanwhile, Mhoja was trying to insert a tiny thermometer up the elephant's rear end. Ridiculous as this might look, his temperature had to be taken, but first Mhoja had to dig a hole under the animal's tail in order to get to the right place.

Men looked small next to this great creature. It was the first time I had been able to stand so close to a live elephant and look him straight in the eye. His were half closed, but his long curly eyelashes blinked slowly from time to time and a big tear rolled down his cheek, as if he were silently crying. He looked terribly sad. He had a little beard of about twenty hairs under his lower lip, and his skin looked like cracked dried-up mud holes. In the crevices were ticks and parasites. Big fat light-colored ticks stuck on to his neck, ears and belly where the skin was thinner; they were about the size of large raisins. Bloody Ear sat through the whole of the operation without moving. Only the tip of his trunk flicked from side to side.

After about twenty minutes Iain injected the antidote, together with a dose of antibiotics, to prevent infection developing in the wounds. We stepped back into the dark shadows of the trees and waited for him to awake undisturbed. The first sign of the elephant coming round was the gentle fanning of his ears. Then he lifted his trunk, turning the tip in all directions testing the wind for any strange smell. A bit shaky in the knees he lifted his huge bulk off the ground and stood up, flapping his ears continuously. Even though we were within hearing and smelling distance, he showed no sign of aggression toward us. When Iain was sure that he was all right we left. Everyone was satisfied with how smoothly the whole operation had gone.

We returned to camp, cool drinks were poured and without delay the men made the final preparations for darting the young bull Robert on the following day.

A roll of machine belting was cut for the radio collar, the transmitter was carefully embedded into a block of fiberglass and left to dry. Strong adhesives were mixed to attach the transmitter on to the collar and then painted yellow and blue. It took all the afternoon to test the equipment. The collar was switched on and the "bleeps" could be heard through the earphones.

While this was happening I looked around. As in every camp, there was always one tree where a lot of life was going on. Under a thick gardenia tree near the kitchen a big wooden box (the safari box) served as an ironing table and around it were six little stools on which the cook and Mhoja could sit and talk with visiting Rangers and drivers. Though its lower branches had been cut off it gave plenty of shade. As it had been trampled on and swept for several years, the ground under it was hard. Near the tree was a large selection of skulls and a few bones, mostly elephant and buffalo, which had been collected around the Park. These were used by Iain to age the animals by their teeth. On the other side of the tree, under a smaller gardenia, stood a green metal hut, which served as a store and still further back, behind a thorny cardiogyne bush, was a whitewashed rectangular mud and straw hut. This was where the cook and the Ranger lived.

The bathroom, which occupied the other half of the kitchen building contained a bath, shower, basin, loo, and plenty of running water, which varied in color from pale to dark brown. But at least, thanks to the wood-burning hot water tank, it ran hot or cold or both, whichever way you wanted it. Blacktailed swallows had made their nests along one of the walls.

I loved this camp the moment I saw it. It had a certain toughness about it. Bare rooms, no decorative things, except the lamp stand and some knives on the walls, no curtains, and each piece of furniture was used. Yet one ate from plates, drank out of glasses and had tea and coffee served in proper cups. There was always cold beer, water and fruit salad in the fridge, there were good books to read, interesting things to look at and one's clothes were washed every day. It represented the minimum, and maybe maximum, comfort needed for a young man to live in the bush.

As the sun was setting, Iain and I had a swim under the falls and then dressed for dinner and drove back through the Park, up to the hotel where he had to entertain some friends. It had started raining, so Howard lent us his covered Land-Rover. By the time we left the hotel, it must have been past 10 p.m. I was absolutely exhausted with my first elephant experience in Manyara. We rolled down the pot-holed corrugated escarpment road toward camp, and the Land-Rover felt as if it were a trotting car.

Below, the Park was lit by the strange light of a full moon covered in drifting rain clouds. The yellow-green Lake, set in a frame of mist and flanked by the dark, quiet forest suddenly resembled a huge steaming oasis in the middle of a desert. When we entered the Ground Water Forest, a flecked black and pink hippo propelled itself down the road. In our headlights it looked like a wine barrel with pig's feet and a tail pinned on it.

We were about four miles inside the Park when suddenly the Land-Rover slumped on one side and came to a jerky halt. There were elephants eating on the slope of the hill about fifteen yards away. "I'm afraid we've got a puncture," said Iain.

"And what about the elephants?" I asked anxiously.

"They're all right. Rhinos and buffaloes are far worse. Come on, let's try and get this tire off."

We looked everywhere for the jack but couldn't find it. Then we tried to drive the car on to the bank, so that we could remove the flat tire, but nothing seemed to work. Finally I was offered the choice of spending the rest of the night in the car, being devoured by mosquitoes, or walking back to Park Headquarters where there was a Rest House. I chose the walk.

By day the Rest House had seemed only minutes away so I didn't worry although I wasn't dressed for walking through a Park. Wearing a flimsy *khanga* (African dress), a belt of red stones with little gold bells around my waist and my loose sandals I jingled and jangled down the road as if I were a circus monkey. The elephants had moved further away but still seemed to me very close.

"Don't worry about them, they'll never hurt us," Iain reassured me as we walked past them. "The best thing to do is to talk all the time, or sing, and your bells will help to make a noise."

Our torch battery was run down and barely lit up a small round spot in the middle of the road, the moon only showed up from time to time, and then through clouds. Branches crackled and these sounds were followed by snorts and barks and the trumpetings of more distant elephants. Twice we came across buffaloes and had to hide behind a tree and throw stones at them and yell, until they galloped away.

When I reached the first bridge I refused to go any further; on it I felt as if I were standing on a fortress; also, my feet were so sore that the idea of more walking made me feel sick. Nevertheless, we walked on. Iain began singing bloodthirsty Scottish war songs about English horses bathing their hooves in Highland blood. As we entered the forest we were surrounded by the long silent ghost-like shapes of trees and I felt like Orpheus on his way to the underworld.

Dwarfed by the blackness I was actually comforted when we met some elephants standing in the road. Noiselessly they slid through the bush and vanished.

The trees around us were far too smooth to climb. It was at this moment that I realized how utterly vulnerable a man without a gun is in the face of his predators. All we had to rely on were our senses and our intelligence. I imagined the yellow eyes of a hungry animal gazing at my body, the smell of my skin blowing into his nostrils. From being man the supreme hunter, we were now potential prey, unarmed and unprotected, very small and very weak in that immense dark wilderness.

In the event, we reached the Park Gate unharmed and walked on to the Rest House, about half a mile away. On the road we met our first rhino. We slid behind a rock into the wind, clapped our hands and threw stones. The rhino, slightly confused, moved off. At last the road was clear and our long walk came to an end on the veranda of the house. It was by then long past midnight. Inside we found big wooden beds, made up with clean sheets. It seemed to us like part of a dream. We slept soundly in this man-made nest until we were wakened by the voice of Howard who had come to look for us early next morning.

As we were driving back through the forest Iain said "I didn't want to tell you last night, but there is a man-eating lion living near here and a villager was recently eaten on the main road." I didn't believe a word as it sounded too much like a line from an MGM movie. When we reached the abandoned car, Robert and Mhoja had already fixed the puncture. They confirmed the story about the lion, and we drove straight back to camp, for breakfast.

The object of the morning's work was to immobilize this fine young bull, who was still hanging around Boa's family, but had been rejected by them. Luckily Howard and Robert had got everything ready, but we were late. Iain was worried that he would not be able to locate Boa. Already the excitement of the coming event tingled through my body. Carefully I loaded all my cameras, and had a lens in every pocket of my jacket, which was specially designed to carry bits of cameras. Mhoja, Iain and I set off in one direction; Howard and Robert in another. We were to keep in close communication with our walkie-talkies.

After failing to find Boadicea from the ground we went back to the strip and flew off in Kix. In less than ten minutes Iain located her and her large family hidden in acacia woods far from any road. I was greatly impressed by the way in which he was able to recognize an individual elephant from the air, it seemed to me an astonishing feat. Now he circled the herd two or three times.

"She's probably heading for the big mud wallow and ought to be there in half an hour," he said. "Let's meet her when she comes out of the woods."

Within a quarter of an hour we were on the ground and back in the car. It didn't take us long to find Boa and her huge family. Her head stood out above the others, daring us to move one step nearer. We watched each other for some time. Iain pointed out the other prominent females to me, Leonora, Slender Tusks, Right Hook and a lovely old cow which we named Giselle after my mother.

Boadicea's family were making little mounds in the cool dust with their trunks. When they had gathered enough sand for a trunkful, they pushed it into the curved tip of their trunk with the forefoot and swished it over themselves as if it were a handful of talcum powder. Even the babies were learning to do this. Boa, ever watchful, stood out and waited to see what we were going to do. About three hundred yards away were three young bulls, who had already wallowed. The tallest, with the longest tusks, was the one Iain had selected for his experiment.

When the dart hit him, the bull ran forward a few paces. Iain and Mhoja came back to the car while the bulls walked in a semicircle around us, remaining in full view. The darted bull lagged behind, throwing an odd trunkful of sand over himself, then he stopped, tottered to one side, regained his balance and walked on until he was within fifty paces of Boadicea. The wind was blowing toward her. Suddenly the whole family surged forward, trunks extended toward the bull, ears perked, the matriarch in front, trumpeting and growling. Boa thrust her tusks against the bull, throwing him off balance and on to his knees. A couple of other females also attacked him as he tried to get on to his feet. But Giselle pushed her way through, and immediately put her trunk to his mouth and tried to help him up. He raised himself with Giselle by his side, always helping and touching him, while the other elephants circled around in a furious state, smelling him, trumpeting and trying to push him out of the way. Iain had never expected such a demonstration. From Giselle's behavior he guessed that she was probably his mother; even though he had reached the age at which he was due to leave the family, when his life was threatened Giselle rallied to protect him; so did a few of the others. It was a strange mixture of aggressive and protective behavior.

By now the bull could no longer stand: his knees bent, he staggered and then collapsed. At this point the trumpeting and movement redoubled. Some of the females charged the car as Iain moved in to try to push them away from the drugged bull, afraid they might hurt him.

Sitting on the roof of the car, cameras hanging around my neck, my hands trembling with excitement, never having seen such a spectacle before, I clicked away; though at times I was so stunned by the action and the noise that I just couldn't take pictures.

Iain had to get Boa away from the young bull and in time she led her family to a nearby tree about thirty yards distant. There she stood, obviously very nervous, making her noises and threat displays.

The moment she moved Iain drove in between the cows and the darted bull so as to keep the angry ladies at bay. Before the bull came around Iain and Howard worked fast and professionally. Meanwhile, Robert and Mhoja took samples and measurements. As soon as the radio collar was securely fixed Iain injected the antidote into one of the bull's veins, and we moved off.

We re-named the young bull "Radio Robert."

Mhoja had pulled a few hairs from its tail and made them into the first bracelet I ever had, made out of hair from a live elephant. I wore it proudly.

For my first evening in camp, I decided that the men really deserved a good meal and that we were going to celebrate the success of these two immobilizations. For me anyway, it was worth a hundred celebrations. In that tiny kitchen Mshaka and I worked for a couple of hours, sweat pouring down our brows. Flames and smoke puffed out of the wood stove making me cry, and all the while I was trying to stop a million insects, attracted by the light, from falling into the food. In spite of all this, we produced a cheese soufflé, roast chicken, peppered potatoes and onions, a ratatouille and, of course, a fruit salad with a bowl of whipped cream from Naivasha. We drank red wine and had candles on the table. Robert had an appetite that could never be satisfied and scraped every last morsel off the dish.

My first visit to Manyara was a revelation of a side of wildlife I knew little about, but I could not stay on for I was needed back in Naivasha. Iain offered to fly me to Arusha on the way home to buy me a pair of proper boots. He said that since I was going to have to do a lot of walking in the bush, it was no use tripping around in sandals, and safari boots were what I needed. On our way we spotted Radio Robert and marked the second cross on the map on which Iain was to follow his journeyings for months to come.

As promised I was back in Naivasha by Wednesday. It had been raining and the baked stale earth looked new and young once more as we landed for the second time on our farm strip. The excitement of swooping down and racing on that field in a little cloth-covered plane, practically stopping at my doorstep, was a piece of life no man had offered me before; but each time we took off and landed on such a short strip, my anxiety convinced me that this was not the ideal place for meetings.

After Iain's departure I walked up and down in the next *boma,* and marked out a new runway which would be much longer and headed into the wind. If I needed boots for walking in Manyara, Iain needed a place for landing in Naivasha. During the next couple of weeks, I got together a special team to slash the bushes, cut the trees and put the telephone wires underground. We even installed a windsock, and celebrated the opening of the new strip with a dozen bottles of beer. Then I waited to hear the noise of a low-flying airplane heading toward our farm. When it came all the thrills of life broke loose.

# 10

## One Day
## from the Sky

For the next couple of months, I spent half the week picking and packing green peppers to go off to Britain by air, selling cattle to the butchers, and supervising the ploughing of fields and the planting of maize. After that it was time to go back to Manyara.

On Wednesdays I would begin the complicated operation of radioing a message to Iain, which might take up to six hours to reach Park Headquarters, from where it would go by a driver or courier to the camp. The first time I tried this my call got through quickly. I managed to hitch a plane-lift to Manyara with a friend, and as we circled the strip I recognized the Land-Rover and two figures standing by it. I was most impressed with how well our method of communication had worked. But that was one of the few times this happened and in the months that followed Iain and I rarely seemed to succeed in getting our messages through correctly.

Adjusting to life in Manyara meant that I had to switch over to Iain's way of living and to his work with the elephants. He had a well-established routine: we got up with the sun and stopped working when it set. Meals were at precise hours; the quality of the meal was unimportant but timing was paramount. To me, of all the meals, breakfast in Iain's camp was the

Approaching the elephants
from the lake leaves them undisturbed.

A mature bull greets
an approaching matriarch
as family units mingle
peacefully on the Ndala River.

## MOTHERS AND CALVES

Top: For the first few weeks, a calf lives on
its mother's milk and rarely strays from her side.
Slender Tusks helps Ndume, born that day, to stand.

Middle: Calves experiment with every movement and posture.

Bottom, left: One baby calf uses its mouth before
it has learned to use its trunk.

Bottom, right: Another sucks its trunk.

# IMMOBILIZATION

Top: A family unit defends an immobilized calf.

Bottom: After the rest of the family left, the mother remained until the calf revived. Calf immobilization was never repeated.

Opposite: After one young bull was darted, an unrelated cow chased his family away and tried to raise him unsuccessfully. She then sat on him. He later recovered totally.

Top: Young cows of related families
embrace after separation.
Bottom: A cow touches the mouth of another
to reassure her in a moment of stress.

# BULLS

**This single bull was driven off when
a Blacksmith Plover demonstrated in territorial defense.**

Inkosikaas covers the retreat of her family.

# DEATH

Top: A baobab, weakened by elephants, collapses on this bull.

Bottom: A cow falls 400 feet after tripping on the steep path to the Marang Forest. After death, all the salts of the body are quickly returned to the soil.

Tragedy.

Opposite: The Torone sister shot by Mhoja after she had attacked the landrover.

**Oria introduces Saba to Virgo and calf.**

Oria, "a girl with long dark hair . . ."

most amazing. It was always served at seven. A radio was switched on for the London Stock Exchange Report which came just before the news. Coming from Italo-French parents, but with an English passport to my name, I thought that only the British could live like this. Iain was a perfect example; eating eggs and crisp bacon with a mongoose on his lap, elephants drinking in the river below his house and listening to the Stock Exchange. No one spoke.

What an extraordinary race the British are! People can criticize them, hate them, love them—they are everywhere, they have stamped an indelible imprint all over the world. A hundred years ago, more or less by accident, they acquired vast parts of the earth. And now? Still some are left, thousands of miles away from their mother country. Here was a Scotsman, exchanging his tweed jacket for a green bush shirt, and his gray flannel trousers for a pair of green cotton shorts and that brown brief-case for a pair of binoculars. Instead of studying English finches he had chosen to live with elephants. Some people would call it eccentric, but for Iain this way of life was perfectly normal. The chimes of Big Ben came over the radio. "Four hours Greenwich Mean Time. The BBC World Service. Here is the news!" All that was missing was a copy of *The Times*. It was a touch of home and the world he had left behind, and very often the only outside contact for isolated men like Iain. After the news the radio was switched off for the rest of the day and we went to work in the beautiful green world of elephants and other animals, with a bottle of white wine and marrons glacés in our lunch basket.

Iain wanted to show me as much of the Park as he could, so that I could get to know it really well and appreciate his work. He hoped I would begin to recognize some of the elephants, but I was far too absorbed with their threats to remember their ear decorations.

We drove for miles along the edge of the Lake towards an area called Endabash. He had told me that the fiercest of all the elephants lived here. On account of the thick bush, it had been extremely difficult to study them. The worst females were the dreaded To-rone sisters and others whose names associated them with memorable charges they had made at certain people: for instance, Grzimek's female and Baldwin's female. Their photographs in the file always showed them charging in a cloud of dust. Iain usually had just had time to take the snap and move off.

As we approached their home, the muddy pot-holed road narrowed, thick bush closing in on us with spiky branches scraping against the sides of the car. Swarms of vicious black tsetse flies attacked us, biting through our clothes which made me jump and smack myself to no avail, the only results were huge red bumps which itched, and made me very nervous.

I knew that at any moment one of these "baddies" would loom out in front of us and charge with a piercing blow of her trumpet. Each time I mentioned this, Iain just told me to keep my eyes alert. However, for the moment, no elephants were in sight. Occasionally, we would pass the neck and head of a giraffe as if detached from its body, sticking out of the bush, and that was all the wildlife we saw.

When we arrived at the river we found it in flood, the bridge half washed away. Iain suggested we get out and walk along the bank following a game trail. Faced with this prospect, I said to myself that perhaps his stories were exaggerated—no more than masculine showing-off to try and frighten me; for how could Iain be so relaxed if this place was really full of "baddies?" I felt better after I had this idea and walked along gaily following the path which the animals used to take them to the best drinking places.

At the mouth of the river, a flock of pelicans were swimming and plunging their heads into the water, fishing as rhythmically and automatically as a trained team. I stood up to my knees in the Lake watching, and as I did so I could feel fish bumping their noses against my ankles. On the other side a few buffalo slept, doz-ing half out of the muddy swamps. Meanwhile, following our tracks, but unobserved by me, an elephant family had strolled down the path as silently as the clouds moved in the sky. Suddenly I heard the noise of water splashing behind me. I turned and saw ELE-PHANTS.

I had been waiting for them all the afternoon, and there they were. I was trapped like an idiot and would never be able to get out of their way in time. Mothers with babies were the most dangerous of all. I knew that. All I could think of was to vanish, and vanish I did. I slipped into the two feet of muddy water. Taking a big breath of air with me, I swam under water as far as I possibly could. My boots kept sticking in the mud, the pelicans moved off, and when finally I lifted my head to catch another breath of air, I turned around to see what was happening.

There was Iain sitting on a log a few yards from the elephants, laughing at me and tapping his forehead with his finger, which meant "You're crazy." The elephants no doubt were also watching me, lifting their trunks to catch a whiff of my scent—not a charge, not a murmur, and here I was in this filthy water full of bird droppings and stinking of fish. I was so over-joyed to find both of us alive that I burst out laughing too, Iain had really achieved his aim. All I could do was to walk out of the mess with dignity, and find out why the elephants had not charged. Thank God, Iain had my cameras around his neck.

I had been right to be frightened, Iain explained, but this family was a harmless one which had made its way down from the north. Jocasta was the name of the matriarch; she had huge uneven tusks. Only a few minutes ago she had looked so fierce.

I couldn't imagine how I would ever acquire Iain's confidence and self-assurance. Elephants were far too big, and my memory was still full of stories told me by my elephant-hunting friends and family about nar-row escapes, and people who had been squashed into pulp by enraged elephants.

In the evenings I had to cope in the kitchen with a

smoking stove which was burning hot, and hardly any utensils. Mshaka was most apologetic about the state of his kitchen, explaining that he had often asked Iain to get him an egg flipper or a roasting pan, but that they never arrived. On one occasion I was looking everywhere for a knife and found a snake curled up in a box. I didn't know what kind it was, but quickly let it slide out and disappear into the bush. At least Iain kept snake serum in camp and I knew that as long as the mongooses were around, snakes would rarely appear.

Since Iain and Robert always expected to have one good meal a day when I was there, and on time too, the only thing I could do was to reorganize the camp. There was nothing wrong with Mshaka's cooking but he needed ideas and a better kitchen.

When I said that we were going to make lists of all the things missing in every rondavel Mshaka's face burst into smiles and he let out a long "Eeeeeeeeeh" and told me "You are doing much good." I promised that next time the plane came back from Kenya I would send him the lot.

Food was a constant problem, especially fresh meat. There never seemed to be enough for all the people living in and visiting the camp. Even the genet cats that lived nearby fed off our chickens which they attacked and ate at night. On several occasions we found a bunch of feathers gone, for the genets pushed their heads through the wire netting and ate whatever they could reach. Since it was inconceivable to throw away a piece of good meat, even if half of it had been chewed off by a predator, the rest of the chicken would appear on the table in a curry or a soup.

We discovered a brilliant green garden of cress which grew all year round in the Mchanga River and it was made into salads and soups. Here was our main source of fresh vegetables and in the market of Mto-wa-Mbu I was always able to find piles of pawpaws, bananas and avocado pears for only a few shillings a pile.

Gradually our camp began to get the reputation for *La bonne cuisine de brousse* (good bush cooking).

In Mto-wa-Mbu Iain and I were known as "Duglass" and "Mama Duglass." Even as far as Arusha and up in the back hills of Manyara people we had never seen before would call out to us "Jambo Duglass —jambo Mama Duglass."

Late one evening coming back from visiting some friends on safari we stopped at the hotel in Mto-wa-Mbu for a meal. There were colorful murals of outsized animals painted all around the rooms by a Tutsi who had escaped from the Hutus. The people in the restaurant were lorry drivers, Mbulu herders, Masai elders and some prostitutes. At a table next to us sat an old Masai. He wore an army great-coat and had an old field hat on his head. Hardly moving, he held his spear in his left hand, ate his soup and *chapati* (dough cake) with his right hand, paid, got up and walked away into the night. We had only enough money to buy a plate of soup and a *chapati* between us and when Iain asked for a packet of milk to drink, which he promised to pay for the following day, it was refused. A man at the other end of the room called the waiter, flicked him a shilling, and said "Give Duglass milk." He waved off our thanks and continued eating. His name was Ali and he had helped build Iain's camp. He was short, well built, and extremely strong. He had a terrific sense of humor and his greatest weaknesses were women, cigarettes and beer. Ali got on with very few people as he could not work normal hours and did not show respect for his employers in the conventional way. One day he told us he was coming to work for us, and as we needed someone to thatch the roof and generally help around we employed him. As a child, Ali had been brought up by a very strict father who made him get up at four every morning to work in the fields. He was so accustomed to this routine that his day always began at that hour, and we could hear Ali's chopper swishing against the grass to the rhythm of a tune he whistled and sang every day. It was his favorite song and he never whistled any other all the time he stayed with us. By 9 a.m. Ali had finished his work for the day, had his meal, washed and then sat around sleeping or telling stories till about four in the afternoon when he started work again.

Most of the people in Mto-wa-Mbu knew of Duglass and his elephants. Whenever there was an opportunity they would come up to him and ask him if he was afraid of elephants. When Iain shook his head and said "No, they're my friends" they would burst into laughter, slap him on the back and say "You watch out, they're bad animals." I loved the atmosphere in Mto-wa-Mbu.

The queen of Mto-wa-Mbu was Mama Rosa, who owned the most popular and profitable beer houses in town. She was about five foot seven inches tall, must have weighed around two hundred pounds and had a half-moon smile that cut her face in two when she laughed, puffing out her cheeks and closing her eyes. She was a friend of Iain's. If she liked you she always helped, and many times when there were too many people in our camp Mama Rosa would lend me her clay cooking pots and give food to help me out.

Each time I arrived at Ndala camp, our life overflowed with activity. Iain was flying every day following Radio Robert, who in turn was following Boadicea. For the first time ever it was now possible to follow a family unit week after week and I tried to cover it photographically as thoroughly as possible.

One of Boadicea's favorite refuges was the Musasa River gorge which cleaves into the Mbulu Plateau. Viewed from above, the gorge disappears between two hills that are matted with straggly, hooked creepers. On foot they clutch your skin and clothes, and murderous bayonet-like, wild sisal plants spear the unwary. From the air, trails stand out like a skein of saffron threads up the hillside, and the rounded bodies of elephants are unmistakable. The radio waves would leap out of the gorge in a straight line to the Yagi antenna lashed to the airplane struts.

Radio Robert's collar quickly became muddy, but after each rain storm enough of the mud coating fell off for the yellow paint to become visible, and Iain always tried to see to which group he was nearest. Most of the elephants soon paid little heed to this noisy bird buzzing over their heads unless they were in open country, where they seemed to feel less secure.

Iain soon realized that he was spending more time driving up and down to the hotel runway than in the air. He now very much wanted to collar and track another elephant in a nearby Park, called Tarangire, so that he could compare the distances and movement patterns. With all this extra flying, it would be essential to have an airstrip near the camp. But first he had to find a suitable place. We followed an elephant path behind the camp until we reached an open area covered in bush with big anthills and some trees. It looked inconceivable to me as an airstrip but Iain said it would be all right.

Shortly after this he was returning from the Serengeti one afternoon, and came in to land on the main strip. Whenever he could he practiced these short landings and as he touched down, put on the brakes, but this time his left wheel had a puncture. Taken by surprise, Kix swung into a loop, which Iain could not correct in time, and off she went into the long grass. Big stones and holes had been left along the side of the runway which Kix hit one after the other, bending the prop and the undercarriage, and damaging the other wheel. That was the end of Kix for several months, while assessors inspected the damage and engineers took the plane to pieces to transport it to Nairobi for repairs. It was a terrible blow for both of us even though Iain hired a plane whenever possible to continue his tracking, and to fly to Naivasha every now and then to pick me up.

Flying was becoming so much part of our life, that very soon he suggested I should have a plane of my own and learn to fly it. He found a little Piper Cruiser tucked away in a hangar in Arusha which was going cheap, and convinced my brother Dorian and me that we should buy it, for £875. When it arrived in Nairobi I thought it was the most beautiful airplane I had ever seen. Nearly thirty years old, tail-wheeled, pale blue and white, with huge white wings, and few instruments. The pilot sat up in front with a wide circular view, and only a stick between his knees to fly the plane with. The plane could carry two passengers on the back seat, had a maximum speed of 100 miles an hour and a minimum of about 45, but because of its huge wings and light weight, it just floated in the air like a gigantic bird.

The Cruiser appeared to us necessary for Iain's radio-tracking and my flying and besides this, with a second aircraft we now obtained more freedom than ever before. If one plane was out of order there was another to jump into and fly off in.

The next time we flew in from Naivasha to buzz the camp, Iain dived down and there below me I saw a straight smoothly graded track, cleared of bush and anthills on both sides. A few impala were standing on it and leapt off as we swept over them. We turned and came in to land, touched down and taxied to the top.

Iain had got together a team of workers to cut the bush and flatten the anthills and had learned to drive the grader, which he borrowed from Parks on Sundays. The strip was not more than 450 yards long, steeply sloped, with a valley and trees on each end. This time, however, the wind was in our tail and we came in like an express train to land uphill which quickly slowed us down. It seemed as easy as one could wish.

Mhoja had made a small enclosure of thorn branches, the same type the Masai keep their goats in, into which we pushed the plane to keep buffaloes and elephants from rubbing against its delicate canvas covering and the lions from chewing the tires. We unloaded the plane and drove to camp, only three minutes away, compared to forty-five minutes from the top airfield. It made all the difference in the world, and it was now possible to do any job in the air and go anywhere at a few minutes' notice. We could also shop in Arusha thirty miles away, collect fresh meat and vegetables from nearby farmers and even pop up to the hotel for a meal.

Iain now began teaching me to fly. At first it was really frightening having to sit up there in front in the cockpit all alone, with Iain shouting instructions in my ear from the rear seat controls as I tried to take off. But once we were airborne, I was so overcome by the beauty and the feeling of flying on my own in space, that I forgot about my fears. Alone with Iain and the wind, I could slide in and out of the clouds and down to the birds that flew below us.

Ndala was slowly becoming my second home. Having made Mshaka happy with a box full of kitchen utensils and crockery, sheets, towels, cloths and aprons, and cleaned out the whole kitchen, I decided to add some furniture to the camp to give it a feeling of bush-luxury. I don't really believe that one has to lead a totally spartan life out in the bush and I like to take certain parts of my background with me wherever I go.

A couple of American limnologists (lake experts), studying Lake Manyara, had left Iain all their packing cases made of American pine wood. This still had a slight smell of pine and was ideal for making our furniture. The Park's carpenter, who was an excellent craftsman, helped us to make some cupboards, benches, a kitchen table and shelves. Since we lived in round houses most of the furniture had to be semi-circular to fit neatly against the walls so that no space was wasted. We began to clean and paint the whole camp and were able to cover the holes in the soft-board ceiling with bits of writing paper stuck on with glue made of flour and water.

These holes had been made by the mongoose when scent-marking. First they had peed and then scratched in it until a big hole appeared. By now Pilipili and

Ndogo had left Ndala and joined up with another band.

I always get great satisfaction from being able to make nice things for one's house out of scraps, instead of buying what one needs from a well-known shop. So we built a sofa in one of the most economic, comfortable and easiest ways to make furniture in the bush. Out of the remaining packing cases Mhoja carved the base. The old inner tubes of the Land-Rover were then cut into long strips which we nailed criss-cross over the top of the sofa frame as springs. A mattress was made to measure and covered in dark purple cotton, the outer edge of the frame was padded and covered with the left-overs of this material, and a long roll for the back was stuffed with straw. It was really comfortable and could seat four.

Kix had now got her wings back and been repainted in a bright new color scheme. Partly to show off our improvements, we invited my sister Mirella and my brother Dorian with their daughters for the weekend. The planeload of four children was flown in by Iain. Mirella brought a car full of food from the farm, fresh meat, vegetables and fruit, plus a heap of colored cushions for my sofa. Unfortunately, after spending a whole day in a hot car the meat had gone bad, so we threw it to the hyenas with reluctance. For the human species living in a Park, good meat is very scarce.

As dawn broke we drove out into the Park to watch life begin to wake. It was the first time those children had been to Manyara. Hundreds of buffaloes spread across the Lake's shore in black muddy mounds, the outline of their horns and ears glittering in the sun. Spoon-billed storks and herons strode through the shallow water's edge, looking for food. Giraffes galloped in slow motion along the beach, as if floating; their legs never seemed to touch the ground. We found Boadicea, Right Hook, Virgo, and other members of her family slowly making their way down hill along the difficult zig-zag paths. As Boa stood watching us menacingly, Virgo walked up to the car waving her trunk up and down as if she were trying to make conversation, and the children talked to her although neither of them could understand what the other was saying. We drove back to camp for breakfast. Baboons which usually spent the night on the top of the Ndala valley slipped down from the cliffs like falling rocks, stopping now and then to eat an insect or a pod, or just to warm themselves in the morning sun.

After a huge meal it was time for our small guests to climb up to the waterfalls and swim in the pools. Iain complained of terrible cramps in his stomach and asked Mhoja to accompany them to Endabash, where we would join them later. I stayed behind with Iain and finished off the sofa cushions.

At about midday Mshaka came to tell me that Iain was very sick, and needed medicine. Mshaka thought he might be dying. I found him sprawled across the mat writhing in pain, vomiting and moaning. He did indeed look as if he were going to die. I didn't know what to do. There were hardly any medicines in camp. I thought he must have food poisoning but we had all had the same meals. Then I remembered that Iain was the only one who had eaten bacon which had also come from Naivasha. Mshaka and I sat by him. When he started to spit blood I realized that I must act swiftly.

I noticed that the spasms occurred every thirty minutes, and calculated that if I could get him dressed and up to the plane in time, he could help me to take off for Arusha and to land at the other end between one spasm and the next. I left a note for my sister "Iain very sick. Am flying him to Arusha. Don't worry." Then I dressed him hurriedly and drove up to the plane. I did all the checks and started the engine. As soon as he had finished a spasm of vomiting Iain fell into the pilot's seat and together we took the plane up off the strip. Then I was on my own. I had only had a few hours of flying practice and I had never taken off or landed alone so I had to work out a plan for landing in Arusha, in case Iain was by then too ill to help me. He looked dreadful, his skin had turned pale yellow and he moaned and groaned as we bounced around in the midday turbulence. I begged him to try to stay conscious just long enough for us to touch down.

When we reached the Arusha airstrip I brought the plane in to twenty feet off the ground, then Iain managed to help me touch down in bumps, after which he collapsed. At least we were safely on the ground and all I had to do now was get him to hospital as quickly as possible. It was, of course, Sunday and there was no one to help me on the strip. I managed to pull Iain out of the plane and left him in a heap vomiting under a wing, while I looked for a car; I found one and at last we got to a small clinic run by a German. "He's all right, he's only been poisoned," the doctor told me.

It was twenty-four hours before Iain was well enough for us to fly back to Naivasha for a few days' convalescence. Then he had to return to Manyara.

He arrived in the camp to find that Mshaka, the cook, had disappeared; he had gone to Mto-wa-Mbu and never been seen again. Iain tried to find out where he was, but only rumors came back from time to time; one of these was that he had been seen walking across the Serengeti because he had been cursed. I was really sorry he had left but I knew that living in the bush sometimes has strange effects on people, it was also possible that Mshaka didn't want to go on working. By the time I got back, Iain had replaced him with Suleiman who had been cook at the camp three years previously and was now working as a laborer on the Park's roads. Suleiman was an excellent cook but his arrival raised a problem: he had brucellosis. "Brucellosis," I exclaimed when I heard this. "I know all about that disease from our cattle. It is extremely contagious." However, I discovered that nearly everyone had brucellosis in this part of Tanzania. They caught it from the local milk supply. In Suleiman's case the disease was chronic and he was no longer infectious.

Our spell of ill luck persisted. I was about to leave

Ndala to return to the farm and asked Mhoja to clear out all the junk in the main room, so that we could paint it. One corner was still stuffed with all the spraying equipment, rolled up mats, and general rubbish, which had been there since my arrival. Mhoja began to tidy it up; as he leaned down to untangle some of the spraying equipment a cobra's head suddenly popped up and spat straight into his eyes. He felt a flash of pain and immediately became completely blind. Holding his hands over his eyes and crawling along the floor he let out a yell for help, crying "Nyoka, nyoka" (snake). Everyone rushed in with sticks and pangas, and killed the cobra. Iain broke open a bottle of serum and washed out Mhoja's eyes, then picked him up, put him in the Land-Rover and rushed to the plane for another emergency flight. Within minutes they were off the ground. By then the pain had lessened but Mhoja said that his whole head felt as if it was being eaten by rats. As soon as they were high enough Iain radioed his "Pan-Pan" message, telling the control tower at Arusha to order an ambulance and to notify the hospital that a passenger was arriving with snake poison in his eyes. This saved Mhoja's sight. He was in hospital in less than an hour. The serum worked and after four days he could see perfectly.

Whenever possible, we would go out on Sunday. Our aims were to get to places neither of us had been to before, land in the wilderness and then walk, or climb a mountain or explore a river. Once airborne we could reach places we had never been able to see till then through lack of roads or time. We could fly over mountains and forests, lakes and plains, or even glide with pelicans and eagles on our long flights back home, racing the sun to catch the last rays of light in order to land.

One day we flew across bare hills, brown and black in a drier year, now turning to green. The Masai, men of cattle, always seeking grass and water, lived in small scattered clusters here and there, like momentary parts of a landscape.

Flying over this sparsely inhabited land as if stalking in untracked space, we saw a road cutting through the scene as far as the eye could see, and we dropped down to a couple of hundred feet. With no windows on the plane, the heat rushed in, the wind blew, everything flapped as Iain searched for a smooth spot to land. Down we came to a few feet from the ground, racing along at high speed, ready to pull up at the slightest danger till he found a good place, went around to land, and we touched the rough uneven ground, running alongside the road. The plane came to a standstill, the engine was switched off, and we remained seated in complete silence. All we heard was the sound of wind running along the surface of the earth. I closed my eyes in a long moment of pleasure.

It must have been about midday for the sun was right above our heads. We got out and stood under the wings, looking for a place to walk to, or a hill to climb. I turned toward the straight track and saw a slim figure with a white cloth over his head, moving along fast, kicking up the dust. It is always strange to see a solitary man in a vast waste; one wonders where he comes from and where he is going to. At the far edge of the hill, behind the man, I saw dust; probably cattle or people from a village snuggled into the mountain I thought, but it was too far off to see.

We stood waiting for the man; now he was running. Perhaps he thought we were in trouble and needed help, indeed why else would a plane land here? Then far behind him I saw other figures, all were running in the wind and partly hidden by the dust.

The man came up and shook our hands, his face sweating, black and shiny. His teeth glittered from a dust-covered mouth, his eyes were alert as if looking for something. He walked around, holding his sticks in his right hand, as Masai do, touched the plane, looked inside and underneath it, and then started speaking in Masai and pointing upward. I could only understand a little of what he said and thought he was explaining that he had seen us suddenly drop down from the sky but he pointed to the hill, and said "long ago."

Then the others arrived. At first only a few came up to greet us. The rest stood a few paces back, sweating and breathing heavily, spitting and coughing, staring, laughing. Finally they came closer to us and to the plane; the wind was blowing its flaps up and down, which frightened some of the women who ran away or fell to the ground. Later, reassured, all came up and shook our hands and stood close, watching us. The door of the plane was open and in threes and fours they looked inside, but ran back each time something moved. The children were told to wait their turn until it was safe to look. The men came up to talk and we exchanged greetings. One man spoke perfect English, some spoke Swahili, but most spoke only Masai.

The men kept on pointing to the hill and telling us about a plane that had come here a long time ago—though some said it was just the other day. It had fallen, killing all the people in it. The men told us they ran to the place, but no one was alive, it had broken in many pieces. We explained that we had not crashed but only wanted to walk in the hills. Two men said they would accompany us, and take us to see the plane. I could not understand what they were talking about for there was no sign of a crashed plane.

Before leaving we put some stones under the wheels, and then followed the two men. Many of the people said they would stay until we returned, and promised they would not let anyone touch the plane.

We followed a cattle trail, where the grass was coarse and long and scratched our legs. It was incredibly hot and I was feeling sick. About 300 yards away from the road we came upon a piece of black and white striped tangled metal, still being pushed along by the wind. To my horror, I realized what it was, and could not believe my eyes that out of all those thousands of square miles we should have chosen this very place to land.

Iain and I stopped and looked. Above our heads we saw vultures twisting and turning in the currents, gliding alongside and over the cliffs. The few remains of the black and white plane were strewn all over the place. Children had played with pieces. Animals, as they passed by month after month, must have sniffed them, kicked them and rubbed themselves against them. The frame of one of the seats still survived, as did a piece of the tail, and bits of the wings. Further along was a cross made of stones, which marked the exact place of the crash. And that was all that remained of Michael Grzimek.

As a young man he and his father had pioneered research in the Serengeti, flying for hours locating and counting the scattered migratory herds in an attempt to establish the natural boundaries of the Park. His death was caused by one of those unpredictable hazards of flying small airplanes in Africa. He hit a griffon vulture which bent his right wing and jammed the rudder cables so that the plane went into a steep dive. Its remains were a sad, abandoned sight.

The lives of the Grzimek father and son had been an inspiration to us. It was through their film and published work, especially *Serengeti Shall Not Die,* that the Serengeti became famous and they were responsible in a large measure for its preservation as the finest wildlife refuge in the world. We hoped to do something of the sort for Manyara.

The Masai who came with us told us he had seen the plane turn sharply and fall, then bounce and break into pieces. Whether he had actually seen it himself or just heard about it, we couldn't tell. I could imagine how elsewhere tourists would have picked up pieces of the plane and taken them home to add to their collections. I was happy that the remnants of Michael's aircraft should stay here in the dust and the grass of the plains he loved. It was better left for the Masai children and the wind to play with. I walked away with the image of Michael's face printed on my mind.

We followed the cattle tracks along the bottom of the cliffs. On one side the Rift rose sharply up to where vultures wheeled and soared on the thermal currents.

Their nests on the face of this sheer cliff hundreds of feet high were tucked into any piece of rock that was big enough for a perch. The birds were safe. From there they could see everything that happened around them. On the other side the Salei plains stretched away into the African haze. It was as if we were nonexistent, so microscopic were we in comparison with our surroundings. There was no present, past or future. It was all there unchanged; yet we were here now, and so alive. Only time was passing by. We walked and walked, through a valley, up a stream, hopping from stone to stone where there was no path. We climbed and looked and explored and wondered. It was the only way to see the country, to try to understand, to learn. We were partly birds, partly humans, partly animals.

The Masai man never spoke to us. When we stopped, he stopped too. When we sat down, he sat down a little way from us. When we reached the top, we sat, looked, and remembered. There were no clouds, the plains were streaked with waves of heat, I saw things turning in the sun. Even the airplane seemed to have melted away and as I sat on that rock in the midst of nowhere, I felt that Michael and the people who lived there were lucky to begin life and sometimes end life in a reversal of time toward wilderness.

When we took off, some of the children were still there and a couple of old men were sitting under the shade of the wing. We looked into their eyes, held hands, said goodbye, ran our plane into the wind and lifted off from the ground, moving higher and higher into the sky, with a growing circle of the world below us. It was part of our moving territory, marked only by the momentary presence of ourselves, and defended by our secrecy. We would never go back there again.

# 11

# Encounters
# in the Forest

When one is really happy one should be able to stop the world from going around, stop life, stop time. Then it's as if time belongs to oneself only and no one could ever interfere.

Despite my happy and exciting visits to Manyara my life was pounded around like a boxing ball in the last months of 1969. We were expecting a baby, but I nearly lost it in an airplane accident. Afterward I was very demoralized; but as the old year turned into the beginning of 1970, my life took a definite turn in a new and unexpected direction. I moved into Manyara to stay and Ndala, the freshly painted camp, was now my home. I slipped into it as if I had never been away. Even my bush clothes neatly folded on an empty shelf with my safari boots, were there waiting for me. The smiling faces of Suleiman, Mhoja and Ali greeted me.

Suleiman brought coffee to the table, Mhoja came to tell me the latest news and I could hear Ali unloading the car, whistling the same tune that he had whistled ever since he came to Ndala. It was part of him, like his shirt or his trousers.

The two big umbrella acacias held up their spreading crowns covered in tiny balls of soft yellow fluff. A breeze rippled through the branches throwing a silent shower of golden flowers over me and on to the barren ground. As I ran to the top of the hill timid eyes watched through the tall feathery grass. From up here I could see the little stream sparkling in the sun and hear the ceaseless flow of water running down the rocks into the warm sand. I could wait for the sounds that I loved to hear, rough skins scraping against rough skins, of silent elephants walking on the sands. When the wind blew up from the river and into my face I waited for the noise of flapping ears and snorting trunks, as the elephants shuffled along one behind the other, with their babies at their sides, up to the ochre-colored pool just below my bedroom. Here they would drink and play and swish cool water over themselves.

I wanted to be able to photograph the behavior of individual elephants and to try and build up a photographic story of their lives, but first I would have to learn how to accept them and be accepted by them. I too would now have to recognize most of these elephants so that I could get to know which were the "goodies," the "heavies" and the "baddies." I wondered if this would be possible; if it were, then I could stay and work with the "goodies" on my own. This was my one opportunity to do something new and to get to know elephants really well.

It was quite simple, Iain explained. The "goodies" just lived their everyday lives, tolerant of anything that went on around them, and anyone was safe with them; the "heavies" were certain big females and a couple of temperamental bulls, that would make most people take instant flight, unless they knew how to approach them and what sort of things they disliked; as for the "baddies" they would make everyone run for their lives; if they didn't they might find themselves upside down in an overturned car, or with a tusk between their knees. I would just have to find out who was who. Iain seemed to know exactly how far he could go with these elephants, but sometimes even he was surprised. I dreaded meeting any "baddies" and every time we drove through the south of the Park, and I heard an elephant trumpet, I was sure this was a death trap, unless we got out of the place—fast. But after following Boadicea and her kinship group for long periods together with Iain, I got to know her and other members of her family well—each had her own personality. With more knowledge about elephants I lost my fear of them.

Virgo and Right Hook were the first to help me get through my phase of anxiety. Whenever we drove near to the family, Virgo would come right up to us, flip her trunk back and forth and stand at trunk's length from Iain.

At that time the trees were in fruit. Mhoja and Iain gathered sacks full of various kind of acacia pods, together with other species like the bitter, hard fruit gardenia and sweet balanites dates to see which the elephants preferred. A variety of these were then spread out near the car and we were able to watch with fascination how fast Virgo could eat them and which fruits she chose first. If Right Hook or others were nearby, she could put three gardenias, which are bigger than tennis balls, into her mouth, and keep another two in her trunk with a wrap-around hold, like a cupped hand over one's arm. *Acacia tortilis* was no bigger than a dried-up french bean; the pods were picked up one by one and blown into her mouth. Most elephants went through the same choosing and eating patterns: gardenia, balanites, albida and tortilis they loved. They also ate the tamarind and *Acacia siberiana* fruit when available. They never ate the yellow fever-tree pods, which are wind-dispersed seeds, or the black and red bead-like trichelia from the forest. The long sausage-tree fruit was also rarely eaten. Whenever we met Virgo and had an odd gardenia fruit in the car, we gave it to her, and this was certainly the beginning and the most exciting part of our making friends. We began to know her character really well and she trusted us. Right Hook who was Virgo's closest companion, became equally friendly in spite of the fact that we hardly ever gave her fruit after the experiments were over. She had a totally different character

from Virgo, far less curious and seemed less observant. Virgo made me feel as if she were watching us
and therefore responded much more to our movements.

Iain decided the best places for my identification
lessons were by the big pool under my hut and along
the river bed. He gave me his family-unit photo files
from which I could pick out other well-known matriarchs of the elephant society. I set myself to become a
sharp observer.

At first Iain or Mhoja accompanied me to the
river to show me how to approach elephants on foot.
Sometimes the wind blew up from the Lake, which
enabled us to creep along the rocks until we were only
a few feet away from them. But often the wind was
tricky in the valley, suddenly changing direction. A
knotted handkerchief, with ash in it, was the best wind
indicator and helped me to dominate my fear by fore-
warning me when the herd was likely to be driven away
by my scent.

Mhoja built me a small hide under the tamarind
tree which offered a patch of shade on the edge of the
river. Here I could sit in solitude for as many hours as
I wished. The hide was built of branches to make it
look like its neighbor the capparis bush; bald, egg-
shaped rocks stuck out of the grass for me to sit on.
In front of the hide the river ran over a flat and sandy
area where, if there was enough water, the elephants
would often stop to drink or just stand around like
people in a piazza, some murmuring and leaning on
one another watching their babies scuffle with other
youngsters.

The elephant I first recognized was a matriarch who
arrived at an unhurried pace, and stopped a few feet
away from my fragile shelter; only my eyes moved,
they went from the elephant to the photograph file and
back to the elephant, as I tried to identify her ears. She
had crossed tusks and must therefore be one of three
matriarchs, Sarah, Anita or Anitoid—only her ears
could tell me which. Anita had a big notch in her right
ear, Anitoid had a similar notch but with square instead

of rounded edges, but this elephant had a string of tiny holes on each ear. She was Sarah, with a family of twelve. She stood about ten feet high, on legs like pillars with cushioned feet, each forefoot adorned by five smooth hoof-like nails and four on each hind foot. These thick nails gave the leading edge of her foot a hard and shiny appearance like well-polished shoe caps. Using the edge of the inner toenails, she scratched the side of her leg with great delicacy. Then as if the sole of her foot were itchy she rubbed it over a rock. I caught a glimpse of the hard pad with its criss-cross fissures, which Iain told me were different in every elephant, enabling skilled trackers to follow one particular elephant through the footprints of a herd. Sarah drank rhythmically, lifting her trunk from the water into her mouth and letting it drop back in the water.

Next to her was another female who was mowing the grass at the edge of the river. With her trunk she grasped one tussock at a time, and then gave a forward kick with her foot, the toenails of which sheared through the fibers as neatly and efficiently as cutting hay with a scythe. Then she popped the little bunch of grass into her mouth. The roots were left in the ground so no earth got in her mouth.

Suddenly the wind changed and a whiff of my scent swept up Sarah's trunk. She wheeled, and, within seconds, loomed up in front of me, trumpeting and kicking up sand, shaking her head, and then looking down as if she were aiming through the crossed tips of her tusks, searching for the intruder. I did not move. This enormous animal was powerful, confident, and coordinated in her movements—there was a certain completeness about her. Then, quietly, looking like a grand old lady who had been offended, Sarah moved away leading her family past me toward the bush. The fifty-two thickly padded feet made hardly a sound.

Iain had warned me never to get overconfident, for one of these elephants could turn out to be a "baddie" I might not recognize in time. Then no handclapping or waving of my arms would deter her from carrying out her threat. For such an emergency I had a special rapid-exit path made behind the hide, from which I could hop over the rocks where she would not have a chance of catching up.

To get good photographs I had to figure out what the elephants were going to do seconds before it happened. The easiest thing in the world is to take an elephant's portrait, with him just standing still. But for every good action picture or to catch the expression I wanted, hundreds of reject pictures piled up. In the end, I learned to sit for hours in the car or in my hide, with my camera at the ready, never getting bored, observing, waiting. I began to understand what they were doing, and why, and this was my reward.

To sit alone in a hide is a great experience. One acquires bush eyes and ears. The faintest sound can be detected and the smallest details sighted. Waiting for the elephants to arrive I had plenty of time to look at the other animals. I learnt many things, such as that only when the baboons came to the river was it safe for the shy bush-buck to come out of hiding and drink. They know then that there are no dangerous predators around. It took no more than ten minutes for the baboons to settle down, then a twig would crack and through the leaves on the opposite bank I would spot part of a face or an eye, and delicately a bush-buck would appear, and wander past the baboons into the shallow water. One or two more would follow, then they would frolic and play with the baboons. Impalas also arrived nearly every day with the baboons, walking up in big golden herds with their ears twitching ceaselessly. The females were grouped together, herded by one male, his head adorned with black, lyre-shaped horns. Most of the time he was kept busy chasing other males out of his territory; only occasionally could he relax for a drink. I never saw lions during the day, but I often heard them nearby. Some days the river was filled with elephants, buck of all kinds, baboons, blue monkeys; even the two rhinos who lived in the Ndala valley would come out or a giraffe might slowly drift along in the haze of the sand heat. It looked as if all the animals had agreed to spend a morning on the beach, playing, washing, drinking and sunning themselves.

The first time I saw Boadicea at Ndala, not a single elephant or any other animal had been to the river during the whole of that day. I went back to camp for a drink. Then suddenly the whole river bed was covered with snorting, rumbling elephants as they went through their slow ritual. None of us had heard them come. There must have been about one hundred including Boadicea's kinship group and several other families strolling up on either side of the river. Instantly I picked out Leonora, Slender Tusks with her son N'Dume at her heels, and Jezebel with her family closely grouped around her. Boadicea was heading for the top pool; Virgo and Right Hook were walking together, there were some big bulls mingling with the families, and a lot of younger ones straggling on behind. Overcome with excitement, I picked up my cameras and the ash bag, and rushed down to my hide, bending as I ran to keep myself concealed. The wind was blowing upstream toward the house, which was ideal.

I found myself in the middle of an elephant world, many of whose personalities I knew. It was like feeling the excitement of sitting in a theater just before the curtain goes up, watching the people arriving, recognizing some and listening to the musicians tuning their instruments. I knew that all sorts of things were going to happen.

The families drifted slowly upstream until they reached the clear water. There were young bulls who dared not come too close to the females and who stood at the water-holes where the river stopped flowing. Since at this season the water was only inches deep and not all the elephants could use the top pool, I noticed for the first time how they began digging holes along the river's edge. The well diggers were usually bulls or old cows. Using their feet as shovels to loosen the earth, they kicked the sand backward and forward, until a wide hole was formed. At times they would dig down three feet or more with their trunks and feet, their toenails acting like a spade. They would push the sand with the side of a foot on to the curved end of the trunk, which they used like a cupped hand to throw the sand to one side. When the sand got damp and the water began to seep into the hole, they used the tips of their trunks, like fingers, to dig a deep, narrow, clean hole. The muddy water was rapidly sucked up and spewed around in circles or blown out like a suction pump and with the same noise. It was amazing how professional they were at the job. Within about a quarter of an hour little wells had been dug all over the place, some only a few feet away from each other.

I could see how each family was organized within the hierarchy that Iain had told me so much about. Not only was there competition between a mother and her offspring, but also between families.

On one side, Jezebel, the matriarch of her family, was drinking rhythmically from her well, while others were standing nearby sucking up trunkfuls at a time and then waiting for the water to seep back. Boadicea's family, having already drunk at the top pool, walked down to where Jezebel was drinking. With hardly a movement of her head, Boadicea took over from Jezebel and so did her family. Even though Jezebel's family had dug these holes, they just moved further up without a sign of annoyance and drank directly from the river. Boa really was a queen whom all respected.

Elephant families walking up and down occasionally stopped to greet each other with their trunk to mouth gesture, while young babies walked up to a big bull and one by one greeted him. In return the bull put his trunk to each little mouth, or touched the babies on their heads in the way in which Masai elders greet their children. A small cluster of elephants stood a little way from Boadicea waiting patiently for her to leave the water-holes, their trunks slung over their tusks, or just hanging like a length of hose from a fire engine. None showed any sign of aggression, except when the young bulls ventured too near. The only ones who never seemed to be able to get any water out of the holes were the smallest calves, who spent most of their time pushing, pulling or walking around their mothers. The older calves either drank elsewhere, or started digging holes themselves.

When Boadicea and her family had had their fill, they quietly ambled off to the flat piece of sand, where they threw trunkfuls of dust over themselves.

Covered in a rough loose-skinned armor the color of stones, rich in ivory, Boadicea's polished tusks stood out like weapons, and I could imagine this great pachyderm preparing for battle. At one end hung a whiskered tail, sought after by man for its few hairs to twist into a bracelet. At the other end hung that masterpiece of the elephant—the trunk. It must be great to have a body of that size and also to be endowed with so rare an organ as a trunk, to do all the work the body needs to keep it always full and clean. Partly lip and partly nose, with two fingers on the tip, it is used as a worker's arm and hand. It has double hoses for sucking in and spraying out water or dust, and can test the wind. It can push down trees or pick off the smallest leaf. It can be as gentle and as loving as the most tender arms, to greet and tickle, to scratch and rub, to smell and caress, always twisting, moving, rolling in an infinite variety of postures. At the same time, it can change into an efficient weapon to kill, and when it detects the smell of man, rears back above the head like a serpent preparing to strike. There was something about the elephants that made me feel close to them. Was it the trunk that made me identify with elephants? Of course it arouses many people's imagination as a sex object, and no doubt some will say that is why I was so fascinated. I have read about an elephant in Egypt who who was in love with a beautiful woman: "One day in the market he brought her certain apples and put them into her bosom, holding his trunk a great while therein fondling and playing with her breasts."

I was relieved that Boa was not near my hide as I was sure she would have smelt me out, chased me away and emptied the whole river bed of elephants, at one signal. But when Right Hook and Virgo walked past me I wanted to go "psst" to attract Virgo's attention. We were daily becoming more friendly with her, and I felt that soon we would be able to walk alongside her. To get to know elephants' personalities, and to be able to sit quite confidently a few feet from them and not feel afraid, was one of the most exciting things about the whole study and our work.

Early one morning, Mhoja called through the window of the Herbarium, telling me to come quickly as he had something to show me. There, curled up in his bottle-green Ranger's cap on the bottom of a tall cardboard box, was a fluffy little female mongoose. Its red eyes peered up at me, with a look half of fear, and half of pleading, because she was so lonely. Even a wild mongoose, separated from the pack and from its mother, needs some form of love from someone. We stroked and scratched her back every half-hour. I was happy to have another mongoose, for Pilipili and Ndogo had disappeared some time ago; perhaps because they were jealous of me, and since then the house had felt only half lived in.

Outside, the rain had brought thousands of grasshoppers on to the long green grass; these provided one of the mongoose's favorite meals. We knew that Widgey, as we named her, would be tame in twenty-four hours, partly thanks to an endless supply of hoppers. Early in the morning when their wings are cold and heavy from the dew, grasshoppers are easy to catch, but as soon as they warm up one can spend hours chasing after them and only catch two or three. We all went out into the bushes, picking grasshoppers, filling up little bags and returning with a vast provision for

Widgey. I don't think she ever ate as many in her life as in those first two days. Her little tummy filled out like a balloon till I was sure she was going to burst. No one walking past Widgey's box could resist giving her a grasshopper; its head was bitten off, then she ate the tasty body.

After a week she seemed completely happy with her new family in her new home. Already she was eating bits of egg, drinking milk out of our cups, chirruping, purring and nosing all around the rooms. When she was not in Iain's pocket she was in my shirt.

On the first Thursday of the month, it was market day for cattle, sheep and goats at Mto-wa-Mbu. Masai, Wambulu and Wambugwe brought their fattest steers and cows, their sheep, and all sizes of goats to sell. One could easily recognize the Wambulu by their shaven heads and scarred faces. The Wambugwe I knew by their piercing dark eyes and solemn faces; they were always on the look out for the evil-eye. Masai women draped in long plum-red pieces of cloth, their heads and shoulders covered in bright beaded jewelry, sat under trees selling milk which they had carried for many miles in their calabashes. This was the day when people exchanged news from across the hills and from the plains. I nearly always went to market with Mhoja to buy a few chickens and eggs so that we could keep our stock going.

A tall young Masai, standing on one foot, leaning on his spear and cleaning his teeth vigorously with a *mswaki*,* called to me: "Soba Mama Duglass" (which means hello in Masai). He was a friend of Iain's. I waved back. He gathered all his sticks in his left hand and dragged a small shiny brown goat, with snipped off ears, behind him.

"Take this to Duglass," he said. I was thrilled with my present and thanked him in Masai.

"Ashe oling . . . Sidai oling" (thank you very much

*mswaki—a little stick cut from a special tree, used for cleaning teeth.

–it's lovely). He helped us settle the goat and some chickens in a safe place in the Land-Rover and went back to his other goats, while we returned to camp with our load of food and animals. I loved the idea of having a goat at Ndala.

"But this goat is going to be eaten in five minutes by some big cat," Iain warned me, shaking his finger. We named her Biba. She was tethered to a small acacia sapling near the bathroom; standing on tiptoe she ate it up to the limit of her nose. At night she was shut up in a strong house which Mhoja had built. Soon Biba became one of the funniest and fattest pets I ever had. Her choicest titbits were Iain's notes and *The New Yorker* which she devoured at such speed that it was practically impossible to save the pages once she started eating them. Any fruit she could find went down just as fast. Bananas were her favorite and she learned every trick to get at where they hung from a beam in our sitting room, climbing on to cupboards and window ledges to reach them.

After a few weeks Biba paired up with Widgey and together they came with us on the long walks, which we took after the day's work. On one of these evening outings along the strip, I noticed some dark spattered patches on the ground. As soon as she saw them Biba shied away and darted off into the bush. Immediately, all my childhood tracking instincts flared up. This was dried blood. It had been splashed over the grass, and the bushes all around had been trampled down. Something quite big must have been killed or wounded that night. Quietly we backed away and slunk down the track for home.

We decided to search the area to try to find the dead or wounded animal. This time, for safety, we took a gun and went in the car. Not more than twenty yards from where we had stood looking at the blood-stained grass, but well hidden in a thick clump of bush, was a dead buffalo. It was half eaten but there was no sign of lions. We turned in a wide circle to go back home and in a dip, about thirty yards from the carcass, we saw two bloated lions sleeping in the shade: Satima and Chongo, suspected man-eaters.

From the window of my little hut I could look out across the river and see that only the tops of the trees had patches of green, everything else was yellow straw and sand dust. Down the grey rocks above us, a line of black water sparkled and fell into the shallow pool, from which a trickle made its way along a sandy bed and stopped abruptly. This was the dry season. The air was dry, the wind smelled of dust, the earth's crust cracked. The two acacia trees stood like huge umbrellas on either side of our banana-thatched house and shaded it from the hot sun.

During the month of October, when all the trees look naked and burned by the sun, the leaves and the bushes wrinkle up, the dry grass crackles and the earth is hot. Then one day you see the tops of the acacia trees covered in little green leaves and every day after that you can count more trees whose tops are becoming green and others filling out with green leaves. This, I learned, was the first sign that the rains would soon be here; in a month, or maybe in two or three.

In the heat of the day it felt as if all eyes were watching and waiting for the woodlands to be covered in a green spray. The animals drifted from one patch of shade to another, eyes and nostrils half closed, waiting for the cool hours to go out in search of food.

Then suddenly, as if all the trees had nodded their heads together up to the limpid African sky, great flat clouds piled up on top of each other and moved around the horizon on a migration of their own. Each day more clouds filled the sky, rolling, tumbling and flying past, changing color and form where the sunshine fell. If there were no landscape to look at and no animals to watch it would not matter, one would just look up at the sky.

The wind from the Lake met the wind from the hills

and all the trees started to bend as the wind rushed and whirled around madly, elephants trumpeted and shrieked, monkeys screamed, bushes bent, branches broke, animals scattered.

This was the wind of rain. I watched the clouds gather and cover the sun. The wind was silent for a moment. The air thickened, the sky darkened, thunder and lightning crashed around us. In camp, doors and windows were banging, dark figures were running to tie things down, firewood was being stored away, chickens were scattering for shelter. Soon the whole place would be under water.

Hot earth and distant rain. The wind dropped and the hot damp silence sat with me and waited. No animals were visible, no noises could be heard except the coo coo of the spotted dove and the plaintive piping of the hornbill. Now and then a huge drop of water smacked the ground. I felt as if heaven lay close to the earth and I between them.

Slanting streaks of grey and white swept up the valley with a rushing sound of rain that grew louder. Above my head the dried leaves of the thatch rustled as the first drops fell and washed away the dust. This was the marvelous sound we had been waiting for. The air grew cooler and the smell of moist earth filled my nostrils. I could almost feel the beginning of life growing from the earth, and I wanted to sing and dance and make love.

The rain came down and pounded the earth. Nothing could stop it now. We took shelter and listened to the drumming on the roof. Where a minute ago there was dry barren earth, now a brown sheet of water swept past and sprayed through the mosquito-netting of the paneless windows, forming puddles on the floor. After an hour the rain passed over to the hills. In the stillness of the valley, the soaking trees shook off drops that fell with loud splatters on the ground. We could walk barefoot across the red muddy compound, jumping and hopping over puddles on our toes. Patches of blue appeared through the cloud-covered sky, sunlight flashed and sparkled on the dripping bushes. The quenched earth sucked in the water and steam rose up from its latent heat.

Far away over the hill I heard a strange rumble and looked up. There too it had rained. The distant rumble grew louder and louder until I could distinguish the noise of water gushing down the dusty valleys and over the boulders. Then the side of the mountain above the top hut erupted, and a thunderous gush of dark brown water leaped over the edge carrying trees and stones with it as it rushed down into the first pool, pushing itself through a narrow gorge between the rocks, and falling in a huge volume of liquid soil on to the white sands of the dry river bed. Where grey rocks and yellow grasses had stood side by side on the sand, the muddy water churned and sprayed, taking possession of every bit of its dried-up bed.

After darkness fell, distant thunder shook the world, and lightning cut across the horizon, revealing in immaculate detail the dark blue lines of mountains far away across the Lake. The rainy season had at last begun.

For three months it rained. The Park lost its pale sun colors and turned into a fantasy of green. Life changed with the rains and so did we. The rains brought food, the rains brought birth. Before the rains only the mothers were fat with heavy pregnant stomachs. The males were thin, the predators were thin. In a month it would be the other way around.

By now I had met a lot of the people Iain was working with and for and realized that some of them were really concerned for his safety. They told him "We've been hunting elephants for thirty years and we know. If you go on like this, they'll get you and you'll die before your time. The elephants will never accept you."

Iain laughed off their fears and tried to convince them he was dealing with elephants in ways quite different to those of hunters.

When our visitors came out driving with us, our acid test of their character was to confront them with Boadicea; seeing the great matriarch, standing tall and fierce, her eyes alight, her ears extended and flapping like witches' wings, her tusks slashing through the bushes, a chill went down their spines.

"What the hell are you doing?" they yelled.

"Please don't shout at my elephants," Iain would whisper back as he sat calmly looking through his binoculars at the other elephants' families.

Because of the rains pouring on to us and the visitors pouring into our camp, I decided to build verandas in front of the houses, so as to give everyone more space and cover.

Ali and a friend of his were repairing the banana thatch and they assured me they would be able to build these verandas in a few days. The Park Warden gave us permission to cut poles. We got them from a tree called "Mbavu ya Faru" (rhino's ribs), whose branches really did look like huge green-grey-white ribs, and they were the best for this kind of building. While Ali and his friend cut thatch, talking and hacking with their pangas, I walked away from the car to pick some wild flowers and bottle-brush grasses. For some minutes there was total silence. I called to Ali. Then, as if a devil had entered his body, his friend started shouting.

"Chui, chui." (Leopard) "Bring the gun quickly ... Chui, chui, bring the gun, bring the gun."

I leaped across to the car and grabbed the gun. I could see Ali and his friend in the tree, but no leopard.

"For God's sake, where is it?" I shouted.

"Right here," Ali's friend pointed to his feet.

I crept up to the tree, two bullets in the .470, my finger on the trigger. "Show me the leopard."

"There," he yelled, pointing to his toe.

I put the gun down and pulled myself up the tree. In a fork, I saw a little nest of leaves, and in it, wet and cold and crawling blindly, two tiny spotted genet cats not bigger than my fist. I wrapped an old jersey

around them and held them close to the warmth of
my body, then looked up at Ali's friend, who was still
standing in the tree, a panga in his hand. "What if the
mother comes back?" he shouted to me. "She will kill
me immediately."

"Don't worry, she will not come back." We searched,
trying to convince Ali's friend that no leopards were
here. So far as we could tell the genets had been
abandoned.

As soon as we arrived in camp we fed them with
warm diluted milk and glucose. Obviously famished,
they sucked hard at the eye dropper which was all I
could find, and I knew they would live.

With these young animals we were going to get all
the experience we needed to bring up a human baby
in the bush, for the mongoose and the genets would
have to be watched over day and night, and taken
with us wherever we went.

One day Mhoja and Suleiman, looking very serious,
came to tell me they had decided I needed a woman
in the camp to help me. Moreover the girl would arrive next morning with John, one of the Park's lorry
drivers. She was his daughter, and a good girl. She had
never worked before, but I could teach her everything. Touched by their concern for me, I agreed and
thanked them.

The girl was called Amina. She was very pretty,
dressed in a tight cotton shift which clung to her
round, hard bottom and she was very lively. Mhoja
introduced her to the members of the camp and
showed her around the place. She knew nothing
about housework and I didn't know how to begin to
teach her, so Mhoja and Suleiman took over for the
first week, until she had settled down to some sort of
routine.

Amina giggled and laughed whenever I told her
to do something. Then she ran back to the kitchen in a
sort of wriggle-trip manner, as if her knees were giving
in at each step, while with her hand over her mouth,

she let out "eehs" and "aays" in a series of short yelps. The result was that everyone in the camp was constantly laughing and the atmosphere was extremely gay.

Amina had never seen elephants before and was terrified as well as fascinated by them. We and our work seemed to fascinate her also, and often when we were sitting at table, having a meal, she would just stand and stare at us, holding a tray or a glass in her hand. Sometimes she sat down with us, leaning on her elbows, smoking and laughing, her eyes sparkling. It took us quite a long time to explain to her that if she was employed here, she couldn't just sit down at table or stand around staring at us. Everyone loved Amina.

After two weeks she had learned how to make beds, sweep the floors, wash the dishes, and set the table. It was about this time that I went to Mto-wa-Mbu and learned that Amina was one of the bar girls from Mama Rosa's establishment. She was certainly not the daughter of John, the driver; and in fact Mhoja and Suleiman had cleverly maneuvered things so that she could help in the camp during the day and keep them company at night. I realized that she would soon get bored, and sadly after a month she asked for her pay and permission to go to the village to shop. She never returned.

Ali told me he knew lots of very good women, and could easily get a replacement but that he would need some time in Mto-wa-Mbu to find the right one. Off he went and sure enough, when Ali returned he had a girl in the car with him. He promised me she was hardworking and would help me with the camp. So pretty Amina was replaced by Fat Amina, supposedly a daughter of one of the Park Rangers, and we were happy to have another maid in the camp. Fat Amina went through the same routine of learning the camp drill as her predecessor, but she was neither as attractive nor as giggly as pretty Amina. Nevertheless, she did her work as best she could and she stayed with us a bit longer. She loved the animals, and always had one of the cats either on her shoulder or tucked away in her dress nestled between her huge bosoms.

But the day came when Fat Amina complained of nausea and giddiness: she was pregnant, and she left soon afterwards.

I was having breakfast when Iain brought me a vulture to add to my collection. The bird was young and must have fallen out of his nest before he could manage to open his wings. When Iain picked him up he was walking on the road in a half-dazed state. We perched him on the windowsill, where he spent that day looking down into the valley.

We called him Auda Abu Taii, after the famous Arab chieftain who swooped out of the desert to pounce on the Turks during Lawrence of Arabia's campaign in the First World War. Somehow, after he had been given that name and despite his bald head and loose purple skin, he took on a certain air of magnificence and lost his repulsive appearance. His eyes were almond shaped and bright as rubies. People and animals alike respected and feared him. If we walked past his perch without shoes he would swoop down and thrust his head toward our toes, hopping after us, pushing himself along with his wings and pecking at our feet until we caught him and put him back on to his perch. I could never leave the genets alone when he was around. Widgey, who didn't approve of this intruder, would stand on her hind legs and growl as loud as a mongoose can, giving out her alarm signals to inform us that something big, bad and nasty was about. She would then dart under a table or a chair and wait for Auda to pass by, so as to get a good nip at him. As for the chickens and birds they listened attentively when they heard Widgey's alarm calls, and immediately went into hiding.

When it came to feeding time, and all the different saucers and meals were ready, Auda would make a flying leap and land with a heavy crash on the table and then totter toward the food. Ruffled out like a furry porcupine Widgey would fling herself at him with her high-pitched attack cry and bite him wherever she could.

In time Auda Abu Taii became a magnificent ornament to our camp, and we grew very attached to him. Then one day he suddenly took off from his perch, flew across the river to the opposite bank, sat on a tree for a while looking at us, and disappeared into the haze where the Lake meets the sky.

Each time I entered the Ground Water Forest in Manyara it always made me feel as if I were living in a fairy tale. It was magical with its tall, naked, grey-limbed trees standing next to yellow-barked fig trees, racing each other up to the sun, covered in an iridescent canopy. Baboons and monkeys jumped through the branches, swishing the leaves like rustling taffeta, and called to each other with chuckles and barks. Crystal clear springs emerged from below the cliffs and flowed in little streams under a shiny, emerald carpet of plants, which looked like tiny palm trees. When one walked through the forest, the sun streamed down like long spider-spun threads. It was cool and translucent, with the same damp smell as an old cathedral. Sweet flowers and the strong scent of elephants mingled and blew in the wind. Anyone who walks through the Ground Water Forest must stop and look and feel the wonder of it, for it is unique. It is alive.

Often we would drift along the wide elephant paths, covered in soft leaves, rotten twigs and elephant dung, a carpet which was the work of hundreds of cracked, thick-soled elephant feet that had walked silently up and down these trails for months. We went barefoot, for there were no thorns or flies and we never bothered about snakes, and on the rare occasion when we nearly stumbled over a rhino or came face to face with an elephant it was easier without sandals to walk away or run quietly, or even to scramble up trees if necessary. Only rhinos really terrified me; we would give way to elephants, or hide rather than chase them and frighten them off the paths. We never felt the need to lift a rifle or pull the trigger in self-defense.

The elephants took care that the undergrowth was kept well eaten and where they had been we could walk from one end of the cleared forest to the other and back on different trails, crossing rivers on huge, fallen logs and drinking from the springs. Our senses became so alert that like hunters, we could smell and track elephants long before we saw or heard them. Then we could follow them, moving with them a few paces behind or to one side. It was incredibly easy to creep down-wind to within a few feet of them. I imagined the multiple ways one could hunt these animals without their realizing that they had their most dreaded predators on their tail.

In the forest there were always unexpected meetings. One day we came upon Right Hook, Virgo and their calves, breaking branches to eat the tender young leaves, not far from where we stood. This was the first time we had encountered Virgo on foot. Deeper in the forest, the other elephants stood around Boadicea. We slipped from one tree trunk to the other, moving up to Virgo, and stood in front of her, semi-hidden by a fallen tree. As soon as she saw us she stopped eating, perked up her ears, and waited, without making a sound. Iain was right in front of her a couple of yards away and held out his hand. It was a moment of great tension. Virgo let out a loud snort, shook her head, clapped her ears in a cloud of dust, and twiddled her trunk in knots, in much the same way as I wring my hands when I am nervous. Iain stood his ground and Virgo seeing that her threats had no effect on him, began a little dance with her trunk curling near his hand like a snake. Then, when Iain took a step forward calling her name, Virgo retreated. Her head went down, she snorted, pulled grass, rubbed her eye with her trunk, used it to dig in her ear, sniffed the air, and kicked up dust, but she never tried to hit him. It looked as if she were playing for time, unable to make up her mind what to do, and meanwhile using her trunk to distract Iain's attention. Plainly, she could not muster enough courage to touch his hand. They stood watching each other for a long, exciting moment. Then Virgo walked straight up to Iain and when she clapped her ears at him he opened his arms making himself look bigger and taller, then he turned and walked back to the log where I was standing.

Meanwhile, Virgo's daughter, who was about seven years old, stood in the background, ears wide spread, watching this extraordinary meeting. Right Hook strolled up, partly concealing herself behind Virgo and extending her trunk as far as she could to sniff at us. She was much the bigger of the two and because they were always together Iain thought she might be Virgo's elder sister or mother.

A couple of times Virgo walked right up to us, stood about four feet away, put out her trunk and moved it around in front of our faces and I heard a long flowing sound, like wind blowing through a tunnel. Then, as if she had nothing more to investigate, she walked away, ripping off leaves to eat as she went; the others followed close behind her.

"I knew Virgo would not try to hurt us," Iain said. "She's a fantastic elephant. I'm sure if we ever had enough time we would be able to tame her completely and even play with her baby."

This was the first occasion on which we had approached Virgo face to face on foot. From now on it was simply a question of time before she, Right Hook and their calves would be able to walk hand in trunk with us. Iain's wildest dream was to be able to ride on Virgo one day and move with Boa's family, making quiet observations from her back, about the family, from within the family and, hopefully, without being noticed.

I was so struck by Iain's ability to deal with these elephants, that I thought it would be a pity if all this was left unrecorded and I decided we had to make a film.

A year had passed and much had changed since my early trips to Manyara. The elephants were so much part of my life now I hardly bothered to turn around when I heard their angry trumpeting. Living amongst animals one becomes more like them. One's hearing and eyesight become quicker and sharper. One's reactions, to stop, to start and to wheel around, grow faster. Some animals live by day and sleep at night, others sleep by day and live by night, and we learned to move and live with them, both by day and by night. We could run, leap over rocks and practically stop breathing. Distances had no limits, time no meaning. Our day began at sunrise and stopped at sunset. There were the dry months, the wet months, the hot days and the cold days.

I knew by the color of the trees, the bushes and the flowers, which month it was. The clouds, rain, dust and heat gave me an indication of the seasons, the sun told me the time. New moons came and full moons went, and when the stars shone bright out of a black sky I knew one month had passed.

Every morning the cock would crow at about four thirty. A red patch would appear on the horizon at five thirty, and the whole horizon would be alight by six. The sun came out half an hour later and when two Egyptian geese flew from the top pool of the waterfall toward the Lake it was seven and time for breakfast and the BBC World News, after which we would go out to work.

At midday the sun would be directly above us, and the elephants would walk under the trees to rest. Then it was time to watch them from the top of a tree.

When the sun fell behind the hill it was five in the afternoon and the elephants would be walking along the Lake shore in the evening light, moving slowly up into the hills. In camp, it was time to cut wood for the hot water boiler and the stove, and begin to prepare the evening meal. It was time also to clean the paraffin lamps and lock up the chickens and the goat. When the Egyptian geese flew back to the top pool there was still enough light to land on our strip. By seven fifteen it was dark.

We had lost the habit of using watches, calendars or telephones. This daily course of nature was all we needed to know.

# 12

# Born
# in the Wild

The mornings greeted us with wispy clouds that drifted
under a blue-black sky, looking as if it had been badly
bruised by thunder. The Park was now thickly covered
in rich, deep green that spread along the ground and
up into the trees. Heavy rainstorms broke, usually
in the afternoon, and lasted for an hour or more. The
clouds swept past and the sun heated up the wet
ground until it steamed and rich smells rose from the
damp earth. On the crest of the hills along the ridges
and tumbling down the sides of the gulleys, the yel-
low-leaved sterculia and commiphora trees shivered
and sparkled. Even the acacia woodland with its thick
covering of blossom had a lush look, and around the
bushes and the wild flowers butterflies danced in circles.

A visitor would be unaware of any problems, but to
a scientist there were problems and they were serious,
for under the thick green cover, and behind the shelter
of the green bush, the elephants were digging with
their tusks into the indigo-colored bark of the *Acacia
tortilis*. They were ripping off thick slices, chewing and
sucking out the juices, often leaving the trunk white
and bare as if the tree's clothes had been torn to pieces.
In a month or less one tree after another would fade
to a paler color, its thin branches would become barren

and finally die. Year after year Iain had seen these trees turn into skeletons. "Soon there will be none left," he said.

Pinned on the elephant board of our working room was a note from Harvey Croze, the elephant man of the Serengeti, inviting Iain to participate in the big yearly elephant/buffalo count. The note read "Please come to help in elephant count, 29–31 May, and bring research tool," which meant his plane. Accommodation would be found for us, but we were to bring our food and bedding.

We decided to go early and spend a couple of weeks in the Serengeti so that Iain could prepare his seminar (which was to take place at the beginning of June) on his four-year study of the Manyara Problem, and exchange up-to-date reports with his fellow scientists. We packed up all our books, papers, maps, food, clothing and bedding and stuffed them into the plane.

It was a very heavy and valuable load, consisting of everything which was most precious to us. On my lap was Widgey, and the genets were curled up like furry sausages, and pushed into one of the knotted sleeves of my jersey, so they wouldn't be able to run away or bite me on takeoff. Kix sped into the wind and lifted higher and higher like a bird in an up current.

Once we were above the clouds of Ngorongoro and had reached the far side of the crater wall, which is over 10,000 feet high, Iain let the plane slide down the slopes as if we were in a giant slalom. Sharp ridges flattened into an enormous panorama which stretched as far as we could see. The great expanse of land below us was speckled with pinpoints of black. These were the wildebeest on the grass plains. With the sun behind us every one of the hundreds of thousand animals on the move looked as if their manes and tails were alight. Young calves stood out white running next to their mothers. I had been told that over a million animals converged during the migration.

I had been to the Serengeti before. First in 1955, when there was only a single Park Warden living in the one house at Banagi. I was working with a small film company making a film called *Toto and the Poachers,* and I stayed in one of the few huts in Seronera, used for the Rangers and an odd visitor like myself. The second time was in 1963 when I was filming the migration. I remember feeling as if we were living in prehistoric times, when animals roamed freely and in great numbers all over the world. But till now I knew nothing of the academic study of wildlife, so the scene was a complete novelty to me.

The Serengeti Research Institute, known as the SRI, is a highly organized scientific center; to house it, a cluster of new buildings have sprouted like mushrooms on a dungheap. They are surrounded by 5,000 square miles of plains and nearly two million head of game. If one loves the African space unspoiled by human beings, the SRI is quite an eyesore, but it represents man's ability to establish a technological center wherever he thinks it is needed. The main building was named The Michael Grzimek Memorial Laboratory. Here animals, vegetation, climate, neighboring tribes and tourists were in the process of being analyzed by scientists and computers so that a plan could be made by which they might live in balance with their environment. I wondered if the Grzimeks ever imagined the birth of this Institute when they first landed their plane on the Serengeti, over a decade ago.

At the SRI there is electricity, running water, modern stone buildings, specialized equipment, and mapmakers, foresters, biologists, ecologists, ethologists and all the other "-gists" that make a center efficient.

Once I was inside the center I forgot about aesthetics and looked at maps and figures and all the meticulous work that was being done there. As an outsider in this academic world I found it difficult to identify myself with the people who worked there. However, the time I spent at the SRI was not wasted. On my first day I learned how aerial photographs taken over several years can help scientists to discover what changes elephants make in their surroundings. Also it was explained to me how the most important causes of death among the game populations can be determined by making a number of laboratory postmortems. I had seen elephants tear down trees, and lions kill their prey, but this statistical methodical collection of facts directed to computer analysis was new to me.

Soon I understood that the dream of setting up a number of Parks to protect wild animals faced a lot of problems. The future of the game was more than an issue of protection from hunters. There was also the question of expanding animal populations and the rapid disappearance of trees; but no one knew whether their regeneration was being stopped by the elephants' unregulated browsing or by the fires which year after year were deliberately started. Scientists were now getting answers to some of these questions. A few years before there had actually been talk in the Serengeti of whether or not elephants should be eradicated, but now, with masses of new data coming in all the time, the problem no longer seemed so immediately serious. Science moves along slowly, creeping from point to point. In the debate each scientist put forward his case, which was often quite contrary to that of the last speaker, but so convincing that I found it difficult to reach any conclusion. For the scientist no idea or generally accepted fact was immune to critical analysis and objection. Even when it came to the question of preserving the Parks they could not agree on a valid reason for doing so. It was left to the idealists, as an act of faith, to say what they believed. Luckily the Africans living in the bush are not involved in all these complications—when things are difficult to explain they say "Shauri ya Mungu" ("It is God's business") and perhaps they are right.

Now for us the elephant/buffalo count was about to begin. Rain clouds massed above us, thunderstorms erupted and water swept over us. Airplanes flew in from other Parks, buzzing the compound for cars to pick them up. The SRI was humming with the anticipation of an important event. Up at the strip one saw new faces, and the pilots were getting their planes ready.

In the evening, Harvey Croze held a meeting to brief all pilots, navigators and counters about the elephants and buffaloes, and to give them their maps and cameras and film for the areas they were going to cover. There were six airplanes and about ten pilots, who flew in four-hourly shifts. Most pilots had to fly twice a day, so that whole sections of the Park could be fully covered on the first day. Planes could refuel and land on isolated bush strips, where fuel had been provided for them.

At the end of two days of exhaustive flying and counting, about 2,000 elephants and 50,000 buffaloes had been spotted from the air.

That evening a big party to celebrate the end of the operation was laid on. Since it was primarily an elephants' count the Crozes' territory was chosen as the site of the feast. Nani Croze filled her ovens with homemade bread and cakes and stirred at sauces for hours, sprinkling spices to barbecue spare ribs of pork, specially ordered by plane from Nairobi. Annie Norton Griffiths and I organized the tent and looked for chairs and tables and things to eat from. The sun sank below the horizon as if it were melting over the plains, pilots flew over us flashing their wings to say they would soon be with us. We poured tankards of cool beer for our hot and thirsty men. The party began.

Under the faded canvas roof of the huge old tent, paper flowers and silver tinsel wrapped around the poles flickered in the bright hissing gas lamps. Large terracotta pots with boiling spicy food and smaller pots with scented wild flowers decorated the tables. Outside the meat sizzled on a bed of red coals. Parties like this were rare occasions and for them we dressed up in all our best bush finery. Laughing faces were tiger-striped with lights that flashed through the canvas opening. Music blared. People danced barefooted on the lawns, where later that night prowling lions, hyenas and jackals would lick up the remnants of our feast. Green was the color that most of the men wore —the bush green clothes of the Parks—added to this a scarf, a colored shirt or long trousers, was an embellishment allowed at a party. Iain walked in, breaking out of this well-established uniform, wearing a long yellow robe, with his blond hair flowing; "You remind me more and more of Jesus Christ each time I see you," John Owen told him. It was our last free-and-easy get-together with all our friends at the SRI.

All that night I heard lions call and galloping hooves go by without ever stopping. Hyenas howled and laughed, music floated from the party into my room, and the noises of the night kept me awake. Outside my window life was continuing in exactly the same way for the wildebeest as year after year they migrated back and forth through the Serengeti. If the rains fell regularly, the population grew. Two hundred thousand calves had been born this year. During the peak few weeks of the calving season 10,000 mothers gave birth each day.

My most vivid recollection of the calving will always be that of the migration as I had seen it on an earlier occasion. I had always wanted to witness and photograph the beginning of life and day. I wanted to see and feel this massive sight of birth, so when visiting the Serengeti one February, I slipped out of the house one morning before the horizon was streaked by the dawn. There were some lions so close by that I could hear them breathe, but I knew they were in a heavenly digestive sleep. My car had no lights, but by keeping the flicker on, I was able to light up the road sufficiently to drive quite fast. It had rained during the night, the track was slippery, and as I entered the plains I kept to the roads to avoid getting stuck. Thanks to all the walking, climbing and scrambling up trees that I had done in Manyara, I was very fit. I wanted to get right into the midst of the migrating world. The noise was unbelievable. Millions of sounds vibrated in the coolness of the dawn. At the first glow, I switched the flicker off and moved against the current of the migration.

The morning burst on to a thousand births. It was a vision of the world's creation; the morning born out of dark, the sun born on to life. Everywhere I looked, long wobbly legs, still steaming with water hot from the mother's womb, stood up hastily, shakily, to learn how to run. There was no time for them to wait.

Surrounded by a hundred thousand of its own kind, only the mother would lower a curious nose to sniff a new-born calf, only she would help with a nudge, or welcome it in the world with a lick of the tongue. From the moment of birth the babies were in danger; all around were signs of death.

The night had been a time for feasts for all the meat-eating kinds, easy kills for a tender meal. Among the births lay the remnants of death. Bones left for the sun to dry. High up in the empty sky, unseen signals passed between the vultures, pointing to the morning's leftovers. The lions' bellies touched the ground, so that they could hardly walk.

All around the calves were running, at first only a few steps, then their legs folded up and they fell to the ground, to get up immediately and run a few more steps. Within minutes, blood and strength rushed into their limbs, preparing them for a life made up of running—for running was essential if they were to survive.

When my car stopped, the animals around stood still, only a few yards away. They stared, obviously wondering what I was going to do. Was I going to eat them? Strangely, I didn't seem to worry them very much. I watched a mother lie down; it took between five and ten minutes for the baby to be born. During each of those minutes she lay on the ground in labor exposed to the jaws of a predator.

As soon as the baby was out, she stood up, made low cooing noises, turned around to smell it, and began to lick it, her ears set forward. I could see the calf's nostrils flare as it breathed in deeply, and blinked its wet sticky eyes. Within minutes, it seemed to know that it must get up as quickly as possible and start running. Its chances of survival would then be nine out of ten. From the moment of birth, until the baby was galloping away at the side of its mother, took no more than fifteen minutes. If then a hyaena should attack it and the mother turned around to defend it, the baby would have only one chance in ten to live. But if the mother decided to keep running they would both probably get away and survive, provided the calf did not get lost in the confusion.

I was told that it was a genetic inheritance that conditioned the turn-arounder as opposed to the runner, and thereby gave it less chance of survival. As an expectant mother, my instinct was to turn around and fight if danger threatened, but after hearing this, I decided I would prefer to run.

Vultures swarmed everywhere, gliding down, wings outstretched, necks arched, legs out and beaks down ready to eat. They dropped like parachutes, and wherever they dropped, there was something to eat. I stood on the roof of the car; though still early in the morning the hot sun glared, and I could see groups of vultures tearing at the scraps of the night's killings or of the thousand births.

When I look at vultures from a distance I feel a strong revulsion for these birds, but like most things in this world, even the vulture has a certain beauty and dignity. We should not condemn him for his habit of eating rotten carcasses or reject him because his neck is scraggy and unfeathered and his head bald and his beak hooked. He is what he is.

That morning, when I was going home, driving slowly through the swarm of wildebeest, I realized when I reached the road that it acted as a barrier. There must have been about 100–200 yards of space between my flow of animals and the next advancing black mass.

Further on I saw three hyenas, walking at a distance from each other, toward the wildebeest on my left. I didn't pay much attention as I thought they were just moving on with the migration, and had surely had their fill, for they looked quite fat. I saw them stop, look around, sniff and move on rather faster. I followed them. I was anxious because a female was lying down, her head on the ground; she was pushing and heaving and I saw that the calf was coming. I said to myself, "This one is not going to make it." Some of the other animals were running but the mother was down wind and got no warning message.

The hyenas closed in, the mother lifted her head, saw them, jumped up and began to run. But the hyenas were too close. They leaped for the baby and pulled it out. I saw it kick, before they tore it to shreds like a piece of paper. I stopped and cried and covered my face in my hands. I drove home thinking how awful a mother's life is.

In the wild, birth depends so much on chance. One new-born calf takes to its heels with its mother and survives, another suffers the fate I had just witnessed. But perhaps it is little different from a human birth: one mother may give birth to twins in an isolated village in the bush, without difficulty, while another suffers a miscarriage in the most sophisticated modern hospital.

When next day we flew over the green scented land, I looked down on the migration. From the sky all the world seemed to be at peace.

After the SRI meeting we flew back to Manyara, gliding between the Rift Wall and the reflecting Lake, which looked as if the sky were hanging upside down. The thick lush canopy of trees was stretching out to feel the sun, branches of fig, fever and forest trees embracing each other, shading all that lived below. As we passed over the acacia woodlands, the green of the long grass under the dead trees and the thick after-rain vegetation covered up most traces of deforestation, as if all of a sudden nature had sprung a surprise solution on us and was saying, "There is no need to worry." We flew low to clear the way on the grass-green strip and dived past Ndala to announce ourselves. The little camp looked deserted; no smoke, no cars, no people, nothing moved except for the water on the sun-splashed rocks. Then came that moment of suspense just before landing and the great sense of joy on touchdown. We switched off the roar of the engines and let the startled silence be our welcome. We were home again. We left the boxes in the plane and walked down the strip. How nice it was to be alone, no cars, no people to greet us, only the genet cats and Widgey darting forward to explore, visiting ants and beetles and crunching grasshoppers as sleek as blades of grass.

On the path we met Kiprono, who had been out cutting wood with his wife Alima, and Biba by their side. He had been looking after our camp while Mhoja was on leave. As we walked we listened to Kiprono's tales about how many elephants had been in camp every night, how many chickens had been eaten, how he had kept the grass well cut, looked after the houses and not let the elephants eat the thatch. I was very pleased at all they had done since we had been away, for I wanted everything to be clean and ready for our next commitment, the great elephant meeting, for which so many scientists were coming to stay to hear Iain give a seminar on the results of his research.

We spent the following days unpacking, rearranging the camp, reading through a pile of mail and papers, ordering food, and finishing the arrangements for the seminar. I had asked John Owen if the guests attending it could stay in the Hotel and Park houses. But the answer was "No." Everyone would far rather camp at Ndala. We were, however, to be provided with as much help as possible: Mhoja would return from leave, two Rangers would come and we would have a lot of cooperation from our Park Warden, David Stevens Babu, who had succeeded Jonathan Muhanga. By 5 June all was ready.

That night we swam naked in the pool, the stars bright, the crickets and frogs singing all around us. Afterward, our bodies wet, we walked down the river drying ourselves in the last of the warm air and listening to the night noises—the rustle of a small animal in the undergrowth, the snorting of buffaloes, the trickle of water. It was the last walk of this part of our life, one I will never forget. A few days later everything was to change.

As usual I woke at dawn. The sun crept around grey walls of cloud, casting gentle waves of light that touched my face. In the basket behind my head, Widgey, Alicat and Amina were chirruping and scratching, waiting to crawl out on to our bed.

I walked down the path through the soft scented air and found Mhoja baking bread. Iain flew off to a farm across the Lake to collect a sheep which had been prepared for our barbecue. Most of the food and drink had to be flown in from sixty miles away. Chairs and tables, plates, glasses and cutlery were to be borrowed from the Manyara Hotel or Park Headquarters. Having only a very small fridge, I had to get all the meat and food ready beforehand, so that it should not go bad. It was quite a problem to lodge and feed sixteen extra people with only one cook and three Rangers to help.

Some of the scientists arrived early; they were immediately given a drink or a cup of coffee, and then put to the task of finishing maps showing the movements and densities of the elephants, and filling in diagrams with colored pencils giving the percentage of elephant damage done to certain tree species. Usually all diagrams could easily be shown with slides; but having no electricity, projections were out.

John Owen flew in and since he was at the top of the hierarchy was given the top rondavel with the best view. Desmond Vesey-Fitzgerald arrived by Land-Rover from Arusha, completely self-contained down to his tin bowl and mug. Harvey Croze came with his wife Nani in a Combie packed full of kids, pets, tents and bedding. We settled them in a camp site along the river under an acacia grove next to Annie and Mike Norton Griffiths, senior ecologist of the Serengeti. Dennis Herlocker, an American in charge of forestry in the Serengeti, came to learn what was happening to the trees of Manyara. David Western, from Amboseli studying the ecology of the Masai and wildlife, drove in from Kenya. Hugh Lamprey, Director of SRI, flew his glider from the Serengeti, twisting and turning with pelicans and vultures on the up currents. David Stevens Babu, Senior Park Warden, welcomed the scientists to Manyara. He had been driving back and forth from HQ to our camp all day organizing the equipment.

Some of our guests brought food, others drink, all came equipped with paper, maps and pencils. There was an electric current of excitement. Tents were going up all over the place. It looked like a pioneers' settlement. Minor accidents occurred; as Mike hammered in the last pegs of his tent he tripped on some roots and spun down the bank into a thorny bush. Hugh, who did not want to be a burden on our tiny bathroom, walked up to the waterfall to wash, slipped on a smooth stone, and slid down the steep rocks, cutting and grazing himself.

The center house was filled with two long tables and chairs, paper and pencils were distributed around them. One end of the room was for Iain and his maps: the other was given to a photographic display of Manyara's elephants. Under a full moon, a big fire was burning. We roasted an entire sheep which had been marinated in oil and herbs. Our dugout canoes were laid upside down to serve as benches and tables. Mama Rosa had lent me large clay pots in which to cook chilied beans, curried rice and ratatouille, which were kept warm next to the fire, and, of course, there were bottles of wine and beer, and drinks for all these men of the bush. The feast went on till about midnight, and after that there were still a few more beds to be made up. At about one o'clock we finally fell on to our mattresses.

Mhoja woke me with tea; it was a cold day, dark and drizzling. There were only two more things for me to do; get breakfast on its way, and then see that everyone was seated by 8:30 so that the seminar could begin.

Suleiman had made pots of tea, and bowls of coffee, and Mhoja was toasting about sixty pieces of bread on his own camp fire. I was in the kitchen frying bacons and dozens of sausages, and scrambling about thirty eggs. Breakfast was served at seven thirty and at eight thirty, on the dot, the meeting began.

When everyone was settled I went to have a bath. I was glad that everything had gone well and felt I could now relax. I was on my way back to my little house when all of a sudden warm water came pouring out of me. I called Mhoja and asked him to fetch Mama Croze immediately. He ran to her tent calling: "Quickly, quickly, Mama Duglass wants you, she's sick." Together they rushed up to my little hut and I told Nani that though I had no pain something very strange was happening to me. "You're beginning your baby," she said. I thought: "This is impossible." She went on, "I'm going to break up the meeting, and you're going to hospital straight away, babies don't wait."

I begged her not to do anything till the seminar was over. We had worked for two months to prepare this meeting, we could not break it up now just because I was having a child, and if Iain was told about me he would be anxious and not be able to concentrate. "Please," I said, "wait till the coffee break. Then when cakes and coffee are being handed around casually drop a word in Iain's ear, something about children being born in the bush, but not to worry about it."

I lay down on the mat on the cement floor of my hut and waited. I knew that owing to some complications I would have to have a Caesarian operation —the baby couldn't be born without one. Annie Norton Griffiths, Alima, Kiprono's wife, and Nani Croze stayed with me. It was comforting to have women around, even if none of us knew what to do. The time passed slowly.

At the coffee break, Iain came in and offered to

take me straight to Nairobi, but I preferred to wait until the meeting was over. I was all right, I said. "Okay casa roho," he answered (this means "tighten your heart" in Swahili) then he hurried back to the meeting and announced "I haven't much time left, so let's get back to the elephants . . ."

". . . At Manyara, certain facts are plain. There is strong evidence that elephant numbers have risen following a drastic reduction in their range."

As Iain walked back and forth from wall to wall skimming over the maps and his notes, the scientists listened intently. It was urgent now to get the seminar over as quickly as possible, but Iain still had many things to say, and this was his only opportunity. Even when the lecture had ended he had to take our guests for a quick round to show them his ecological experiments.

Several trees had been planted to demonstrate the different growth rates of acacia seeds which had been picked out of elephant dung, and of others that had been picked up at random and planted in different types of soil. All the scientists came to look at the trees, measurements were taken of the growth of the trunks. I thought all this was going to go on for ever. I could hear remarks and questions.

"Very interesting," said one. "So you think that if the seed goes through the gut of an animal, it has a greater chance of survival and may grow into a healthier tree?" "Yes," replied Iain.

They were standing just outside my window considering the survival rate of acacia seeds, but no one popped their head in to ask, "What chances of survival have you?"

At last the meeting ended. Bottles were opened. Nani and Annie were getting lunch on to the tables. Everyone congratulated Iain on his excellent seminar and the imminent arrival of his baby.

I dressed and walked down to the main house accompanied by the Ranger's wife. All the Africans were sitting under the shade of the gardenia tree. They looked concerned. I waved to them and smiled, "It's all right," I said. "I will bring you a baby tomorrow." Their black faces split into wide white grins and their eyes laughed. "Mungu ta saidia," ("God will help"). "We will wait for you, God will send you a child."

My heart was pounding with anxiety and the joy of being in the midst of the bush where I belonged. Whether or not I got inside the white walls of a clean hospital room for this baby to be born was now a question of chance.

Iain and I drove to the strip. Everyone came to wish us farewell, car following car, filled with bush people, children and animals. When we got into the plane each in turn came to kiss me goodbye—all the people, the genet cats and the mongoose. The plane had no self-starter but Hugh Lamprey spun the propeller, the engine roared, wind blew into my face, the doors were locked, we raced down the narrow runway and climbed over the trees and up over the great Rift Wall.

John Owen was waiting for us at the Manyara strip with his bigger and faster plane. We changed over and flew in the heat of the day along the route I knew so well.

Hanging on to my stomach, as the plane dropped and heaved in the empty sky, a great wave of pain started pushing through my body, and then disappeared only to start again five minutes later. Nairobi was still very far away. This, I thought, is where I need that British cool, to pretend that nothing unusual is happening. During my other anxious flight with Iain when he was poisoned I had fixed my eyes on the place to come, watching it gradually get bigger as we approached, and I had been able to forget the fear of turbulence and the anxiety for the sick man at my side. Now I needed an image to fix my mind on. Through the light's strange rose glow, I sighted Lake Natron to the left where long lines of red crusts float on the water. I loved this desolate Lake.

Suddenly I heard voices crackle above my head.

Contact had been made with the outside world. "This is East Air Center, your doctor cannot be found, it is Sunday and he is away for the day. We will try to get you an ambulance."

We arrived at Nairobi at two thirty and, as we had flown from Tanzania into Kenya, had to go through immigration and then find a taxi, for there was no ambulance to meet us. I did not mind, I only wanted to keep my strength for later; this was my first baby and I felt my heart flicker with waves of panic. "It'll be all my fault," I thought, "if anything should go wrong, because of the way I've been living, never giving a damn about the thing that mattered most—our child—and now entirely dependent on the help and competence of others for our survival."

An hour later I was on a hospital bed, and Iain was ringing everyone we knew in Nairobi telling them to look for our doctor.

At six thirty he arrived—Adriano Landra, my friend, a tough, confident and capable surgeon, with a smiling round face. I knew then I was going to make it.

"Come on, roll her out to the theater," he said, holding my hand as he talked to the nurses and to Iain.

Needles were stuck into me from all sides. I stared up at the huge white lamp above me. All around me, I could see masked faces with white caps looking down at me. They resembled people from Madame Tussaud's Chamber of Horrors. I recognized Iain by his black-rimmed glasses between his white mask and cap. He had on a green apron, his arms were bare and he stood next to Adriano. We looked at each other for a long moment. I heard the doctor say,

"Okay you can put her out."

And to me:

"Now count up to ten slowly." I counted till a whirlwind shook my brain.

Slowly I woke. I heard voices. The room was full of flowers. I could not move for pain. I looked for Iain and found his face, his hair still tousled and covered in dust and sweat from the day before. All my family was there too. "You've got a daughter, she's fine, she's in the premature unit, she weighs five pounds three ounces."

My window was open, I looked up at the moon. Now I knew what it was like to give birth. I was lucky.

The news was sent to my home and the Africans there named the baby Saba (Swahili for "seven"), because she was born at the seventh hour on the seventh day of the week, on the seventh day of the month, and she was the seventh grandchild.

# 13

# To Look
# and to Learn

When Saba was three weeks old and weighed nearly six pounds I was allowed to leave Nairobi and return to the farm where I was to spend another two weeks so that she and I could build up our strength before returning to Manyara.

Iain flew us to Naivasha. Many of the African women came to the airplane, some dressed in their beautiful tribal costumes and covered in jewels. They brought eggs and chickens for me and the baby, singing and swaying in a semicircle around the plane. Some came up to kiss me, and to kiss Iain's hands because he had given me a child. This was an important event, calling for a big celebration. The following day, Masai men asked to see me. When they met me, they took my hands in theirs and spat on them. Then one, the eldest, began the traditional spitting ceremony, during which he spat all over me, opening my shirt and spitting into my bosom to take away all the devils and all the evil eyes so that my milk would flow continuously. He also spat behind my head, then on his hands and touched my forehead. It was a shower of spit. I couldn't stop it because this was the biggest honor that they could give me, because for them the most important thing in life is to have a child. Life must continue and it can only continue for you through your children.

For about ten days, women of different tribes drifted over from the village into our house in groups of four or five, and came up the stairs to see our child. She was sleeping in a straw cot covered with a mosquito net and they looked at her, and said, "Aaaah mzuri sana." (Which means—"Aah, she's beautiful.") Reson's wife presented us with a chicken, kissed us both on the cheeks and then with one arm raised to God, and covering her mouth with her other hand, she thanked God for saving us. "Everyone is happy on the farm for you, Oria. Everyone has prayed for you and the child."

"But I made a big mistake," I said, "It should have been a son to carry on the line."

"No, no, it is God's will, the next one will be a boy."

Each day brought me new strength until I was able to walk over the hills and ride a horse. A few days later we packed our plane once more with supplies of food, baby clothes and a small straw cot, and took off in the early afternoon. Looking back, I saw my anxious parents, two figures standing close in an empty paddock watching us vanish along the blue path of the sky.

Back at Ndala camp it was as if life were beginning again with all the excitement of the unexpected. Exactly six weeks had passed since my baby was born. Wild flowers filled the rooms and the floor was sprinkled with lilac and vermilion colored petals picked from the Park to welcome us back to our world. Everything was clean and polished, food was cooking and all the animals were there for me to hug.

Mhoja took Saba from my arms, laughing and welcoming her to the bush. A baby was as important as the elephants. Widgey, Alicat and Amina had grown into beautiful strong animals. The genets were jumping from shoulder to shoulder, sniffing Saba from time to time. Only Widgey was unsociable: she would never look at us after we had been away. Iain let the corks

go with a loud bang and champagne flowed in the
glasses. We drank and laughed, hugged and kissed each
other, caught for a moment in a net of happiness
by the subtle fingers of life.

Before my return, Mhoja, Suleiman and Ali had
been to Mto-wa-Mbu to find me an "ayah" and she
was already being trained by them. Her name was
Maria. She was a mature woman with a warm smile and
her face was decorated with beauty scars across the
cheeks, which is typical of the Wambulu tribe.

We carried the bags, basket and baby up to our little hut, and followed by all the animals sat down on
the mattresses, and emptied Saba's few possessions on
the floor. She was given her first bush bath propped up
in a yellow basin half filled with warm brown river
water.

Maria, who had no children of her own, had served
behind a bar in Mto-wa-Mbu, but told me she now
only wanted to look after Saba and did not want to
have anything to do with men any more. We went
down to dinner. On the center of the table was Iain's old
lion skull now covered over in candle wax, so that only
its white teeth showed up in the candlelight. Nothing
else seemed to have changed in Manyara. It was so
simple to come back with my child under my arm as if
she were just a continuation of my wild family. Out
of my four babies, I didn't know which one I loved
most, because my wild adopted ones seemed as important as my own. Before this, I could never believe
Iain when, as a zoologist, he tried to convince me that
to have a baby was the most natural biological function in a woman's life. I was sure that it was going
to be terribly complicated and that my whole way of
life was going to be shattered.

But now, all I felt was a very strong protective instinct like most other mothers.

I had never been interested in childbirth or child
rearing. I was also quite old to have my first child, but
instead of buying the usual Dr. Spock's book, which
I was told was the mother's bible, I was tutored by

Iain on the importance of the mother-child bond, as shown in a study of the rhesus monkey which had recently been completed by a Cambridge professor. I knew very little about primate behavior but since then Iain had told me how important it was to learn about such facts, and I listened earnestly.

The most significant thing about the rhesus monkey was that tactile contact was essential for the baby in the early stages of its life. So far as I could understand, it had three definite points of contact by which it could cling to its mother simultaneously. It could clutch on to her fur with its two hands and hang on to her nipple with its mouth. Since I did not have a furry body and had a far less developed baby than the rhesus monkey it was up to me to do the hanging on.

The best method I could think of was the one the African women use. They carry their children strapped up against their body with a piece of cloth. This assures safety from animals and gives the baby as much body warmth and contact as it can get. An African mother does not have to be the wife of an ethologist to understand the importance for her baby of tactile contact.

I was much impressed by the experiments with a rhesus monkey in which the baby had been deprived of its mother at an early stage of its development, missed the phase of essential tactile contact, and had grown up into a maladjusted animal, unable to form mature adult relationships. Iain insisted this must not happen to our child.

Since I was living with animals, I hoped to learn something from them. Had I been living in a city, these ideas would probably never have entered my head, and I am sure that my baby would have been wrapped up in beautiful clothes and slept in a frilly white cot under a mosquito net, with lots of mothers coming to see her and saying: "What a sweet little dress she's wearing!" But how much of its mother's touch would that baby have had during a day? Inevitably I began to wonder whether it would be possible for me to bring

up my child in a more natural way than our society
has taught us, in which hygiene is often overempha-
sized. Was I going to be able to learn something from
animals that lived around me and how much would
this affect us?

Waking up in the morning, the first rays of sun
peeped through the window. The air was cool. There
was only the noise of water running down the rocks
behind us. A bird was singing, another whistling.
I opened my eyes sleepily, stretched and looked
around. It was still too dark for me to distinguish the
trees in the Park, but an orange light was already
touching the slither of water below our house, and
walking along it were the dark shapes of elephants.
All night long they had been trumpeting, growling
and moaning in the avenues of the woodlands.

I pulled on my trousers and jacket, crept out of our
rondavel and ran down the path along the top of the
cliff. I had not gone more than ten yards when I
heard grass ripping. I stopped dead in my tracks and
peered through the shadows into the bush. The first
things I saw were two white tusks and I heard the
munching of grass. The animal was only a few feet
from me. Relieved that it was just an elephant, and
not a buffalo, but not quite sure what he was going to
do, I kept one eye on him and skipped past. He must
have been slightly surprised, as he stopped chewing
for a moment.

In the kitchen, I found Mhoja making tea. A big fire
was burning in the stove, puffing out clouds of smoke.
I told him that I had practically run into an elephant
near my hut and he said that they had come to welcome me back. When he got out of his door earlier
that morning, he too had nearly had to crawl under
one. We laughed. I did not believe him, but I knew
he meant to tell me that elephants had been very close
to his house.

On the slopes behind our camp other elephants
cracked and ate branches. They were Portia's family,
belonging to Sarah's kinship group, who frequently

came to eat around there in the mornings. As the sun rose, the orange, red and yellow streaks disappeared and a dazzling round spot of light slowly lifted from the Lake. The river sparkled like glass. It was exciting to see so many elephants here at this time of the morning, for I knew they would be staying in the woodlands for the rest of the day. After having been away for so long, I was longing to go out among them again.

The elephants ambled over, one family at a time, black moving figures with only their trunks outlined and an occasional gleam of tusks. The wind was blowing and the dust rose as they walked. One family left the river and another came toward it. As they passed they greeted each other, a few members lifting their trunks to the others' mouths. They were probably related families but I could not make out who they were, although by now I knew most of the major matriarchs in the Park. I felt as if I were a part of the scene and had a certain delight when recognizing some of them.

It was the same feeling I have when I suddenly pass by friends in a café in St. Tropez or at the Thorn Tree in Nairobi after having been away for some time. I wanted to smile, or nod my head and say "Hello, it's great to see you again!"

I walked back to our rondavel with a tray covered in red and yellow cups, a pot of tea and a big jug of milk. It was about 6:30 in the morning. One wall of our room was blazing with sunlight. On the floor, sleeping in different corners and beds, were five bodies that had to be woken. Iain and I shared a mattress in the middle. Next to us on one side, slept our baby in her straw basket, and on the other, in another straw basket cuddled up together, were the genet cats and the mongoose Widgey. All the bodies were stretching, yawning, making their own peculiar noises. The room came to life.

I sat on the floor with my tea tray and began pouring our safari tea, which always had a taste of smoke and powdered milk. Widgey, followed by Alicat and Amina, jumped into their cups, chirruping and mewing as they pushed their heads in to get to the milk. Afterward, they had been taught to go outside and pee, which they did reluctantly. Usually they were accompanied by Iain, for we shared the upbringing of all these babies and they seemed to have imprinted on both of us as parents. Saba had to be fed too; this was never a problem, since I had plenty of milk. This was lucky, as in camp the water was dirty and making up bottles of milk and keeping them sterile would have been a problem. Even Biba walked up to the house to join us for tea as soon as she had been let out of the pen.

On entering our room, she began eating the nappies, even though she knew this was forbidden food. It took us about ten minutes chasing her around the camp to get back a half-eaten nappy. This first early morning family tea gathering gave us a feeling of being happily alive.

Whenever I moved through the camp all the animals followed me. With Saba safely strapped on to my back and usually secured by a *khanga,* a colorful piece of African cloth, I could walk wherever I wanted to. Biba would run along in front of us, with Widgey making her safari noises in a series of fast "ti-ti-ti-ti-ti-ti" sounds. The genets, being night animals, were frightened to move from house to house by day and dashed for the undergrowth as soon as they were in the open; I was always afraid of losing one of them. I loved walking with all these animals down the little winding path covered in sand. The breeze blowing up from the river brought the smell of smoke and bushes mixed with bacon and coffee.

Birds and butterflies flew from branch to branch and flower to flower. Familiar sounds of wood-chopping and of barking baboons running down to the river to drink, drifted through the camp. The whole of the Ndala Valley was alive with activity as the day began.

It was always amazing to see how each animal was perfectly adapted to its own particular way of life and environment.

So were we to our own particular way of life, which few people were able to share, and which, therefore, remained very intimate.

Maria did not stay long as she had a row with Suleiman, refusing to comply with some mysterious request he made at four in the morning, prefaced by the English words "Let's go." She departed in tears. I desperately needed some help to look after Saba, for during the coming weeks we would be filming. Luckily my sister Mirella found me the perfect person. We flew to Naivasha to pick her up. She was a Seychelloise, Madame Violette Thesée, middle-aged with decades of experience of looking after babies. When she heard that she was going to have to get into a tiny airplane, fly out into the bush and live in the midst of elephants, she bravely settled into the back seat, clutched her rosary, closed her eyes and prayed all the way. Violette's arrival was greeted with tremendous enthusiasm by everyone in camp.

She did not mind how much work she had to do, provided she was paid the right amount of respect and had a proper escort, for she was convinced that every lion, leopard, buffalo, elephant and rhino in the Park had a personal desire to end her life, and she was not taking any chances of meeting one of these terrible beasts. In the evening when Violette went to bed, a great ceremony always took place. Mhoja went first with his gun, followed by Violette; then came Ali, with a torch, and Suleiman in the rear armed with a panga. Accompanied by lots of talking and shrieks of laughter they all made their way to the top house.

In the afternoon, Violette did her ironing under the gardenia tree and held court. She had a powerful character with a tremendous sense of humor. Word soon got around Parks so that in the evenings before the lorry drivers or Rangers returned to headquarters, they would stop by for a cup of tea and listen to some of Violette's stories. The gardenia tree was the gathering place of Ndala for all of us. The camp at last became a complete unit.

Maybe for those who live in towns or cities in Europe, our lonely camp might seem to be set in a valley of silence. For me, it was intensively alive; there was life everywhere, peeping through the long grass, hiding under bushes, or dozing in trees. Birds in the sky fought with other birds, or pounced on mice and insects. A bateleur eagle hovered above us waiting to drop on to one of our chickens. Few things were ever safe outside; babies of any kind, pets, chickens, even food, needed to be guarded. Snakes, scorpions, tsetse flies, mosquitoes, eagles, mature genets, leopards, lions, buffaloes, all visited our camp by day or night. I had to be constantly alert. Only the elephants were no trouble.

We were in the midst of violence, but it was one of necessity. One got used to killings in the wild and it helped others to survive. We were not living in fear, on the contrary it was a great joy to be part of Manyara, only we had to be alert like every other animal, for predators.

Shortly after my return to camp I felt a twitch of fear running up my spine as I dozed in the sun. It was the beginning of the dry season. The leaves and the trees looked worn and faded. From lush green the grass had paled to light sienna, and there was a dry trembling rustle everywhere. I heard something stirring in the bush, turned, and to my horror, saw rising up like a periscope from the grass behind me, the flat head and long body of a yellow and grey cobra. My sense of being a protective mother went completely astray, I shot out of my chair leaving my baby asleep in her cot on the table and rushed for Mhoja. He came armed with sticks and pangas. "Don't ever leave your baby like that," he scolded me, "Don't you know snakes like milk and are attracted to small babies by the smell?" I was very ashamed of myself; I was not going to let this happen twice, so I asked him to burn the bush around the camp area straightaway. This flushed out two puff-adders, but we never had snakes in the camp again as long as the bush and grass were kept short enough for Widgey to explore everywhere.

As time went by, we became used to nearly everything, and adjusted our lives accordingly. As long as Saba was never left alone during the day and slept with us at night, nothing could happen to her. Biba, the goat, knew better than to stray far, unless she came for walks with us. The genet cats had to be watched, particularly at night, to protect them from other predators or from the territorial genets who lived in that area; only Widgey was more independent and could usually defend herself against anything. Her little red eyes were vigilant. If she thought something was dangerous, she'd stand on her hind legs, her fur ruffled out, her ears twitching and give her war cry, a sort of treble growl. This was a warning for all of us, and many a time we were able to save a chicken from the claws of an eagle because of it. Once we even chased away a buffalo who was walking down the path. It was always worthwhile checking Widgey's war cries, even if most of the time they were muttered against the cook.

At night, and even when we went away, we never had to lock doors or windows, for no humans could get in to steal or harm us. So, in a strange way, though we had to protect ourselves against wildlife, we knew that wildlife protected us. We could not have found better guards or night-watchmen than elephants, lions and buffaloes. They kept all human prowlers far away.

It was only when we began to make our film on elephant behavior, with a French cameraman, that all our problems started pouring in.

Our isolated life was suddenly invaded by the world of competition, which hit us unannounced. We were menaced by our own species. Perhaps because we had been living among other species for such a long time we were not properly tuned-in to people and our life deteriorated. But it counted for part of the vital experience we needed for the future. We had to learn to be far more on our guard in the midst of people, than with elephants or other animals which diverted our attention.

The first unhappy incident was the disappearance of Amina, the genet. One evening while she was playing hide and seek with Alicat and Widgey, she hit a window, dislodging the pane, and fell outside. She probably rushed under the nearest bush and remained there, motionless. However much I called and put out food, nothing would make her come back. We never knew whether she had returned to the wild or been killed. Alicat and Widgey then became very close companions, grooming each other, sleeping next to each other and eating and playing together.

One still night, we awoke from the depth of sleep, to hear a piercing shriek—Mhoja yelled, "Ali na kufa, Ali na kufa" (Ali is dead). I stepped out into the blackness and hurried down the path following the dim light of Iain's torch, unable to understand what had happened. Alicat had got out of the kitchen. Blood was on the ground and on the branches of the thickly matted, spiky cardiogyne bush. I found Widgey walking around, picked her up, and we started to search for Alicat. Being a male he must have ventured on to the territory of the other male genet cats. We looked and looked for him, until we gave up all hope.

Four days later as we were sitting around coffee after dinner, a very thin, limping, smelling Alicat stalked in. He smelled dreadfully of rotten meat. His whole lower jaw was broken, the bones were sticking out covered in pus. One of his legs was badly hurt and he had sores on his body. He went straight to Widgey, to seek comfort, but she turned her head from him, and walked away not allowing him to come near her.

The only hope was to get Alicat to Sue and Toni Harthoorn as soon as possible. They were the best wildlife vets we knew in East Africa, treating wild animals as individuals whose lives were important.

They amputated the broken tip of Alicat's lower jaw and set the back tooth, vital for his survival later, should he live. The operation was a complete success. Slowly life returned to Alicat, his wound healed and they helped him learn to eat with half a lower jaw, using a syringe at first, then teaching him how to catch butterflies and other types of food.

Alicat made a new home with Sue and Toni, and I shall never forget the work they put in to save his life. Few people could understand what we all felt for this animal. After all, we had snatched him from the wild and brought him into our lives and had not adapted him to cope for himself in his own territorial world.

Soon afterward we had a similar experience with Widgey. One of the sequences of the film was to take place in Marsabit, in the north, where we were to film the famous Ahmed, who had the longest tusks of any elephant in Kenya. The film unit departed in their car, and we packed all our belongings into our tiny plane, Iain and I in front, with the baby on my lap, Violette, the cameras and our luggage in the back. When it came to finding a place to put Widgey and her little round basket, there simply was no more room. Widgey knew we were leaving without her. As soon as the engine started, she screamed and struggled, biting Mhoja's hand and jumping out of the car. She ran towards my side of the plane, jumped on to the wheel, and waited for me to open the door. The wind from the propeller was blowing her off, but I could still hear her pleas.

By the time we returned to Manyara, our morale was low for we had had great difficulties with the film crew. But in camp things were far worse. We found Widgey demoralized, very unhappy, with a skin disease, and covered in ticks. Each time I tried to pick her up, she turned her head away or bit me as if she had been betrayed. It took a long period of talking and touching to convince her that Iain and I still loved her. We treated her, but each day her health deteriorated until finally there was only one thing left to do: take her to the Harthoorns. They examined her, and found that she had mange, tick fever, and possibly also rabies. They could not tell, until the tests had been completed. This was very serious. Every single person in camp had been bitten by Widgey, except Saba, and we had passed the safety time for being cured. We might be in danger of dying of rabies. I had visions of all of us going mad and foaming at the mouth with only the .470 to finish us off.

Only Saba seemed happy and well. She was getting fatter and stronger every day, smiling and reminding us of the important things in life, many of which we were forgetting. We waited for three anxious days. At last a radio message came to tell us that Widgey was better and that the tests were negative. After a week she had recovered from the tick fever, her mange was healing, and bits of her fur were growing; but she still had a long way to go before complete recovery.

One day at Ndala River, Iain said to me, "You won't believe it, but the Torone sisters are here." I had been waiting to meet these "baddies" about whom he had told me so much. There were four big females with their offspring; they were extremely aggressive, charged on sight and without warning, and each time they visited the Park caused havoc.

Iain had only seen them three times since he had been in Manyara. I was dumbfounded, I could imagine them charging up the river as soon as they caught our scent, and attacking the camp like great tanks. But instead, here they were drinking peacefully, with their young ones by their sides; the wind blowing steadily from them to us. Taking the identity photographs and a camera, we crept along the river to within fifty yards of them—the famous Torone sisters whom I had never seen before, and we were able to get portraits of each one.

During the next three days we heard stories of tourists having been chased by elephants. A report came from the Park Warden that a Volkswagen with Canadian tourists and a guide had been overturned by an elephant. Luckily, no one was hurt, and the car was only slightly damaged. At least the Canadians would be able to go home and tell their tale of adventure for years to come. We showed the guide the Torone photographs but he wasn't sure if they were the same elephants.

The first warning came as we were driving along the bottom road through the Ground Water Forest in the evening. A loud shrill trumpet sounded, followed by a swish of bent bushes, then silence. There, hiding behind a tall, white tree trunk (as if she were trying to make herself invisible) stood a big Torone female, head high, trunk down, peering at us over the tips of her tusks, one foot swinging ready to pounce on us. We were only a few yards away. Iain and I looked at her fascinated. Her eyes burned with hatred as she watched us. Then she came at full speed, determined to get us. Deliberately we drove only a few feet in front of her, to see what she would do. She must have run for at least two hundred yards, trunk turned under, head aiming at the back of the car and eyes fixed on us. It was a terrifying sight, and I realized how easily this gigantic animal could squash us all into pulp, should the car stall. She was so determined to get us that she even ran straight over a bridge without noticing it, a thing which Iain said he had never seen an elephant do before. As we came out of the forest she swerved off the road, trumpeting and thrashing the bush, throwing up branches and dust, a demonstration of what she probably intended to do with us.

It was very frightening, and Kiprono, the Ranger who was crouched in the back of the Land-Rover (the same Ranger who had been with Iain when the rhino knocked him down) was petrified and yelled to Iain, "Kwenda tu, kwenda tu, huyu mbaya sana" (go on, go on, that one is very bad). I had a camera in my hand, but the circumstances were so overwhelming that I couldn't take a photograph. It was the first charge of an Endabash "baddie" I had seen. For over a year I had kept my eyes open and my ears alert whenever we were in the Endabash area, but until now I had never encountered one bad elephant.

The next day we were driving home and were about three hundred yards from the house, when all of a sudden a fanfare of wild trumpeting burst from the trees; we heard the sound of elephants crashing through the bush, and there they were, this time all four of them converging on us with their young. It was our second warning that the great sisters were around. Iain said "Quickly, Oria, load the gun." Then he stopped the car, but kept the engine running, as he wanted to try to understand their behavior. I begged him not to, but he insisted, saying he must know if they were inhibited. All stopped together in a tight, closed group just twenty yards behind the car. Heads held high, their tusks aimed at us, trumpeting, growling and wielding trunks that looked like weird weapons, the sisters paused, seeming uncertain. Even the babies and teenagers were glaring at us. Iain whispered: "It's all right, you see, they *are* inhibited." He and I and the elephants watched each other tensely, neither knowing what the other was going to do. My heart was beating fast. I sat facing backward, and tried to stop my knees from trembling by locking one arm against the back of the seat. I was ready to shoot above their heads if necessary. Then without any warning they turned and disappeared in the undergrowth of the acacia woodlands, and the safety of the approaching night.

After this there would be no more walks along the river or roads without a gun. Any time, anywhere, one or more of the Torones might be out like a flash to get their hated enemy. They must have been shot at a great many times for the smell of a human being or the sound of the car to arouse their immediate hostility.

Next morning Iain wanted to make some observations on the eating habits of elephants, and found a group not far from the camp, so he asked Mhoja to come with him with the gun. I stayed in camp having a multitude of things to do. Suddenly I heard a shot, followed by another shot, and then those terrible sounds of frightened elephants and of branches and trees cracking and breaking under their weight. It seemed to be happening not far from the house. I rushed down the drive, but couldn't see anything, only sounds filled the woodlands. I was really scared; I didn't know what to do. I thought "If Iain has had to shoot, something terrible must have happened because he would never shoot an elephant, unless he himself was nearly dead." I retreated to the gardenia tree, waiting with Violette and Suleiman, my eyes scanning every foot of the forest.

After ten minutes the car returned. With tears in his eyes, Iain said "We've shot one of the Torones! I didn't want her shot, but Mhoja has the right to shoot if he thinks the animal is too dangerous." The front of the car was bent and ripped where her tusk had gone in, and one side of it was crushed. The car had no bonnet and both of them might easily have been killed.

Iain had been taken completely by surprise. He had been looking through his binoculars, taking down notes on what Jezebel's family were eating, when from the right Torone sister Number Four burst out from the bush, jumped straight over a tree trunk and rammed her tusk into the car above the mudguard, then swept up her head ripping the metal and pulled her tusk out again. Iain reversed away but couldn't do it fast enough, she came in for another bash and, as she was picking up the Land-Rover, Mhoja shot her, right through the head. She collapsed practically on top of the car, then he shot once more—the *coup de grâce*. It was probably inevitable that she would be shot sooner or later; everyone was in danger when the Torones were in the Park.

We went immediately to the scene of death. A pool of blood was forming under the head of the dead elephant, a red thick liquid pouring out of the one small fatal hole made by the bullet of a .470. Her tusks were marked with green paint from the Land-Rover. Her breasts were full and she must have been suckling a calf. We wondered if it might come back to her. I took some pictures and then climbed into a big acacia and waited. There were elephants all around but nothing happened.

After several hours, we decided to do a postmortem and try to find out if there was any specific reason for her aggressiveness, like old bullet wounds. The corpse was well hidden from the road, so we could conduct our investigation beyond the inquisitive eyes of tourists. Soon we had heart, lungs, liver, and assorted organs laid out in neat piles, but there were no old wounds or diseased organs which could explain the matriarch's crustiness.

One cannot help being impressed by the size of an elephant—huge intestines some about one foot in diameter tumbled out, still hot and smoking. A thick red carpet of coagulated blood covered the ground all around us; it made me realize how many years it took for everything to grow to that size, and within a couple of hours all life had spilled out.

I had never seen the inside of an elephant before. We wanted to know if she were pregnant. Running along the back of her body cavity was a white tube that emerged from the pelvic girdle. Its front end thickened and split into two horns at the end of which were the ovaries, about the same size and consistency as sheep's brains. We carefully dissected these organs, slitting open the tubes along their length, examining every inch minutely. We were rewarded with the discovery of a little elephant no bigger than my little finger nail. It was still in the fish stage of development with gill pouches, but had four perfect elephant feet, and a tiny pointed nose which could have been the trunk. We put it in a bottle of alcohol and kept it.

Every day I went back to the scene to watch the slow disintegration of this huge elephant corpse, black with flies, and crawling with worms. The stench was appalling. Iain wanted to see how quickly all the salts and minerals would return to the soil. I watched the first vultures arrive and settle on a nearby tree, necks outstretched and bent, looking like old men in winter coats sitting on benches at a murder case. Then the tall long-legged, pink-necked, black-cloaked marabou storks flew in and gathered on the corpse, walking up and down in slow motion, with their wings tucked behind their backs, as if pausing before giving their verdict. Hundreds more vultures arrived and glided on to the corpse to compete for food. They became so gorged with meat and offal that it was as much as they could do to flap up into the nearest tree. Normally an elephant's skin would be too thick for them to pierce, but our dissection had allowed the white-backed vultures to insert their long bare necks far into the carcass and pull out all the soft parts they could reach. The tips of the ribs stood up like blood-streaked fingers. Some marabous picked at dried-up scraps and aggressive lappet-faced vultures screeched and fought for the strips of meat which they tore from the bones with a twist of their broad beaks. Some scavenger had gnawed the tip of the trunk in the night.

As the days passed, the body began to shrink. Lions found it and chewed through the skin to get at the remaining bits of meat. The intestines and stomach were ripped open and their fibrous contents mixed with blood to form a putrefying black pool, which sank deep into the soil and eventually dried to a crust. The tusks fell out of their sockets, and soon there was only the dried-up thick skin draped over the bones, and of course the flies. It was indeed a sad sight to see the brave and fierce shrill queen shriveled up into a rotting heap.

The death of the Torone sister made me realize once again how fragile is our existence, the prisoner of chance. The smallest event can change its whole course and so it was when the shrill queen met Iain and Mhoja. The signals for fight or flight flashed in her brain, she made the wrong decision, charged and met her death.

If life is so finely divided from death by the uncontrollable workings of chance then at least we should turn toward life and live it to the full. We are born, we survive, then we die. I believe our lives have no purpose in the universe beyond what we create for ourselves.

Being such a restless creature, I have never been able to accept the stability and security of a well-planned existence—a situation I have always tried to avoid. I hate to stay in one place, feeling the years sliding away toward old age—wasted. Security and stability interfered with the force of my nomadic cravings by which I could experience the real pleasures of life and especially the taste of space. As a child I had always longed for a miracle to change me into a Masai. When I grew older I travelled away in search of life. Yet each time I went somewhere, in the depth of my mind was a call beckoning me back to Africa. Here were my roots; here was where I belonged.

To have found a life among the elephants was an opportunity, a card was thrown at my feet and I picked it up. I now had a companion with whom I could share this life, and the urge to wander was constantly fulfilled by the work and the way we lived. Together we could drift into limitless dreams playing life against death. We could come back to earth and work; we could face the problems, the difficulties, the blows. We could stand up to the world and then laugh into its face. Everything was alive and real. We could feel the sensation of the first rain, with a sensual delight, and even enjoy the cramps which sitting motionless in one spot entailed. When the wind blew dust into our faces and sun burst over us from morning till dusk, we could smell the African space and listen to the music of the wild.

With the birth of Saba, inevitably the bonds between Iain and myself deepened. I loved the isolation of Ndala. I was surrounded by space, and was living a simple life with time enough to look after my family. We were strong and healthy, with a challenging aim and plenty of stimuli to create a balanced existence. We never experienced the humdrumness of suburbia.

We lived in a small clan, only six members of our

own species among five hundred elephants—a whole society for us to investigate, which fascinated us. We knew each other's capabilities and limitations, we got on well together; we had explored every corner of the Park and survived there without all the worldly trappings of society. We were part of a continuum with the elephants, and our behavior often showed the same motivations as theirs in similar situations.

I was not afraid of elephants any more. I could stand up to a charging elephant and call his bluff with a wave of my arm, then walk away. It was not bravado. I just knew what I was doing. It was up to me to recognize danger and to get out of the way, or else I would fall to a really hostile elephant's tusks, in the same way that they would fall to a hunter's bullets. I could not help feeling a great admiration for them. I was drawn to them. Was it their size, their power, or their gentleness that attracted me? I could not tell. I just knew that I loved being surrounded by elephants and that this experience brought me great joy.

On moonlit nights when the elephants came up the river to drink, we would often lie on a rock close by and hear the trickle of water as it slipped over the sand and into their trunks. Huge dark shapes, making sipping-squirting-spilling noises, stood motionless and then wandered on past us. On these special nights, I could absorb the long hours of nothingness in the half-light of the moon, where there was no sadness or boredom, and where I was nourished by silence, and felt rich in my simple way of life.

By photographing elephants day in and day out, I soon discovered that they showed many of the old-fashioned virtues; loyalty, protection and affection toward each other. As we lived far away from our own species and became so deeply involved with the elephants, we both consciously and unconsciously drew parallels between their society and ours. The bond with my child, the tactile care of each other, the trust in leadership, the group defense if one of us were in trouble, all these increased.

For elephants, the unity of a family is one of the most important things in their lives. I was deeply moved by the constant affection and care which they showed every day within the families; mothers, daughters, sisters, babies all touching and communicating with each other in a very loving way. Stability seemed to be the key to their security. Unlike us they do not have male parents or companions living with them; but perhaps for elephants this is an advantage because they have to deal solely with female problems. They frequent the males only when they need them for mating, which is after all the purpose of survival: to reproduce the genes, and when the bulls arrived, the same greeting and touching ceremony took place. The matriarchs not only perform the usual maternal tasks, but also the roles which we tend to think of as male— leading and defending the family units extremely efficiently. Whatever the reason, these female-led families remain united and extremely stable.

I was no elephant expert, but at least during all the months that I lived with these animals, I was able to get a glimpse into the incredible complexity and sophistication that elephants show in their everyday activities. I not only learned to understand and especially to respect them, I also longed to protect them. I could not bear to watch someone lift a gun to an elephant's head and blow its brains out, for sport or for man's greed. What a waste of life.

Months of living with and observing these animals, taught me something that no text book could ever do. As a result I now felt a great deal more civilized.

Few people in the world have studied the behavior of wild animals, in their own habitat, especially those considered to be dangerous. To be able to spend years living in the bush, often alone, requires both tremendous dedication and a love of adventure and of the wild. Scientists making behavioral studies usually get two-year grants, after which they have to dash back to their universities and write up their findings. Only a few are able to return and continue their studies in long-term research projects. Yet this is when they could really get to know the animals individually and have enough time to form closer relationships with them. Jane Goodall has shown this with chimpanzees, Diane Fossey with gorillas, and Iain with elephants.

When meeting elephants face to face, we found one of the secrets was always to keep still, to make no noise, and then to move very slowly toward or away from them. Elephants like Virgo and Right Hook, and well over a hundred others, accepted us as harmless. But even after five years of living with them, only Virgo actually came into friendly body contact with us. The others always stood a few feet away. When Saba was three months old, and before our departure from Manyara, we met Virgo and her closest relatives one evening. I walked up to her and gave her a gardenia fruit, in a gesture of greeting. She was a trunk's length from me, took the fruit, put it in her mouth, and then moved the tip of her trunk over Saba in a figure of eight, smelling her. I wondered if she knew that Saba was my child. We both stood still for a long while, facing each other with our babies by our sides. It was a very touching moment. I feel sure that Virgo will remain a life-long friend of ours, even if we do not see each other for years.

In Manyara I experienced a feeling of completeness and serenity, which I had never encountered before. With Saba's birth stability and security had taken on new dimensions, and instead of avoiding them, I embraced them. They gave my life maturity.

I knew that once I left our life with these animals and returned to live in a city, it would be hard to find the intensity of these relationships again. Like millions of other human beings, Iain and I would have to face an overcrowded and over-complicated environment and be ill-adapted for the complete change of living. Yet like those millions we also would survive.

Our time was running out and soon we would have to go. I was deeply aware of the intensity of each day as it went by. The sun faded behind the hill and long shadows lay in belts across the valley. In front of me was the river I had looked on a thousand times. No one was around, no one was walking on the sand. I knew that everything I loved most was here, silently saying goodbye. Beyond were the trees holding the secrets of their destiny, then the lake, and the mountains, and into the empty universe life moved around and took us with it like a speck of dust blowing in the wind.

# III

## Iain Douglas-Hamilton

# 14

## Facts of Life

By the side of the road an elephant calf less than a year old fiddled with its trunk among the dust-powdered leaves, scarcely looking up as we clattered around a corner and past him.

"There's an elephant calf all alone," shouted Oria.

I stopped the car and turned around. The elephant calf had not moved. It hardly seemed aware of its surroundings. There were no other elephants within two miles. I remembered vividly how the lion, Dume Kubwa, had killed and eaten the orphaned calf at Lindbergh's camp. This one was now alone and in dire peril.

"Let's catch it and see if we can help it," I said.

There was a rope in the back of the car and I quickly knotted a loop in the end. Then I advanced very slowly towards the calf with the lasso open in front of me. The little animal, which was male, was so oblivious to his environment that he never noticed me until I was standing almost within arm's length of him. Then he awakened with a start and made a brave attempt to defend himself. He flared his ears and lunged forwards, which gave me the chance to drop the loop of rope right around his head. He turned and rushed into the bush, pulling Mhoja and me behind. It was all we could do to hold him. Then we bandaged his eyes

after which he calmed down. Oria drove back to
Ndala camp, which was very near, for reinforcements,
and soon with the help of Suleiman and a friend who
was staying we hoisted the elephant into the back of the
Land-Rover. He was small but very heavy.

The only place large enough to put him was our main
living room, covered by the veranda between the two
lower rondavels. We gently lowered him here on to a
mattress and then released the bandage from his eyes.
He stood up, shook his head and went berserk. The
water filter was sent flying, my desk overturned, he
trampled on upset papers, and barged into the fridge
which teetered on the point of balance, luckily remaining upright. When I went into the room to try and calm
him down he charged and chased me around. Even at
that age he weighed between 250 and 300 lb, and I
did not want him to pin me against a wall. In the end
after several hours he remained so much wilder than
expected that we felt that perhaps there was not so
much wrong with him after all and the best thing we
could do would be to return him to the nearest elephant
family hoping that they would take care of him.

Accordingly we bundled him into the Land-Rover
once again and drove down to the Bagayo River, where
the nearest elephants were. We released him in sight of
a family unit and he ran towards them. They greeted
him with deep rumbles. The cows sniffed him all over,
putting their trunks in his mouth, until each had in-
vestigated him. When they moved off he went with
them.

Over the next two days we were able to make contact, but we noticed that although the mature cows tolerated this calf none of them would let him suck. Only
a twelve-year-old female paid him any attention. Without milk he grew weaker and weaker. On the second
day he was lying down while the others ate. The young
female tried to lift him on her own while the others
ambled on. When this failed she appeared torn between her family and the calf. She walked off a hundred
yards with the group but then rushed back to the calf,

excited and trumpeting. She stayed with him all alone until her family were out of sight, then finally abandoned him and rejoined the others. We drove up to the calf, but when he saw me approach on foot in a last desperate surge of energy he mustered enough strength to get on his feet and quickly disappear into the bush. We were never able to find him again, and I assume he died.

This incident impressed on me yet again how much the survival of young elephants depended on the group, and this was also true of older animals. As a rule baby elephants were very well looked after in the family units, but perhaps this one was ill and unable to keep up. Usually cow elephants are very maternal even to strange calves. A friend of mine, Simon Trevor, once found a calf whose mother had been shot and when he released it, a wild unrelated family adopted the calf and some cows even suckled it. So too did Eleanor, an adolescent female reared from calfhood by the Sheldricks in Tsavo. Several examples of how she has greeted abandoned, debilitated calves with intense rumbles of internal emotion, and has nursed them back to strength by the essential tactile contact, and a tenderness that can only be described as love, are recorded in Daphne Sheldrick's book *The Tsavo Story*.

After Oria joined me at Manyara and during the tracking of Radio Robert, I kept pondering on what would happen to the Manyara elephants if they remained at such a high density. I wanted to find out whether or not elephant numbers were in any way controlled by social behavior. If I could show that elephants by some behavioral mechanism were capable of limiting their numbers below the point where they irreversibly damaged the habitat (which many people thought they were doing at the time), then it might not be necessary to shoot them in order to save the trees.

There were several ways in which such control might work, as it did with other species of mammals. In a classic laboratory study J. B. Calhoun showed that the antisocial behavior of mice increased with density to such an extent that reproduction eventually became completely inhibited. The mice neglected their young, failed to court and mate properly, and even resorted to cannibalism. Their experimental community dwindled in numbers to the verge of extinction.

The overcrowded mice had been particularly aggravated by their territorial natures. It was a far cry from mice to elephants, but recently Richard Laws and Ian Parker had written a paper which raised the possibility that elephants might also be territorial and that social factors, as yet undefined, might contribute to the slowing down of the reproductive rate which they had recorded in the high density areas of Murchison.

Manyara had the highest known elephant density in Africa, which I had now confirmed in my aerial counts. Therefore if antisocial behavior among elephants were related to density, it would be expected to appear here in its most extreme forms. I proposed first to study social problems within the family units and bull groups, and then to answer the territorial question by summarizing all my information on movements and elephant home ranges.

Radio Robert was one of the chief instruments of this study. In passing from family to family within the Boadicea kinship group, he opened up a new world; a complicated web of social interactions to unravel.

We were able to keep good records, for whenever Oria came down, at first for weekends, and later to stay, she took pictures while I made notes. Furthermore, at this time Simon Trevor and his wife Laila came to make a documentary feature film on the natural history of the African elephant. I invited them to set up camp next to mine under an acacia tree. Every day while Simon filmed, Laila quietly dictated notes on the exact behavior into a tape recorder. This was a vaulable additional source of information.

Simon had formerly been a Warden in Tsavo East under David Sheldrick, and was a naturalist cameraman who placed himself well and patiently waited for

the action. He had already filmed elephants striding
through the long grass of Murchison Falls, glowing
with the red dust of Tsavo, walking through the mists
of Marsabit, digging for water in the sands of the
Ruaha; and for all the family behavior and hopefully
for a birth, he had come to Manyara. I gave him the
photofile, to take with him daily, and a list of cows
which were due to have a calf. Several of these belonged to Boadicea's kinship group and when I offered
to lend him the radio-tracking equipment from time
to time he accepted eagerly. He knew enough about
elephants to recognize Boadicea's threatening bluff
for what it was.

Within Boadicea's kinship group it was possible to
see many sorts of relationships between females, for
the adult cows seemed to hold each other in varying
degrees of affection. By recording the nearest neighbors of each elephant on many separate occasions I
was able to work out sub-units within the family structure. Boadicea, even though rarely at rest for long,
stood nearest to Giselle more often than anyone else.
Virgo and Right Hook were also closely associated,
two young cows Diana and Calypso went together,
but more independent than any other was a young cow
named Isabelle, with an ear outline like the Gulf of
Suez. She often wandered apart, with none but her
three calves. Her eldest calf was a teenager who was
growing up fast. This daughter was greatly interested
in her mother's latest three-month-old calf, and we
were alerted to her maturity and possible pregnancy by
the sudden development of her breasts.

As the dry season wore on that year, mud wallows
thickened and cracked, creepers hanging on the bushes
shriveled into curly brown shreds, and the Ndala
waterfall dwindled to a trickle and sank into the sands
at its foot. Food and water for the elephants, although
still abundant, became scarcer. With scarcity came
competition and antisocial behavior. Cracks and
stresses appeared within the family unit solidarity.

Isabelle seemed to annoy the big cows more than the

others. She had no special friend much larger than herself, as Virgo had Right Hook. I saw her receive a sharp jab from Giselle, a shove in the ribs from Right Hook, and a head swing from Boadicea that made her drop a branch which was promptly picked up and eaten by the aggressor. At the water-holes she tended to stand apart, and this separation extended to the family's feeding formation. With her went her own three calves. In effect they had formed a consistent sub-unit with Boadicea's family unit. She in turn reacted to antisocial behavior by becoming more independent.

One evening, returning from Naivasha, we were met by Simon who told us that Isabelle's calf had just produced her baby, and he had filmed its earliest hours, though not the moment of birth itself. We named the baby Bottlebrush, because of his fine bushy tail, and his teenage mother we called Laila, after Simon's wife. Bottlebrush was filmed as no other calf had ever been filmed before, and became the star of the film *King Elephant,* never failing to bring the house down when he played, or wallowed, or inadvertently trod on his trunk.

Both the elephant Laila and the youthful grandmother, Isabelle, were transported with maternal feelings for this calf, but its arrival seemed to accelerate their drift away from the rest of Boadicea's family unit. Sometimes it was hard to know if they were still in contact with the main unit.

The day came when they were a little removed in this fashion and Boadicea made one of her forced marches down to the swamps at the mouth of the Endabash River. Isabelle, her three offspring and her grandcalf remained behind, all alone in the Ndala woodlands, quietly browsing and drinking, with no competition from elderly cows. This was just as exciting as originally finding that the family units were stable. I now knew that stability was not absolute and that large family units might split.

When Boadicea, Leonora and Jezebel returned with

their families a few days later, Isabelle associated with them just as before, but from then on whenever the mood took her she would break contact and move off on her own as an independent family unit, just as Leonora and Jezebel did.

There was nothing at Manyara to suggest that the splits and social aggression I saw between cows caused a higher mortality or reduced numbers in any other way. Rather they illustrated a delicate balance of advantage, where a young cow, in choosing the right distance from the senior intolerant matriarchs, managed to get the benefits of independence, the ability to get water, wallowing and feed without competition, without forfeiting the benefits of group protection, should she or her offspring run into trouble.

Family units within kinship groups were almost always within earshot of each other and would swiftly combine to beat off any attack by a predator. The swiftness of this response we saw when Simon Trevor provoked a really good threat charge for his film. We sidled up to Boadicea's family unit in his Toyota landcruiser camera car and stopped thirty yards away. Then Simon got his camera ready, cupped his hands, and with a heave of his diaphragm, gave an excellent imitation of a lion's roar. Immediately pandemonium erupted among the forty-eight strong kinship group. Every head swung around in our direction. Isabelle came rushing in to stand shoulder to shoulder with the big cows. Then led by Boadicea, they staged a magnificent charge on a broad front. Even the invariably placid Leonora was there in the forefront, an imposing, angry giant bearing down with her long tusks raised and ears out while Simon's camera whirred. They swept up to within ten yards of the car, then stopped and peered around as if the target they had found was not the one they had been looking for. Boadicea, weaving and foot-swinging in her highly agitated manner, did not dare to come any closer, but found a heavy log on which to redirect her aggression. She picked it up and hurled it with great force. It whizzed past my head and struck the roof of the car. Whether this was accidental or deliberate I could not say, but if this time it were done by chance it was the sort of behavior that could be learned and repeated and if repeated often enough other elephants might even imitate it.

The combined response was typical and another time I saw them chase the lion, Chongo, and the Chem-Chem pride of lionesses; the elephants shrieking and bellowing while the lions ran low to the ground giving vent to furious growls. The elephants did not stop until the lions ran up a tree, where they were finally safe. Stephen Makacha once saw elephants catch a lion cub at the foot of a tree, and, while the lioness looked on helplessly, they stamped the life out of it. As lions killed elephant calves when they had the opportunity, so did elephants kill cubs.

Strong bonds between cow elephants are the cement of elephant society on which the survival of the younger animals depends. This made the splitting of Isabelle from the rest of the family unit particularly interesting. The gulf between young and old, an elephant generation gap, was apparent in many other family units. Two actually split up in the same way, remaining in association afterward, and five more showed splitting tendencies with well developed sub-units but never actually separating by more than one kilometer, which I considered to be about the limit at which elephants could remain in contact with each other by rumbling.

It seemed to me that the bond between a mother and her daughter could go one of two ways. Either it would weaken, marked by intolerant outbursts from the mother; I imagined that Isabelle was Boadicea's daughter though I couldn't prove it for certain. Alternatively the bond might develop from the overriding attachment between baby and mother, until it becomes a permanent bond between two adults, reinforced by all the shared experiences and dangers which need coordinated action to overcome. This I imagined to be the case between Leonora and Slender Tusks, between whom I never saw even the mildest intolerance, though once again I couldn't be utterly sure of their relationship.

I developed a hypothesis that elephant group size resulted from a balance between the spacing of competition and the clumping of mutual protectiveness. If these are the two major factors affecting elephant group sizes, then it would be expected that if the danger of predation were high, the groups would tend to be large; and if food availability were low the group sizes would tend to be small. At Manyara family units tended to stand further apart during the dry season when food became scarcer. This tendency was never very strong because the food supplies always remained adequate, depending not on rainfall but on the underground waters supplying the forests and swamps.

The work of scientists and Wardens in other places is consistent with my hypothesis. Elephants in the Serengeti formed large herds in the wet season when food was plentiful and competition presumably low. Large groups were also found by Richard Laws and Ian Parker on the periphery of the Murchison Falls National Park, where the elephants came into conflict with human predators. In contrast, under the conditions of extreme drought which hit the central part of Tsavo in 1971–72, when food availability became critical for individual survival, family units fragmented mainly into sub-groups of three to five animals, and large groups were not observed. After the drought, however, when the bare earth was once more covered in grass, the elephants banded together in huge herds of 200 or more animals. Since many of the matriarchs appear to have died it seemed as if small groups of leaderless elephants were impelled to join up with others by a feeling of insecurity. This whole extraordinary event is described in *The Tsavo Story,* by Daphne Sheldrick.

Whatever occasional bullying the young cows may have received it was nothing compared to the treatment meted out to Radio Robert. His presence was decidedly unpopular, and he only had to come within forty yards for some irate cow to shake her head at him, and if in the course of feeding a cow came quietly up behind him, he was liable to be startled by a jab delivered out of the blue. He still had an open wound in his left ear, oozing an aqueous fluid, where he had been tusked during the immobilization operation. None the less he faithfully followed the family, playing with any of the youngsters who wandered far enough for him to meet them without entering the matriarchal danger zone.

He had reached the traumatic stage where a young bull is forcibly rejected by the adults of the family. Eventually, the same would apply to N'Dume, after a calfhood in which the little bull would become more and more obstreperous and sexy until eventually the cows would turn against him. A series of attacks would gradually drive him away and, like Radio Robert, he would linger on the edge of the family for perhaps several years.

Radio Robert had been in this satellite condition ever since I first came to Manyara. All this while he was meeting many others of his own age and sex, in a similar social condition or already independent, but all with a long way to go before being fully grown. Much of the day he was occupied in settling his position in the loose shifting hierarchy that would become established between these young bulls. They were often so absorbed in their struggles that I could approach them quite openly without them noticing.

The final break between Radio Robert and his family came almost imperceptibly. Like Isabelle and Laila he was increasingly tending to linger. The family had gone to the thickets along the Endabash River, and one day when Boadicea turned north the young bull turned south and ventured by himself into new territory right outside the normal range of his kinship group. He went straight south until he reached the Marang Forest escarpment. I was waiting with great excitement to see if he would climb up and disappear in the tall trees next to the Endabash waterfall when suddenly the transmitter packed up for good. I did not see him again for several months and have no idea where he roamed during that time, although as usual I saw Boadicea's group frequently, even without the radio-tag. Somewhere in his wanderings he also managed to get rid of the collar with its expensive, almost irreplaceable radio transmitter.

Radio Robert was late in leaving his family. While still attached he had outgrown some of the younger mature cows, and if they dared to threaten him without the matriarch to back them up he would turn on them and chase them away. He would even threaten the matriarchs themselves if he could choose his ground so that he was at the top of a steep bank beyond their tusk reach.

His relationships with mature bulls were friendly, and there was no question of challenging them at a waterhole or over the ownership of a succulent branch. It was only with his own size class that he had furious fights, and sometimes these could result in deep gashes across the trunk as the combatants locked their tusks and lunged and slashed at each other. Once the relative strength of every other bull had been learned his mature relationships seemed to be governed by the same sort of balance between aggression and affection which controlled interactions within the family units. Play-fighting continues between bulls for as long as they live and probably provides a social mechanism for them continually to check their position in the adult hierarchy.

Bulls, despite their independence, are still sociable and are rarely found more than a mile from another bull or family unit. Beyond a general desire to be near other elephants they don't seem to mind which elephants are their companions, and associate freely with other bulls and cows and calves once they are too big for the matriarchs to chase them away. The largest purely bull herd I saw at Manyara was fourteen strong, but this was unusual, and did not last long. None of the eighty bulls which I knew individually appeared to have any significant preference for any other individual of either sex, apart from brief associations during the time that a cow came into oestrus. There were no permanent attachments between mature bulls and family units, contrary to reports which have appeared in many books about elephants.

Serious fights between fully adult bulls I never saw, although one bull I found dead with what appeared to be a deep tusk wound penetrating his skull. Occasionally sounds of loud trumpeting and breaking branches came from the woodlands, and when I caught a glimpse of excited bulls it appeared that a fight was in progress. As a rule adult bulls appeared to have an understood hierarchy based on size, and mild threat gestures were usually enough to resolve any conflict. Tolerance between bulls declined only at times when a female came into oestrus, but even then smaller bulls moved rapidly out of the way when threatened by one larger.

In their relations with cows and calves mature bulls were sometimes aggressive. A large bull approaching a family unit might put his ears half forward in mild threat and sometimes the cows and calves ran away. More often they turned to greet him by extending their trunks toward him or placing the trunk in his mouth, possibly in appeasement. One cow a few years ago was actually killed by a bull in the Addo National Park in South Africa after being darted by one of the Rangers. Although she was sick and aged and the incident was described as a mercy killing, it is probable that under the effects of the drug she failed to respond to his approach in an appropriately submissive manner. Bull intolerance toward females and young is however atypical and their behavior is usually gentle.

If bull behavior were to affect or control elephant numbers it might do so through sexual behavior. A hypothesis put forward by Sylvia Sikes was that herd dominance in most of the Parks of East Africa had been disrupted by overcrowded conditions or by excessive hunting of ivory-bearing bulls which had left only young bulls of equal status, with the result that the young and highly potent bulls all got a chance to mate and the breeding rate had consequently gone up. I was interested to test this as far as possible by observation at Manyara.

Normally, when a bull entered a family unit he would sniff the genital area of each cow one after the other to sample their sexual condition. Cow elephants are receptive for about three days during their oestrous cycles, which last about 2–3 weeks. If a cow becomes pregnant she will not usually be ready for more sex for another 3–4 years; if the bulls are to propagate themselves they need to miss no chances. The exception to this rule was Diana from Boadicea's family, whom I saw flirting with a bull by backing into him and smelling his penis. She was already ten months pregnant, for only twelve months later she gave birth to a large calf. An oestrous cow may be followed by up to ten bulls simultaneously. Elephants become excitable at this time and trumpeting and growling are frequently heard. The bulls may show a copious secretion from the penis which lasts on some individuals for several days. I found that among the wild elephants of Manyara courtship is virtually absent. Whether this is general for other populations I cannot say, but in restricted surroundings elaborate play-fighting of captive African elephants has been observed immediately preceding copulation, by the ethologist Wolfdietrich Kühme.

Despite the fact that he has the largest penis of all terrestrial mammals, weighing about sixty pounds with its skin, the bull elephant is not the greatest lover in the animal kingdom; not, that is, on the four occasions on which I was lucky enough to witness the act of coition.

One of these happened fifteen miles north of the Park boundaries beyond Mto-wa-Mbu on the edge of the Kitete Chini swamp. I had located a group from the air and followed them up on foot in order to find out if they were elephants from the Park. There were two cow-calf groups of thirty and twenty-five animals, and they all turned out to be complete strangers. Within these groups were at least five large males including two from Manyara, one of whom was the old broken-tooth male named Cyclops. I was pleased to see that the jagged ends of his tusks had smoothed down and in time the injury would grow out. He had just been wallowing and suddenly without any warning he began to chase a young female, who ran before him away from her group. He caught up with her, after about fifty yards, and trumpeting softly, pushed her hind-quarters with his trunk. Then he laid his head upon her back and levered himself upright, with the help of his chin and trunk, until his forefeet were straddled on either side of her spine, his trunk hanging straight down to the right side. Papyrus fronds masked his lower regions, but I could see pelvic thrusts which lasted for thirty seconds during which time he emitted deep growls. Then it was all over and the rest of the group rushed up trumpeting. As soon as the cow became disengaged she was chased by another larger cow. The group milled around. Ten minutes after the mounting two more large males joined this group. The excitement continued. I lost sight of the original female but several elephants backed into others, trumpeting at intervals, and the whole group set off in a tight clump with the males on the outer edges moving warily of one another.

On another occasion within the Park, Oria and I were able to watch the mating of a well-known cow, whom, at a time when I had run out of names, I had called Innominate. She belonged to Queen Victoria's family, which after Boadicea's was the one I knew best. It was a sunny morning in the acacia woodlands. At the moment we arrived Innominate burst out of a bush closely pursued by a large bull. As he rushed after her his penis dragged along the ground, about four feet longer than normal. This organ is proportionately very long in the elephant, as it needs to be in order to reach the vulva of the cow, which uniquely among terrestrial mammals is situated well in front of the hind legs. When fully erect the penis is flexed in the shape of an S by special muscles which move it independently of pelvic thrusts. As Oria and I drove after them in the bucketing Land-Rover, the bull's male organ began to flagellate the air, jerking up and down like a club. Innominate fled another 200 yards before he caught up and reached for her rump with his trunk. Immediately she stopped, evidently responding to the touch. He reared up and straddled her back, with his hind-quarters edging forward until his legs were bent and almost squatting. The penis beat at her belly searching for the vulva. Eventually, the tip became hooked in the opening, presumably touching her seventeen-inch erectile clitoris. Intromission was brief and accompanied by deep groans from the bull, while Innominate remained silent and passive. After only forty seconds he dismounted and the rest of Victoria's family arrived and rejoined Innominate with much growling. All the elephants then calmed down and began to eat grass with the bull in their midst. We observed no more sexual activity throughout that day. The group moved into the shade of a dense clump of *Acacia tortilis* and remained drowsily inactive or feeding. Four other family units were sharing this patch of wood with them. During this time a second bull approached Innominate twice, but although she appeared to be more aware of him than the other females she made no attempt to run away, neither did he try to court or copulate with her. Meanwhile, the first bull remained within a hundred yards, apparently uninterested, not it seemed, wishing to rejoin her. We saw no antagonistic behavior between the two bulls. In the evening the family walked out into the open but the bulls did not even follow them and nothing more in the least sexual happened before darkness fell.

The next day I found them again. Innominate was still fully integrated with her family and no bulls were following. I believe I must have seen her right at the end of her oestrous period.

The other occasions were less dramatic. But the same excitement was evident. I never saw bulls fighting for cows, but from accounts from other parks I learned that sometimes more than one bull may mate with a cow while others look on, but as her oestrous progresses, one bull, usually the largest, after some threat displays or actual fighting, establishes his dominance and the primary right to mate.

There is no doubt that the bond between the cow and the bull was a very temporary phenomenon at Manyara. There were no "sire bulls" with permanent attachments to any particular family unit or kinship group, nor was there any tendency among the largest bulls to establish such a relationship. The bulls mated and then their function was over. They went off on their own or with other bulls and bore no responsibility for the raising and care of the young. Bull society was fluid, constantly changing with no rigid hierarchy to disrupt. For this reason I think it unlikely that shooting the large bulls would have the effect of speeding up the breeding rate.

In their response to danger every bull usually looks after himself, which makes it all the more remarkable that bulls do sometimes help others which have been wounded, just as cows defend a member of the family unit that collapses. There is a widespread belief among hunters that when a bull becomes old and feeble with a heavy load of ivory to carry around he is attended and protected by certain young bulls known as "askaris" who permanently look after him in his senility. Partly with the object of investigating this legend I visited Mount Marsabit to see the giant old bull named "Ahmed" who until his death at 55 in 1974 was believed to carry the largest ivory of any living elephant, but his tusks really weighed only 148 lb. each. It was said that, like squires, younger elephants awaited the call of Ahmed, the largest of them all; but in the few days I spent with Ahmed on Marsabit mountain I saw him alone without any "askaris." The Wardens, Bill Woodley and then Peter Jenkins, who took care

of his safety and protected him from poachers, told me
that they had often seen him with other bulls and cows,
both young and old, but these meetings were most irregular. They had not noticed recurrent associations
between Ahmed and any other individual, that struck
them as significant, nor did they, who knew him so
well, notice any other behavior suggested by the "as-
kari" concept.

These observations are consistent with what I found
in much younger bulls at Manyara, and were later
confirmed by Harvey Croze working with known bulls
in the Serengeti. The belief in protective young "askaris" probably originates from the experience of hunters who, when trying to get close to an old tusker
with heavy ivory, have been charged by a younger,
probably more alert bull in temporary association.
However, a threat charge is part of any elephant's defensive repertoire, and the behavior of the younger
bulls can be explained in terms of self-interest rather
than altruism.

The first chance I had to get comparative data on
elephant movements and social structure came from
the Serengeti. Howard Baldwin modified one of the
surplus lion collars for elephant use. Harvey Croze
was delighted at the chance of plotting the movements
of one of his elusive Serengeti elephants which were a
byword for shyness or aggression when approached too
closely. We mounted a big operation which despite its
size went smoothly. Myles Turner brought along his
heavy artillery and stood behind my shoulder in case
anything went wrong, but our victim went down quickly and the matriarchs of the large group to which he
belonged made only a perfunctory attempt to lift him.
When we drove up they fled, and he was duly radiotagged.

The next morning Howard, Harvey and I flew up to
find him in my plane. He was standing on the edge of
a family unit of about ten that was part of a larger
group. As we circled, the females of the family who
were agitated by the noise of our engine, redirected their

aggression on this hapless young male, who seemed to want nothing more than to mingle in the defensive circle of the cows, and press his flanks against the others. The cows joined in a sortie against him and he was driven further away from the security he appeared so much to desire.

Exasperatingly, the collar lasted no longer than another four days. The technology of radio-tracking, although highly effective for animals like ground squirrels and grizzly bears, we found wanting when applied to the rigors of elephant life. The Serengeti bull had moved much further and faster than a Manyaran elephant during the short observation period but the behavioral observations, although tantalizingly similar, were much too short to confirm whether the Manyara social organization of elephants was generally applicable.

Fortunately a further chance to get comparative information was available just across Lake Manyara in the newly proposed Tarangire National Park. It was a superb wilderness of tangled elephant paths and baobabs which was within easy reach of my airplane from Ndala camp. The elephants proved to be far more elusive than the Serengeti elephants and it took ten days to put a radio collar on one. He was a young bull, and was attached to an easily identifiable family unit of eleven. I located him twenty-two times in a three-month period, and each time he was with the same family, although once again he was the recipient of the same aggression seen in Manyara and Serengeti. With his family was a second family numbering exactly twelve, which contained a large female with only one right tusk. Sometimes the two groups amalgamated and at other times they joined larger clusters of elephants similar to the temporary feeding assemblages of Manyara. All in all, the relationship between these two families, so far as I could tell from their movements and spacing, was identical to the kinship structure that I had found at Manyara.

Bulls also appear to be as independent of the cow-calf groups in other areas as they are in Manyara, and in some areas they may occasionally form much larger purely bull herds, such as one of 144 reported by Ian Parker in Tsavo. In some ranges bull areas exist where few or no cows are to be found. Seronera, the Ngorongo Crater floor, parts of the Kruger National Park and parts of Tsavo are examples. It also appears that where elephant populations invade new areas the bulls are the first to arrive.

In summing up elephant social behavior there did not seem to be any that led directly to decreased reproduction or to increased mortality. Elephants seemed to get along fine with each other despite their density. However there was still the possibility that they might tend to spread out more if there were any form of territorial behavior.

# 15

# Diminishing Ranges

Late one evening, months before Radio Robert's collar stopped working, I found Boadicea, Leonora, Jezebel and their families just south of the Bagayo River, where the escarpment sloped almost straight into the Lake. The road ran beside a white sandy beach lapped by the soda water and flecked with foam, and the elephants were walking along it in a steady determined way toward the flat bushy expanse of Endabash. I drove past them for a couple of miles and met an equally large mass of wild Endabash elephants, coming in exactly the opposite direction. There seemed little doubt that the two parties would meet head on. Unfortunately, the light was fading fast and darkness fell before this happened.

Early next morning I searched for Radio Robert and the others. Half an hour's flight over Endabash brought no success, so I swept the north, my ears straining to hear the bleeps, with the volume of the receiver fully turned up. The Piper Cruiser's wing dipped as I banked over the Musasa River Gorge, then as the plane swung vertically above the depths, my ears were suddenly swamped with the insistent electronic chirrup of the radio-collar, so loud that I had to snatch off the headphones. I sideslipped into the heart of the gorge, and elephant bodies flashed past the window. Leonora, Giselle, Slender Tusks, Boadicea, Jezebel, Radio Robert with his yellow collar, they were all there.

What were they doing up here? From the usual pattern of their movements I had expected them to spend the morning feeding on the banks of the Endabash River and then spend the heat of the day in the swamps at the river's mouth. Had Boadicea turned tail and fled from the approaching horde of Endabash "baddies?" This sort of observation made me consider very carefully territorial behavior among elephants.

Boadicea was an active matriarch seldom staying in an area for more than three days. Then she would make a long march of ten miles or so and take off for a new area to the north or south with her family trailing behind her. In the course of every month she covered her entire range, which entered the Ground Water Forest in the north, coming within two miles of Mto-wa-Mbu, but no closer; and extended south as far as the Endabash River, which she crossed but never went more than a mile or two beyond. Between these extremities she ranged from the Lake shore to the escarpment heights. However, she did not climb up to the Marang Forest, nor did she go outside the Park, except up the Musasa River Gorge which was the only place her group ran the risk of meeting hostile human beings.

I wondered why it was that Boadicea did not use the whole of the Park area that was available to her. Were there territorial limits beyond which other elephants would not let her go, or was she avoiding the boundary zones where she might meet man? This question involved gathering as much information on the ranges of all the other elephant families and bulls in the population. Only then could I assess the importance of space to these elephants and the role of the Marang Forest.

The culmination of the movement's study was the radio-tracking of one of the timid but fierce family units that lived mainly in the Endabash area. My acquaintance with many of these was limited to brief glimpses of massive heads and ears, or of bushes and branches being bent and broken as they fled. For all I knew they might trek all the way by devious mountain paths through the Marang Forest to the great Eyasi Salt Lake. After failing to recover the collar from Radio Robert I begged Harvey Croze to let me have one which Howard Baldwin had sent him, since I had little time to go before I would have to leave Manyara and write up my findings, and he kind-heartedly sent it to me. Harvey came over to help me put the collar on, but we ran into great problems. The elephants were so shy and dangerous. We could not afford to expose ourselves to any counterattack, which limited our freedom of maneuver in a way that would have been quite unnecessary with a northern group. Eventually rather than wait for an Endabash group to venture north we took them on their own ground. But we were quickly defeated, not by the elephants, but by the Endabash River itself which flooded across the causeway and swept my car down river when I tried to cross. The last day Harvey could spare was spent retrieving my sunken car. Another attempt led to an extraordinary incident. I had immobilized a young bull when a cow from an unrelated family unit chased away his parental family unit, tried to raise him, and when this failed, turned around and sat heavily on top of him. There seemed to be no reason for this astonishing, irrelevant behavior, beyond the thwarting of the cow's protective drive.

Finally with our darting team down to the bare minimum, Oria and I, with Mhoja and Suleiman, successfully immobilized and attached a collar to a young Endabash cow, who belonged to the matriarch Jane Eyre's family. It was the first cow I ever tried and I only did so because she lagged far behind her unit and presented an ideal opportunity. Now at last I could radio-track a mysterious Endabash elephant. In fact as we were sitting working on top of her, to our horror Jane Eyre quietly returned and towered over us, her down-turned tusk making her look like a giant and evil-intentioned rodent. I jumped up, spread my arms and shouted. Fortunately, she was half-hearted in her rescue bid, and retreated before my demonstration, leaving the prone body of the young cow to our mercy. It was a surprising way to behave. I expected that, like the other matriarchs, she would make a determined defense of a fallen member of her family, particularly another cow. But we could not tell what was going on in her head. Perhaps she was near panic-stricken with fear to confront her mortal enemy face to face, perhaps her bond was weak with this junior cow, as it often appears to be between young and old in elephant society. The more I had to do with elephants the more I realized that however much I might attempt to seek for rules and generalities to describe their behavior there would always be exceptions to every common response. The young cow was named Radio Evelyn after a great friend of mine whom she had charged several months before.

It was the time when I was preparing to give my seminar and to deliver my recommendations to the National Park authorities. This involved a great deal of analysis of my results and I could not afford to spend much time in following Radio Evelyn, now my marker for Jane Eyre's group. I was only able to locate the elephant twice a day, so I took off every morning and flew along the escarpment currents in the dawn, the mists hanging below in bands of white on green that changed into swirling seas of red-gold as the sun rose. A twenty-minute flight was usually enough to take off, locate the unit, and land back at the Ndala strip. The rest of the day I pored over notebooks pulling out figures, then as the sun sank behind the scarp, setting pillars of cloud on fire over the Lake, I made my evening sweep to see how far they had wandered.

Jane Eyre was a much less active matriarch than Boadicea. Most of her time she skulked in the Endabash thickets moving half a mile or so during the day. At night however she came alive and moved greater distances than Boadicea. It was a curious reversal of the twenty-four-hourly activity cycle, and was probably caused by her fear of man. The development of nocturnal behavior as a response to persecution was also adopted by lions in the Kruger National Park at a time when they were shot on sight as a matter of policy. When the shooting stopped the lions reappeared once more, eventually to become the greatest attraction for the public. In Parks like the Wankie in Rhodesia the nocturnal behavior of elephants persists, even after they have been protected for several years, possibly as a tradition passed down to the calves from their elders who do not forget. Jane Eyre had possibly met her unfortunate experiences at the hands of the farmers and may well have been driven into the Park as a refugee. She avoided the southern farmers during the three months I tracked her. Instead she would go to the foot of the escarpment leading to the Marang Forest, almost as if seeking for a way to get there without passing near to human settlement.

Jane Eyre never crossed out of the Park during this time, but she brought me into contact with many strange elephants that I normally would not have seen. On one morning flight I spotted a huge skew tusker on the shoulder of the Marang Forest escarpment high above the Park. Her left tusk was large and curved, but bent straight out from her head. It was surprising that it had not broken, for it must greatly have impeded her movements. Below, the slope ended in a sheer circle of cliffs, at the foot of which Radio Evelyn and Jane Eyre paced back and forth. I never expected to see that strange cow again, but that very same evening I saw her on the shores of Endabash. She was within a herd of a hundred tightly-packed elephants, a very rare sight in Manyara, and all of them were strangers so far as I knew.

That settled my doubts. There must still be some way for elephants to move directly into the Park, for I did not think they had passed through the Italian's farm in the time available.

Next morning I went with Mhoja to the foot of the escarpment. The Marang Forest was wrapped in cloud and soaking mist, and steady unrelenting rain fell on our heads and trickled down our backs. Twice we thought we had found a possible route only to be rebuffed by smooth vertical cliffs, and unscalable waterfalls hidden by overhanging trees. Then eventually after passing through atrociously thick sage brush we found a network of elephant paths that dwindled to one, which narrowly wound higher and higher between giant boulders and precipices. The air grew cooler but the rain stopped. Trees on either side were festooned with thick hanging lichens. We reached the level of the mists and then to our delight the slope eased and we entered the tall forest. We followed a ridge into the dark green labyrinth, along which, totally concealed from aerial view, was the largest elephant trail I have ever seen. It was smoothly beaten down and must have been at least twelve feet wide.

Having found this path I went back to it many times, and waited to see elephants coming down or going up. I found there was a continual flow of elephants across this crucial boundary. The Manyara Park was in no way an isolated, self-sufficient ecosystem. Now I could easily visualize the acute crisis which might occur if the foresters' policy should change and they should start shooting elephants in the Marang Forest. Those elephants if driven into the Park would probably more than double the already crowded population.

This possibility once more focused my mind on the important question of territoriality. If outside elephants wanted to come into the Park and stay there, would the residents allow them, or would they defend their own home ranges against invasion and drive them out?

At the end of my radio-tracking I was also to put together all my observations of the sighting and movements of known elephants and compare the area covered by each family and how much it overlapped with other families. There were forty-eight family units and about eighty independent bulls and between them I had well over 5,000 records of their positions on different days spread over four and a half years.

The ranges overlapped extensively with one another. There was no question of the elephants carving up the available area into mutually exclusive parcels of territory, as so many territorial animals do. Yet there was not a completely homogeneous mixing either, and each family unit did not roam equally throughout the whole Park. Most of them preferred certain areas. Boadicea stayed in a central area of 20 square miles. Radio-tracking in her case confirmed the range maps I had made from accumulated sightings.

Jane Eyre spent far more time in the south, even though her range did overlap with Boadicea. Other groups hardly ever came out of the Ground Water Forest in the north, restricting their movements to a fraction of the range available to them. Most of the family units covered most of their range every month, although in the dry season those whose range included the *Acacia tortilis* woodlands tended to spend more time in forests and swamps to north and south. In effect there was a continuum of ranges from north to south, each group ranging about two to three miles inland to the beginning of the settlement above the escarpment and between three to fifteen miles along the length of the Lake.

The aerial counts showed that far from avoiding each other, the elephant families were always more clumped than would be expected by chance movements. When I analyzed their distribution by superimposing a ¼ km² grid on the Manyara map I found that on average the entire population would be found in only 7% of the squares. This clumping is even clearer in areas like Serengeti, where you may fly for hours without seeing an elephant, then suddenly encounter ten to fifteen families all within the space of a square mile.

What was puzzling was the differences in size and position of the various home ranges. Two units known as the Aphrodite and Ori families lived in the extreme north of the Park and scarcely ever ventured south. The Ori family unit had the smallest home range of any. I never saw them outside an area of five and a half square miles. Why they did not venture into the acacia woodlands and participate in all the good food there was to be had there was a mystery to me. Her range still overlapped with twenty-eight other family units, but she only used one-sixth of the Park.

The Aphrodite and Ori family units were also exceptional in that they were very seldom seen in company with others. This may have been partly due to the fact that they were almost always seen in conditions of poor visibility in the forest and an associated group might easily be missed. Nevertheless, I wondered if they were actively avoiding other elephants, and if that was why they were restricted to a small area near the *shambas* (farms) of Mto-wa-Mbu. There was nothing in their behavior to suggest this. On the rare occasions when I did see them in company with other elephants there were no territorial displays of hostility.

Even when the dreaded Torone sisters came northward on one of their forays they seemed to coexist quite happily with the peaceable family units they met on the way. I once saw the Torone sisters from a distance in the twilight, leading their group of thirty across the open point of the Musasa River, where its delta fans out into the lake. They passed straight through a concourse of northern-dwelling family units, without any trumpeting or menacing noises or gestures on either side. The next day they and their group tagged on to the slow movements of this large feeding assemblage, and it seems from this and other examples that when a strange elephant or family unit comes to a new area it simply joins temporarily whatever groups of other elephants happen to be there, without any territorial manifestations.

It appears therefore that elephants influence the movements of others more by attraction than repulsion. However, there still remains the mystery of the self-imposed restriction of the two family units Ori and Aphrodite. If they were not avoiding other elephants then why did they always stay in their little pocket handkerchief of forest? The answer possibly is that elephants are very conservative creatures with a strong attachment to the home range to which they are accustomed. It may be that both Ori and Aphrodite used to range through the area that only recently has become the village of Mto-wa-Mbu. Certainly they persistently visited the banana plantations after dark, and enjoyed the alien fruit which they found. So damaging did these nocturnal excursions become that the Park's reputation began to suffer.

There was only one way we could try to reduce the antagonism that the elephants caused when they trampled and ruined the villagers' crops without shooting them. Vesey had for some years experimented with an electric fence along the boundaries of the small Ngurdoto National Park (now called Arusha Park), and using an ordinary stock fence operating a standard voltage he had succeeded in conditioning the elephants to avoid it. Jonathan Muhanga, the Park Warden, tried installing one at Manyara to protect the village of Mto-wa-Mbu, but it was broken so repeatedly that finally he abandoned the attempt. I conducted some experiments to find out what actually happened when a family unit encountered a fence, by stringing an electrified wire across part of the acacia woodlands. The first family unit to arrive, when they had approached to within about ten yards, immediately perceived this wire and cautiously advanced to investigate it. A young cow touched it with her trunk and gave a squeak of pain and astonishment. Then the matriarch touched it, received a shock, bellowed with rage and tore up the fence line carrying away about a hundred yards of wire draped over her tusks.

Jonathan Muhanga was succeeded by David Stevens Babu, an efficient young graduate from Mweka College of Wildlife Management. David had all the breaks mended and then organized daily patrols down the electric fence line, which stretched from the Park entry road, parallel to the main road as far as Mto-wa-Mbu and then down almost to the Lake shore. For most of its length it ran next to the Kirurum River that marked the Park's boundary with the village. Elephants and other animals had to cross the river, before arriving dripping wet before the fence. Consequently, although the voltage used was no greater than for any stock fence they received a terrific jolt. Through David's persistence in mending the fence the number of breakages slowly declined as more and more of the Park elephants learned what would happen if they touched it. Learning was almost certainly speeded by elephants observing and imitating the pained reactions of those that were actually shocked. The fence became effective not only against elephants but also against buffalo, rhino and hippo.

Once the Manyara elephants had learned the fence's unpleasant properties they avoided it like the plague. I remember one moonlit night when David Stevens Babu tried to chase some elephants out of the *shambas* before they did so much damage that the villagers would insist we should shoot them. We could see them easily in the maize on the wrong side of the main road. We crept up on them and hurled a thunderflash which detonated in a shattering, loud explosion. The elephants fled precipitately back across the road and toward the friendly Ground Water Forest which started just on the other side. Unfortunately, the electric fence barred their way, and rather than touch it they ran parallel up toward the Park entrance until they reached the place where the fence ended; only then were they finally able to bury themselves in sheltering vegetation. There was absolutely no doubt that they had learned what the fence could do to them, and they had no intention of giving it the chance.

However sad it was to restrict the elephants in this way it was for their good. Unfortunately, Aphrodite's family unit made a habit of slipping around the end and wrecking the magistrate's bananas almost every night. David Stevens Babu came under pressure and

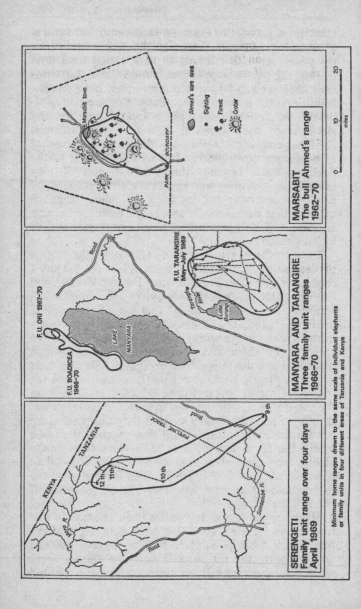

**SERENGETI**
Family unit range over four days
April 1969

**MANYARA AND TARANGIRE**
Three family unit ranges
1966-70

**MARSABIT**
The bull Ahmed's range
1962-70

Ahmed's core area
Sighting
Forest
Crater

Minimum home ranges drawn to the same scale of individual elephants or family units in four different areas of Tanzania and Kenya reluctantly agreed that one would have to be shot to placate public opinion. One elephant was bound to die and rather than risk the death of a matriarch I took the shot myself and killed an adolescent bull in Aphrodite's family. It was the only time I ever shot an elephant, and when I saw the sudden collapse of this marvelous organism which tumbled down a steep bank like a deflated paper bag, I found it incomprehensible that people should do this for pleasure.

Good public relations were a cornerstone of Parks policy and it was sometimes hard to convince the villagers of the national importance of wildlife when they suffered its depredations. Every year saw some sensational but unpublicized incident. A fisherman was bitten in half by a hippo, a smallholder was gored by a wounded buffalo which chased him into his house, broke down the door and killed him, a woman was horned by a rhino on the main road. It was David's job to soothe down the feelings and also his duty to destroy the offending animals. The worst fears were aroused when three people were eaten by lions, only the heads, feet and hands remaining in the morning. David set an ambush when the fourth person was killed. A lion came back to feed on his prey and a bullet ended his life. In the morning he was revealed to be Satima the young male.

When the Manyara elephant movements and ranges were compared with other areas it became evident how minuscule they were.

The range of the Tarangiri radio-elephant of 127 square miles, was six times as large as Boadicea's and twenty-three times as large as that of the Ori family unit. The Serengeti bull had only been tracked for four days before the radio packed up, but in that time he had covered a distance of thirty-five miles—that was about double the widest distance across the Tarangiri elephant's range. It was impossible to work out the area of his range from such meager data, but Harvey Croze, from aerial monthly recce flights which plotted the distribution of elephant groups, believed that Serengeti elephants had ranges of as much as 1,000 square miles. More recently Dr. Walter Leuthold, a scientist working on the long-term radio-tracking study set up in the Tsavo National Park informed me that some elephants have ranges of over 1,200 square miles and as much as 80 miles across. At any rate the range of the Tsavo elephant is at least 220 times greater than the range of the Ori family unit and 60 times greater than Boadicea's, which gives an idea of the adaptability of elephant behavior to different conditions.

There is no doubt that if it were not for man's pressure on the boundaries the home ranges of the Manyara elephants would be much larger; although for the present food is abundant and they don't yet need to wander far. The greatest threat to their future lies in the ever-tightening circle of settlement, cutting off any possibilities of dispersal should the ecological cycle turn to an unfavorable phase. If ever elephants dared to venture back into their former range, conflict with man would be inevitable.

The electric fence protected elephants from men and men's crops from elephants only along the Park village boundary, but elsewhere the advancing agriculturalists were near to the Park boundary with no safety barrier. One incident sticks in my mind which illustrates the fate of those elephants which tried to break out or go crop raiding.

Searching for Radio Evelyn one day I spotted a dead elephant above the scarp with some raggedly dressed men cutting it up with axes and pangas. Swooping low over their heads I saw them duck and run for cover, but I could not tell whether they were within or outside the Park, as the boundary was poorly marked here and the cut line had long since become overgrown and indistinguishable. I sideslipped over the lip of the escarpment, sinking through layers of uprushing air, and came in to land like an express train with the usual strong wind in my tail. The Land-Rover was parked there, so I raced to the house, scooped up Oria, a gun, Mhoja, some cameras and set off at high speed to the point below where we had seen the dead elephant. Oria was very pregnant but managed to slog up the steep, deeply cut elephant trails lined with numerous thorny bushes, that scratched and clung to our flesh. It was high morning when we reached the ridge. I sent Mhoja on ahead to see if he could catch any of the poachers. Oria was very weary, but we staggered on, until we caught up and found Mhoja reclining against an ant hill, his gun cradled between his knees looking at a grim spectacle. About twenty Wambulu tribesmen surrounded the corpse of a young bull elephant. Tusks, ears and trunk had all been hacked off. The guts were spilled all down the side of the hill and large puddles of blood congealed around the body.

"Why didn't you arrest them?" I asked.

"It was the Game Department that shot him."

Mhoja gestured at a lanky figure dressed in a khaki uniform, a jersey, a red beret with a brass buffalo badge and khaki drill shorts. The beacon marking the boundary was 200 yards back along our path. Apparently the bull had been eating the crops along with many other elephants for several days. The game scout had cycled ten miles from Karatu and laid in wait until he could make the ritual sacrifice that would satisfy the *shamba* owners for a while, and perhaps scare away the family units that had witnessed the killing for a few weeks. The young bull had run back straight for the Park as soon as the bullet hit, apparently knowing where safety lay, but had collapsed just before reaching his destination.

So the killing was legal. There was a festival atmosphere among the Wambulu crowding around to get their pieces of meat. An old man, whose crops had suffered the worst damage was carving monster steaks and distributing them to everyone in turn. We were given a steak about four feet long. The first meat to be hacked out were strips on either temple, and they were carried away complete with eye and eye lashes and cooked on a fire that someone had got going. The men were a wild-looking lot, speaking a strange Cushitic tongue.

Their language sounded so odd that the Swahili speakers of Mto-wa-Mbu called them Wambulu, the ones who mumble. Their own name for themselves was the Iraqw.

This was not the first time I had seen protein-hungry men butchering a Park elephant, but this incident sharply outlined how the elephant problem had developed at Manyara. As soon as I returned to camp I pulled out the 1958 aerial photographs and looked at the place where the young bull and his associates had devastated the crops. There was no trace on the photographs of human habitation or agriculture. All these Wambulu settlers had moved up near the boundary within the last decade. Only the ravages of the elephants kept them at bay now, but with increasing land pressure no doubt they will move right up to the Park boundary within the next decade, and as population pressures increase, the Park itself will become increasingly desirable and hard to justify unless it brings benefits to these local people.

# 16

# Death

To me the death of an elephant is one of the saddest sights in the world. The day I met Torone Sister Number Four unexpectedly in the Ndala woods she was an epitome of vigorous life, a powerful strident member of her species, the growth of scores of years had fused her skeleton and muscles into a marvelous organism, coordinated by a brain conditioned by decades of experience. Motivated, at that instant, in defense of her family, she bore down, like a mighty battleship going full speed ahead, upon Mhoja and me. Next second, separated only by a pinpoint in time and the deadly passage of lead through living tissues, she was a collapsed mound of flesh, a colossal lifeless wreck, with a tiny hole in her head from which came a thin trickle of blood.

To a statistician the only significance of death is in its effects on population dynamics and the causes of death are analyzed for their relative importance. For human beings and for elephants death remains significant in the behavior of the survivors. In life individuals of both species are tied by strong family bonds and frantic attempts may be made to save a sick or dying relative.

Many great zoologists including Charles Darwin have thought that animals possess strong emotions and I have little doubt that when one of their number dies and the bonds of a lifetime are severed, elephants have a similar feeling to the one we call grief. Unfortunately science as yet has no means of measuring or describing emotion even for human beings, let alone for animals.

It is perhaps not surprising that attempts to assist a dying elephant may continue long after it is dead. Mhoja and I searching for more elephant paths up to the Marang Forest one day heard the loud bawling of an elephant calf in distress about a hundred feet up the Endabash escarpment. It was coming from our left, so we cautiously worked our way across the face of the scarp until we were very close to the source of the noise. Peering through the foliage I could make out the head of a cow at a curious angle to the slope. Her eye was open but she didn't move. In front of me a tree jutted out, and by swinging up into its branches I was able to get a better view.

Now I saw quite clearly a scene of great natural drama. The cow, an adult, was lying on her side down the slope; one of her hind feet was wedged between a boulder and a thick tree and she was hanging from it. Her head was bent backward at an acute angle and she was stone dead. Next to her stood three calves of different sizes. The eldest was moaning quietly but every so often gave vent to a passionate bawl. The second just stood dumbly motionless, its head resting against its mother's body. The smallest calf, less than a year old, made forlorn attempts to suck from her breasts. Then the eldest knelt down and pushed its head and small tusks against the corpse, in a hopeless attempt to move it. I watched them for fifteen minutes repeating these patterns of behavior until suddenly they caught my wind and wandered slowly away.

On closer inspection I found that the cow was still warm and that no flies had settled on her, so the accident must have happened only a short time earlier. Trees which had stood in the path of her fall were broken and boulders dislodged. I backtracked the path of her descent to a point about 400 feet up the slope where I found her last footprints. It appeared that she had stepped into a pig hole covered in vegetation, lost her balance and rolled out of control down the precipitous slopes. There were several cliffs and in places it looked as if she had bounced down them leaving the vegetation undamaged. The calves must have had some difficulty in finding her afterward, for the nature of the terrain would have forced them to make a wide detour. It seemed that they were not aware that she was dead, although they must have known something was wrong. Perhaps they could not adjust immediately to the finality of her death.

Similar behavior has been well authenticated elsewhere. Shortly after this incident Harvey Croze and a photographer friend of his witnessed the death of an old cow in the middle of her family unit in the Serengeti. Her dying dragged out over an afternoon in that lovely rolling northern country, not far from where we had darted the young bull. Harvey first noticed her lagging behind the family unit; when she fell they all clustered around her, putting their trunks in her mouth, pushing against her and trying to raise her. The most prominent was an independent bull who happened to be with the cows and calves, and he at times kept the others at bay while he attempted alone to aid the dying elephant. She died there among her family, and they stayed with her for several hours longer. The bull in his frustration at failing to raise her, indulged in totally irrelevant behavior. He mounted the dead cow as if he were attempting to copulate, before finally moving off with the others. One cow, presumably she had a particularly strong bond with the dead animal, stayed longer than the others, only withdrawing reluctantly at nightfall.

A more extreme attachment to a dead animal was witnessed by Bill Woodley, the Warden of the Aberdares National Park in Kenya, who told me he observed cows and calves defending the body of a young female for three days after it had been shot, and even more bizarre is the account given by Rennie Bere in his book *The African Elephant* of a cow who refused to abandon the decomposing corpse of her new-born calf, and carried it around for days resting on her tusks. The only other animals I have heard of doing this are baboon mothers who may carry a dead baby for a week or more.

Such a responsiveness to inert bodies is of obvious value in saving a member of a group who has temporarily collapsed. The helpers may also later benefit from the sick animal's recovery when it resumes its role in the family unit's life. It may participate in the communal rearing and defense of the calves, or if it is the matriarch herself, may continue to lead in times of stress and benefit the family unit by drawing on her accumulated stores of experience. A zoologist brought up in the theory of natural selection must always try to explain such apparently altruistic behavior in terms of the helper's own advantage, or in cases where one animal sacrifices itself to save another, such behavior must statistically tend to perpetuate the genes which prompted it, by increasing the chances of survival in a closely related animal that carries those same genes. What is far harder to explain in these rational terms is the value of the extraordinary interest which elephants sometimes show in corpses even when they are decomposed.

After ten days of rotting in the woodlands Torone sister Number Four was reduced to a foul black cavity enclosed by a bag of skin, with bones sticking out. The tips of her feet had been gnawed by hyenas and some of the metacarpal foot bones were missing. I paid her a visit every day to watch the return of all the salts and minerals to the ground. In the rains this process was speedy and within a few more weeks I expected to see grass and herbs sprouting from the dark fibers that had once been her stomach contents.

On the tenth morning a large number of elephants came up from the south to the Ndala woodlands. I was curious to see what they would do if they found the corpse, so I parked the Land-Rover just behind the carcass, with a clear view, and awaited events. After a little while a large matriarch named Clytemnestra appeared with her family unit close behind her. She was a fierce inhabitant of the south whose range overlapped in many places with that of the Torone sisters, and she must have known Torone Four when she was alive. As soon as she caught sight of my vehicle she brandished her ears and looked sideways in my direction. Having made this aggressive flourish she continued quietly on her path. Over the four years I had known her she had calmed down a great deal and was now almost used to quiet vehicles. The tourist explosion and the ever-increasing stream of cars through the Park even down in the wilder regions was gradually having its taming effect on all elephants except for the irreconcilable Torones and a few others. Clytemnestra continued for several paces, and then all of a sudden she caught a whiff of the corpse blowing toward her on the wind and spun around. Her trunk held out like a spear, her ears like two great shields, she strode purposefully toward the scent, like a medieval olfactory missile of very large proportions. Three other large cows came right behind her, heads suspiciously raised, until they closed around the corpse. Their trunks sniffed at first cautiously, then with growing confidence played up and down the shrunken body, touching and feeling each bared fragment of bone. The tusks excited special interest. Pieces were picked up, twiddled and tossed aside. All the while they were aware of my presence at ten paces' distance. Never had they come so close to me before. One of the young cows took two paces in my direction and tossed her head angrily; the others reacted to her mood, and the spell cast by the corpse was broken. They made perfunctory threat displays and moved away. But for my proximity I felt their investigation would have gone on longer, and I cursed myself for being too close.

Before this incident, I had heard of the elephant's graveyard, the place where elephants are supposed to go to die. This persistent myth I knew to be untrue after discovering elephant corpses scattered all over the Park. I had, of course, also heard that elephants took a special interest in the corpses of their own kind; it had sounded like a fairy tale and I had dismissed it from my mind. However, now after seeing it with my own eyes I collected every reliable account I could find and the earliest I discovered came from David Sheldrick. In 1957 from Tsavo he wrote:

> There is now fairly convincing evidence that elephants have a strange habit of removing tusks from their dead comrades. In Tsavo East over the past eight years, the Warden has recovered a great number of tusks from elephants—which had died from arrow wounds or from natural causes—and has found in many instances that the tusks have been removed and carried anything up to half a mile from the carcass. In other cases, the tusks have been shattered against trees or rocks. Quite obviously, no hyena could manage to drag or move a tusk weighing up to 100 lb. for no purpose. The lack of teeth marks, and the fact that some of them are smashed, showed it could only be elephants that resorted to this practice.

Sheldrick's deductions were quoted by Alan Moorehead in the *Sunday Times,* but later debunked by Richard Carrington in his book *Elephants* as an attractive piece of African folklore . . . simply based on tribal gossip but not supported by any eyewitness accounts. However, similar reports persisted, such as the following from the Uganda Parks in 1958:

> An elephant with a badly damaged foreleg had to be shot near Paraa. Immediately afterwards, the body was approached by two other elephants. Both circled the body very slowly, after examining it in great detail with the extended tips of their trunks, which were never allowed to make actual contact. One then

made a systematic but unsuccessful attempt to draw
the tusks.

More recently, Simon Trevor, after leaving Manyara
to finish his film in Tsavo, witnessed a similar spectacle
and filmed it. Elephants approached a corpse, which
had little left apart from skin and bones. They sniffed the
tusks and bones systematically and then carried them off
into the bush. They did not however smash the tusks.

Clytemnestra's exhibition and these reports convinced me that it would be worthwhile setting up a
crude experiment to test if elephant bones really did
have some special significance for live elephants. I
couldn't believe that the behavior I had witnessed was
a coincidence. I found an elephant carcass and transported its skin, tusks and bones to the Ndala River
pools. There were a large number of family units in
the area and one by one they came down to drink. In
most cases as soon as they became aware of the bones
they showed great excitement, raising their tails and
half extending their ears, grouping around and carrying out a thorough investigation, picking up some of
the bones and turning others with their feet. They
usually became huddled in a tight circle so that I
couldn't see what they were doing, except when an
elephant raised a bone above its head. These reactions
in six out of the eight groups that came near the bones
by the river made it all the more puzzling that the remaining two groups simply walked over the bones as
if they weren't there.

Later, when making our film about the Manyara elephant research project for television, I made a similar
experiment in the Ndala woodlands. This time I set
out the bones on one of the most commonly used woodland trails, and with the camera crew retired a little
downwind where we could get a good view through
our long lenses without disturbing the elephants. The
corpse belonged to a bull which had been shot in the
farm nearest to the south of the Park while raiding

some maize fields. After waiting for about twenty minutes a large group of cows and calves appeared led by a familiar tall gaunt matriarch. It was none other than Boadicea with her kinship group. It seemed at first that they would pass the corpse. Then a breath of wind carried its smell directly into their trunks. They wheeled *en masse* and cautiously and deliberately closed in on the body. Shoulder to shoulder the front rank drew nearer, ten trunks waving up and down like angry black snakes, ears in that attentive half-forward position of concern. Each individual seemed reluctant to be the first to reach the bones. They all began their detailed olfactory examination. Some pieces were rocked gently to and fro with the forefeet. Others were knocked together with a wooden clonk. The tusks excited immediate interest; they were picked up, mouthed, and passed from elephant to elephant. One immature male lifted the heavy pelvis in his trunk and carried it for fifty yards before dropping it. Another stuffed two ribs into its mouth and revolved them slowly as if he were tasting the surface with his tongue. The skull was rolled over by one elephant after another. To begin with only the largest individuals could get near the skeleton, such was the crush. Boadicea arriving late, pushed to the center, picked up one of the tusks, twiddled it for a minute or so, then carried it away, with the blunt end in her mouth. The rest of the group now followed, many of them carrying pieces of the skeleton, which were all dropped within about a hundred yards. Virgo was the last to leave, and catching sight of me she came close by with a rib in her mouth, and waved her trunk as she went past. It was an uncanny sight to see those elephants walking away carrying bones as if in some necromantic rite.

A curious variation of the elephant's interest in bones is related by George Adamson in his book *Bwana Game*. He was obliged to shoot one of a party of bull elephants who had chased the District Commissioner around his own garden. The bull was shot at the scene of his misdemeanor, and after allowing the local Turkana tribesmen to cut off as much meat as they could, Adamson had the carcass dragged about half a mile away. That night some elephants visited the body, picked up a shoulder blade and a leg bone and returned them to exactly the spot where the elephant had been shot. It was impossible to prove that they were his companions of the previous day but unless the replacement of the bones at that spot was a coincidence it seems that the place of death held some significance.

An observation of Ian Parker further supports the idea that elephants may be able to recognize the place of death even after the carcass has been totally removed. He was once herding by aircraft a small family unit during a cropping operation and they were moving steadily toward the gun party on the ground when suddenly they changed their course and headed for a discolored patch in the soil. Parker realized that here was the fibrous content of an elephant which he had "utilized" three weeks previously. Despite the elephants' nervousness caused by the aircraft they all stopped when they reached the spot and made a thorough investigation with their trunks, huddling together for a few minutes before moving on to meet their fate.

As curious as the smelling and removal of bones is "burying" behavior. I have never seen this but it has been so widely and consistently reported, often by reliable witnesses, that it must be accepted as fact. This behavior is elicited by fresh corpses or even by animals not yet dead, and it is not confined to elephant bodies, as the following examples will show.

George Adamson has written of an old woman he knew who was buried alive by elephants. She was a Turkana and one evening, when walking home with her son, he stopped behind a bush bidding her at the same time to follow the route ahead. She was half-blind and soon strayed from the path. After wandering until nightfall she lay down under a tree and fell asleep. She was woken a few hours later by an elephant standing over her playing its trunk up and down her body. Paralyzed with fear she lay motionless. Presently other elephants came and, trumpeting loudly, buried her under a great pile of branches which they broke off from trees near by. The old woman was not found until next morning when her faint cries attracted a herder who released her from the imprisoning branches.

Professor Grzimek has recorded four second-hand accounts of elephants, both bulls and cows, killing human beings and later covering them with vegetation and soil. The most interesting of these accounts concerns a bull—it took place in the Albert National Park of the former Belgian Congo in 1936. A tourist approached this bull on foot with his camera. Despite warnings from a number of the National Park staff that the elephant was well known to be extremely dangerous, he persisted in his attempt to get some pictures and the bull charged. Unfortunately the man had a bad leg and was not quick enough in getting away. Just as he turned to flee the Park employee took a last snapshot. The tourist was swiftly overtaken and the elephant smacked him down with a blow of its trunk. Eye-witnesses allege that he was dead before he hit the ground, but to make sure the elephant knelt on him and drove a tusk through his body under the shoulder blade. The survivors returned after the elephant had left and found that the tourist's body had been covered in plants. I was lucky to meet the avenger of the tourist, Professor L. Van den Berghe who later tracked down the bull and destroyed it. It was discovered that the cause of his bad temper was a deep ulcerated wound, full of pus, in his head, which had obviously been caused by a bullet.

Burying behavior is not restricted to human bodies. In a Kenya Park report of 1956 a description exists of a rhino carcass which from tracks nearby appeared to have been dragged some distance by elephants and then covered up with grass and branches.

Another reliable observer, George Schaller, saw burying behavior in the Indian elephant and describes it in *The Deer and the Tiger*. Schaller had tied a buffalo to a tree as bait for tigers. A mother tiger killed it and waited while her cubs ate. Soon an elephant appeared from the undergrowth. The cubs ran off and then the elephant broke down branches and covered the remains of the buffalo.

Accounts of elephants burying their own kind are well authenticated. Myles Turner once made a living by taking out hunting parties. On one safari a client shot a large bull elephant out of a herd of about six. The survivors immediatedly surrounded the dead animal, and stood over him. Myles told his client that the elephants would disperse after a few hours; meanwhile they could retire a little and have their lunch. When they came back some hours later one bull was still by the corpse. The hunters managed to scare it away. Then they advanced to the dead beast and found to their amazement that the other elephants had covered the large wound in its head with mud, and had piled earth and leaves on the body.

A similar observation, this time of cows and calves, was made by Irven Buss, one of the first scientists to study elephants' ecology. In Uganda, he had planned to immobilize an elephant and fix a radio on it. Though he was never able to do this he secured some unique observations. The first animal he darted was a cow and he gave it an overdose. The other members of the group closed up in a defensive phalanx with the result that he was unable to administer any antidote and presently the cow died. The leading matriarch took the group away, but then returned to cover the dead cow with branches and grass.

Lastly I must include the experience of the ethologist Wolfdietrich Kühme who made some observations on three captive African elephants at the Kroneburg Zoo in Germany. The bull when it became aggressive used to throw straw and objects at him over the railings which restricted it. Once Kühme lay down just out of its reach on the far side of the railings. The bull thereupon threw straw at him until he was almost completely covered.

In spite of the fragmentary and incidental nature of the evidence, it is clear that elephants often show more than a passing interest in decomposed carcasses of their own species, even when little remains but the smell. One can only speculate about the survival value in any of this extraordinary behavior. It is possible that the olfactory exploration might provide information about how the animal died which could conceivably be of value, but at the present stage this must remain a conjecture.

I have simply no idea why elephants carry bones. The special significance of the tusks which seemed apparent both to Simon Trevor and myself is equally mysterious, although of all the organs of the body they remain much the same in death as life, curving shafts of ivory, perhaps still with some signal effect. As with the burying behavior I shall know no more about it unless I or someone else conduct some controlled experiments designed to unravel exactly which stimuli elicit these responses, and then try to find out why. These phenomena are certainly not beyond the realms of experimental investigation. It is not enough to say that an elephant possesses a "sense of death," and to leave it at that.

However mysterious and fascinating the bones and burying behavior might be, the relevance of death to the ecological problem could only be discovered through statistics, particularly in trying to answer the question of what controls the size of the population. I had shown that the breeding rate was healthy, but the net changes in population size, so important for the future of the Park, would also depend on immigration, emigration and the death rate.

In my sample of known family units I was able to record deaths in exactly the same way as births. If an

animal disappeared and failed to reappear I concluded
that it was dead, even if I could not find its body. By
the time the elephant conference came up to be held at
Ndala I would have enough mortality data to inform
my colleagues of the way in which deaths and births
affected the size of the population, taking into account the effects of movements in and out of the Park.

The relative importance of different causes of death
to elephants was also very much in my mind. This has
hardly been studied in the wild. The few figures
which exist are mainly concerned with shooting elephants for sport, ivory, meat, or crop protection. Nothing exists on the numbers that die from disease.
Anthrax, rabies and arteriosclerosis have all been diag-
nosed and the manuals about how to care for domestic elephants written by Indian and Burmese civil
servants list so many diseases that elephants may be
prone to, that one is left with the impression that, for
all their size, they appear to be exceedingly delicate
creatures. The old matriarch that Harvey Croze saw
dying in the Serengeti succumbed to a streptococcus
infection of her mucous membranes.

At Manyara I was able to locate fifty-seven elephant
corpses in various stages of decomposition. Some I
spotted from the air, or by following the descent of
vultures, others from the reports of Rangers or tourist
guides. Unfortunately many of the corpses were too
disintegrated for me to be able to find out the cause of
death or who they were, but in other examples the
causes were obvious. Accidents took their toll; in addition to the cow who fell down the scarp there was a
bull who became hopelessly stuck in one of the swamps
of the Ground Water Forest. It was impossible to
extract him and he was shot by the Park Warden.
Across the Lake in the Tarangire National Park another
bull met his end when a baobab, which he had been
in the act of eating, fell on top of him—this is not an
infrequent cause of death in those areas where elephants weaken the trunks of these enormous trees by

their persistent tusk chiseling. If an elephant survives to old age the ultimate terminator may be tooth wear and decay. When the sixth set of molars is ground to stumps, as I found in the mouth of one old cow, the mastication of certain rough, but necessary types of food becomes impossible and death follows. Fighting is rarely fatal though I found one bull apparently gored to death by another, with a deep tusk-sized hole that pierced his brain. Predation by lions is still an important risk for calves. Twice I have observed lions eating small calves, and the one at Lindbergh's camp was definitely killed rather than scavenged. Starvation, the ultimate controlling factor for many animal populations, had not yet made an appearance at Manyara. The Park elephants were remarkably healthy. Few were out of condition or suffering from disease. Some had skin growths or abcesses the size of tennis balls on their bodies but these usually sloughed off after a few months. One female had hundreds of wart-like growths that covered her trunk but this was a very rare condition. Typically the thighs, back, shoulders and fore-limbs of almost every elephant were well padded with flesh. I never saw Manyara elephants looking like the walking skeletons that were later to make their appearance and to die in thousands in the Tsavo.

In Manyara's history the shooting of elephants has played an important role. Before the Second World War the area was famed for good hunting, but not of elephants, since there were few large tuskers. After the Park was established the first Warden killed any elephants that entered the village of Mto-wa-Mbu in an attempt to "teach" them the boundary. To the south even larger numbers were eradicated in the mid-1950s as the European farmers moved in to take over the new wild areas granted to them. Many were shot below the escarpment in an area about the same size as the Park. The survivors fled into the Park or up the scarp to the sheltering Marang Forest.

Even while I was there many elephants were killed

that strayed out of the Park boundaries into the *shambas* that pressed in closer every year. The Game Department, responsible for all wildlife outside the National Parks, were organized to protect crops by shooting. Other elephants were speared by the Wambulu. I once found a young female with a deep wound clean through her trunk, obviously caused by a spear. Every time she took a breath she blew frothy bubbles out through the straight cut edges of the wounds. Luckily she was a healthy individual and after a few weeks the holes closed up and she appeared to regain the full mobility of her trunk. From several corpses I recovered the heavy spear blades of the Wambulu.

Most shocking was the discovery of an entire family unit of seven that had been massacred inside the southern game fence. I found them where they had fallen, the matriarch and her six offspring one on top of the other. Mhoja dug around in the soil and uncovered a .470 bullet. This was not the work of tribesmen justifiably defending their crops, but we never found out who the poachers were, who used heavy caliber sporting rifles inside a National Park.

The greatest killer of Manyara's elephants, even after ten years of protection, was still their ancient enemy man. Statistically his effects on the scale I observed were not in the least harmful, although illicit hunting, if allowed to proliferate, would still be the greatest threat to the survival of these elephants. The ecology of the Manyara Park depended entirely on the tolerance of man, the key factor in all elephant problems. Not only is modern man more tolerant, but he has stopped primitive hunting, which must have exerted profound effects in the past. The modern African elephant, *Loxodonta africana,* is a species not much older than man himself, even though its ancestors can be traced in the fossil record with greater ease than man because of their massive body size. The past, the present and the future of the African elephant is inextricably tied up with that of man, and no ecological study ignoring this factor can be realistic. To understand the elephant problem in its entirety I realized that I would have to pursue a study of the elephant's history in relation to mankind, as far back as it could be traced.

# 17

# Man the Killer

A group of elephants was moving across the face of the escarpment and I was watching them through binoculars. All was peaceful until one dislodged a stone that rolled down the slope past an immature bull. He suspiciously raised his head and shuffled down the scarp, thoroughly alarmed, waving his tail high in the air behind him. His feeling spread like quickfire and almost immediately the whole family were tearing downhill, crashing through bushes. This noise seemed to make them even more frantic and total panic gripped them as they fled helter-skelter into the forest, little ones and adults running blindly, smashing any woody vegetation in the way, trumpeting and growling. It was apparently an example of blind terror, and I had witnessed its accidental cause—a rolling stone.

Another time, when tracking Jane Eyre's family unit, I stopped half a mile upwind of them. There was a light breeze blowing and they were heading for a clear spring at the foot of the scarp. Suddenly, all their trunks swung up above their heads like mobile chimney stacks, the elephants about-faced and fled ignominiously back along the path they had come.

Some observers have been astonished by the timidity of elephants, but perhaps the creatures have sufficient historical cause for fear. Not only has man hunted them for at least twenty thousand years, but predators, far more formidable than man—until he invented firearms—were pursuing elephants from the earliest times.

Among these were the sabre-toothed tigers of America and the scimitar cats of Europe and Africa which preyed on elephants in the Pleistocene era. They were heavy carnivores with strong front paws and huge, stabbing teeth whose remains have been found in cages surrounded by the bones and teeth of young mammoths, which seem to have been their staple diet. European elephants had also to fear cave lions and cave bears which were certainly larger than the predators of today. Probably the heavy armament and thick skin of contemporary elephants have been developed by natural selection. Only the most strongly armed, and possibly also the most timid matriarchs, survived to pass on their attributes to their descendants. Man, too, may have played a part in the elephant's evolution.

Even Stone-Age man was a great hunter. Evidence of this comes from a discovery made in the nineteenth century by a palaeontologist named Maska of a camp of mammoth hunters in Czechoslovakia. The camp lay between two mountain ranges where herds of mammoths probably concentrated during their annual north to south migration. The success of these hunters can be measured by the fact that bones of 900 mammoths were uncovered at this one site; killings on such a scale may well have hastened the retreat of the mammoths to Siberia and their extinction there.

The fossil evidence has come mostly from Europe and North America, but there is little doubt that the ancestors of the African elephant suffered similar attacks, first from dangerous predators and later from Stone-Age man.

Even today, there are many efficient hunting techniques which probably predate the Iron Age. These include stampeding elephants on steep hill sides until they fall, driving them into marshes where they get

stuck in bogs, burning them to death when they enter
long grass, and digging pitfalls.

The first recorded observations of African elephants
made by man are rock etchings. A number of them are
to be found in the Sahara which, in that early period,
5,000 to 11,000 BC, was not a desert, but bore vegetation that made it a suitable habitat for elephants. At
Ain Safaad in Algeria, one of these etchings depicts a
cow elephant drawing her calf under her belly for protection as a leopard, just beyond the reach of her trunk,
tries to grab it.

During the reign of the Pharaohs the chiefs of the
Sudan paid a tribute in ivory to the rulers of Egypt,
but apart from a wall painting at Thebes dated 1,500
BC and a painting of a domestic elephant led by an
Indian mahout on the tomb of Rhekmere (1,200
BC), there are few references to elephants in this
period. This may be because, by then, the Sahara
desert had grown much larger, and as a result very few
elephants were left in Egypt and what is now Libya.
There were, however, still plenty in Tunisia and Morocco. In 500 BC, Hanno, a Carthaginian navigator, saw
them on the Atlantic coast.

Alexander the Great was probably one of the first
Westerners to encounter domesticated Asian elephants.
For thousands of years the Indians had trained them
for war. At the battle of Hydaspes, King Porus used
200 elephants against Alexander's army and according
to the historian, Arrian, "the elephants themselves,
partly enraged by their wounds, and partly for want
of riders, no longer kept any certain station in the battle, but running forward, as if madness had seized
them, they pushed down, slew and trampled under-
foot friends and foes with no distinction." Alexander
won the battle but it was a near thing, and though afterward he was contemptuous of the use of elephants
in warfare his generals were deeply impressed, more
particularly Seleucus who had commanded the infan-
try upon whom the task of resisting the elephant attack had chiefly fallen.

It was however after Alexander died in 322 BC and his empire broke up that for a brief period elephants became of such importance that records were kept from which their abundance and distribution can be deduced. All Alexander's chiefs, or Successors, as they were called, received a share of the elephants captured in his campaigns. But a feud broke out between Seleucus who held the Eastern lands and Ptolemy the master of Egypt. Seleucus therefore commanded a monopoly of the elephant supply.

As a result Ptolemy was unable to import elephants from India and sent out an expedition to capture and train African elephants. His successor Ptolemy II established a settlement on the Red Sea, Ptolemais Thermon (Ptolemais of the hunts), for this purpose. African elephants were caught here for the first time in written history, and shipped to Memphis by way of a canal which ran from the head of the Gulf of Suez to the Nile.

At this time elephants were regarded as so valuable to strategy that Ptolemy's officers tried to persuade certain elephant-hunting tribes to stop killing them. The answer was a categorical refusal.

The area around Ptolemais Thermon must have been quickly denuded of elephants for, within twenty years, the main hunting settlement was moved a hundred miles to Adulis, in what today is Ethiopia.

The domestication of the Ptolemaic African elephants continued throughout the Third Century BC until the battle of Raphia (217 BC). In this battle the African elephants, which may have been young or members of a small subspecies, were ranged against a superior force of larger and less nervous Indian elephants. Ptolemy was victorious and captured many elephants that were more efficient than his own. After this no more references appear about the Red Sea training stations, although these elephants were still killed for their ivory.

In the same century elephants lived along the Afri-

can coast of the West Mediterranean, at the foot of the
Atlas Mountains, and all through the domain of
ancient Carthage. The Carthaginians had close trade
relations with Egypt, and probably heard of Ptolemy's
successful experiment for later they too used elephants
as tactical shock weapons, deploying them in battle
against the Romans. Their trainers, however, were Indians according to the contemporary historians who
refer to them as "Indi."

In the battle of Tunis (255 BC), a Roman army under Regulus was annihilated by a charge of Punic elephants. The elephants with which Hannibal crossed the
Alps in winter were drawn from the same stock, but
only one survived the ordeal.

In the final decisive battle of the Punic Wars, at
Zama, near Carthage (202 BC), Hannibal used eighty
elephants, but after years of fighting the Romans had
learned how to deal with them. Scipio Africanus drew
up his troops in open order, leaving lanes through
which the elephants could charge. As they did so,
they were harried, on either side, by Roman troops.
Scipio won the battle and captured all the elephants.

After this, though the Romans continued to use elephants in minor wars, they came to be regarded as
obsolete weapons which were as great a hazard to
their own men as to the enemy; for, subjected to flank
attacks and red hot sling bullets, the elephants stampeded in any direction.

Some 270 years later Pliny refers to elephant catching as a bygone custom:

> It was formerly the practice to tame them by driving
> the herds with horsemen into a narrow defile, artificial-
> ly made in such a way as to deceive them by its length;
> and when thus enclosed by means of steep banks and
> trenches, they were rendered tame by the effects of
> hunger; as a proof of which they would quietly take
> a branch that was extended to them by one of the
> men.

But this did not mean that the North African elephants were left in peace, for Pliny was writing at a time when ivory traders were already making inroads on their numbers and distribution. He wrote:

> At the present day, when we take them for the sake of their tusks, we throw darts at their feet which are in general the most tender part of their body . . . Large teeth, in fact, are now rarely found, except in India, the demands of luxury having exhausted all those in our part of the world.

Sir William Gower wrote in his history of the African elephants that by the Sixth Century AD the North African elephants had been exterminated in Algeria and Morocco.

There is, however, evidence to suggest that the training of African elephants did not die out with the Ptolemies and the Carthaginians. For as late as AD 533 the Negus of Ethiopia received Justinian's envoy at Axum, sitting in a chariot drawn by four elephants on the road from Adulis, the old elephant training center. Also, Arabic historians mention the year AD 570, when the Negus sent an army of Africans, supported by elephants to attack the Koreish of Mecca, as "the year of the elephants." In the event an army led by the Prophet's grandfather defeated the Negus's troops.

I have not been able to find any reliable accounts of man's treatment of African elephants in the Middle Ages. The medieval bestiaries show elephants with stiff legs and monstrous trumpet-shaped trunks, and are valuable only as a tribute to their authors' imaginations. It was not until the fifteenth century that the Portuguese discovered the Guinea coast, and before long they, and the Spaniards, Dutch, French, Danish and English who followed them, were taking away quantities of slaves, gold, spices and ivory, disrupting age-old patterns of existence for man and beast in West Africa. Yet most of the trade was done through intermediaries and even by the eighteenth century the interior of Africa was virtually unexplored so that Jonathan Swift could write:

> Geographers, in Afric maps,
> With savage pictures filled the gaps,
> And o'er unhabitable downs
> Placed elephants for want of towns.

The maps were probably accurate enough, for other than in desert regions, the elephant probably roamed over the whole of Africa south of the Sahara, apart from the Cape Colony.

In the year 1635, the Dutch, led by Jan van Riebeeck, founded The Cape Colony. At that time elephants were to be found as far south as the Cape of Good Hope, and were numerous around Table Mountain.

We have seen that even before the invention of firearms man was capable of exterminating elephant populations in North Africa. Armed with the primitive wheellock or matchlock he became a hundred times more efficient as a killer. The Boers were unrestrained hunters and, equipped with guns so heavy that they had to be steadied on a forked rest or supported against a ramrod, they went out in pursuit of ivory which they sold to the Dutch East India Company.

It was a dangerous occupation and many a Boer was tusked or trampled to death, but the profits were so substantial that the hunters' ranks always filled up. Some Boers became professional elephant hunters with the result that the virtual extinction of elephants in South Africa was accelerated.

By the 1830s elephants were scarce in Cape Province and only in the Addo and Knysna forests were there any herds left. At this point the British Government, which now ruled the whole colony, prohibited elephant hunting, thanks to which the Addo and Knysna herds, though now very small, survive to this day.

Meanwhile British, Boer and Hottentot hunters were

penetrating the elephant strongholds of the North and as firearms improved first with the flintlock and then with the rifle, so did their killing power. Between 1835 and 1860, the heyday of the "game sportsmen," the veldt was teeming with life and virgin to rifle fire, so these hunters managed to exterminate most of the game in the Transvaal and Bechuanaland (now Botswana).

The hunter-explorers were followed by the Trek Boers, many of whom hunted for a part of the year in the veldt and spent the rest at their homesteads. When the Free State and Transvaal Boers had disposed of the elephants in their new territory they began to look for ivory in other regions.

In the heart of Bechuanaland, Livingstone recorded the slaughter of 900 elephants in the vicinity of Lake Ngami in the space of one year, 1849. No large slow-breeding mammal population could resist such slaughter. Not only were small parties of English and Boer hunters combing the entire subcontinent for elephants, but in tribal lands traders were supplying guns to Africans who, throughout the year, with patience and local knowledge, followed the elephant herds and wore down their numbers.

The traders who had gone up country to buy the ivory, would return to the coast in ox wagons loaded with tusks. By 1860 elephants were scarce and by 1885 little remained of the once innumerable herds south of the Zambezi River. The few isolated pockets of survivors were probably led by cunning and timid matriarchs, conditioned to detect the slightest hint of man's presence and avoid it. Then the ivory hunters crossed the Zambezi and began to make inroads on elephant populations in the interior of Africa.

The slaughter, as one commentator, H. A. Bryden, put it:

Took place in territories over which British rule had not been extended . . . if Great Britain had suddenly extended her sway from Cape to the Zambezi fifty years earlier the elephant might have been saved. Nothing else could have preserved it from extinction.

This comment, written in 1903, reflects a sense of the appalling, almost accidental, loss of elephants and of most of the rest of Southern African wildlife. This uncontrolled exploitation by bloodthirsty "sportsmen" and unscrupulous ivory traders, speedily eliminated the elephants in those parts of Africa which they were able to reach.

The next chapter in the fate of the elephant was to unfold in a vast tract of Africa to which the rule of law was extended before the spread of firearms had completed their deadly task.

The first hunters armed with firearms who arrived in East and Central Africa behaved in much the same way toward elephants as had the Boers and the British in South Africa. They were Arabs and Swahilis who, while engaged in the slave trade, also sought ivory. Many slaves returning to the coast carried tusks on their heads.

Even when the slave trade was suppressed the general opinion remained that elephants would be exterminated in most parts of Africa except for places which were particularly inaccessible, such as the primeval forests of the Congo basin, which were sparsely inhabited by dreaded aboriginal tribes. These were thought to be the only elephant haunts still untouched by hunters and likely to remain so.

Many British and German officials in East Africa deplored the wholesale killing, particularly of elephants, and hoped it might be controlled by suitable regulations. As early as 1894, official concern at the decline in wildlife in the previous decade was expressed by Sir Harry Johnston. Then in 1896 when the East African Protectorate was declared, the Marquess of Salisbury requested a report from the British East African and Uganda commissioners on the desirability of closed seasons and specially reserved districts. He also ordered that a regulation should be introduced requiring all hunters to apply for licenses, the cost of which should be high enough to act as a check. German administrators introduced similar measures and sanctuaries in their territories.

At last the threat to the game aroused international concern. In 1900 a conference was convened by Great Britain and Germany, and attended by representatives of other powers with the express purpose of endeavoring to protect the fauna of Africa "from the destruction which has overtaken wildlife in Southern Africa and in other parts of the globe." Perhaps they were stirred into action by the recent extermination of millions of buffalo on the plains of North America. The treaty was not ratified for some years and even then not all the parties signed, but, for the first time, in most of the European colonies in Africa, laws were passed which gave some hope for the future of the elephant and many other wild animals.

Among the measures requested at the conference was a limitation of the size of ivory which might legally be dealt with in trade or export.

The British and German governments also agreed on certain principles. Among them were prohibitions on killing an animal under one year old, or females with young, and on the wholesale trade in hides, horns and ivory. A further recommendation was a ban on the export of elephant tusks under 10 lb weight. Heavy duties on tusks between that weight and 30 lb were imposed and licenses for all hunters whether native or others were introduced, and so was a closed season for some game animals. Finally the creation of game reserves was proposed.

A far-sighted German administrator, Major von Wissman, suggested that wherever possible the resident tribe in each area should, through its chief, be made responsible for elephant hunting, and for preventing hunting by any outsiders. A similar proposal was made in a British Colonial Office paper to the effect that "Native chiefs should be given a pecuniary interest in

the preservation of game as well as in the enforcement
of the game laws." Unfortunately, both these ideas
were well in advance of their time. If they had then
been put into effect, the future of wildlife would be
much more secure today.

In the Belgian Congo, in addition to the sanctuaries
established at roughly the same time as in British and
German territories, King Leopold of Belgium personally
supported an elephant project of great originality. He
wanted to domesticate African elephants and use them
for forestry and agriculture after the tradition of the
East. One Indian elephant and an Englishman walked
their way across Africa from the Indian Ocean to the
Belgian Congo. They formed the original nucleus for
the elephant school, which, after more than seventy
years, several changes in location and many tribulations, still survives today at Gangala na Bodio.

Up to the turn of the century the history of the
African elephant showed a steady trend toward extinction; after this the picture becomes blurred. The new
game laws took time to bite in the countries in which
they were applied, and even then they could not be
enforced until adequate police forces or game depart-
ments had been built up. Illicit hunting was controlled
patchily, more effectively in some areas than in others;
as a result elephants were safe in one place but continued to be killed in others.

Together with a measure of protection, some natural
factors played a significant role in reestablishing favor-
able conditions for elephants, but they too acted un-
evenly. The first of these was the cattle plague—
rinderpest—which swept down Africa in the last decade
of the nineteenth century. The corpses of immense
numbers of cattle, wildebeest, buffalo, waterbuck and
other antelope littered the plains, even hyenas, vultures and other scavengers could not dispose of the car-
rion; elephants, however, were not susceptible to the
disease. For pastoral tribes, such as the Masai, the
rinderpest outbreaks were catastrophic. Their whole

economy and culture depended on cattle, of which about 90% died. Smallpox, famine, and internecine warfare further reduced the Masai and they abandoned many of their grazing grounds.

This may have had profound ecological effects. The herders no longer burned the grass every year to prevent the bush from encroaching on their pastures, which in consequence were probably invaded by bush and young trees, and became an ideal habitat for elephants. This new landscape also suited the tsetse fly which spread carrying a disease deadly to cattle, trypanosomiasis. Thus many of the cattle people were barred from returning to thousands of square miles which they had previously inhabited. Even today much of Tanzania is closed to livestock for this reason.

In other parts, particularly in Uganda, the tsetse carried an even deadlier scourge, sleeping sickness, which affected human beings. In the early twentieth century the only answer the colonial authorities could find was to move entire populations from the fly belts and resettle them elsewhere. In this way huge tracts of land were left vacant for elephants, among them the Murchison Falls National Park and its environs.

In areas where disease had removed or diminished human influence, and where the game laws were strictly enforced, it was not long before the elephants found themselves free from persecution, and living in plenty. In such circumstances animal populations almost invariably increase and it is reasonable to suppose that, for the first time in centuries, in large parts of Africa elephant births exceeded deaths. Records of the time do not give us any figures of the increase in elephants, but potentially elephant populations under good conditions can increase at the rate of 4–5% per year, which is close to the rate of the fastest growing human populations.

In the more densely settled areas, however, or where the enforcement of game laws was lax, elephants probably continued to decline. Modern medicine, the end of slavery and the cessation of inter-tribal warfare allowed human populations to expand—a trend which has continued to the present day. In the 1960s the Wambulu population above Manyara increased at an annual rate of 4½%.

This has led to the final phase of elephant history, similar all over Africa and reflected in microcosm in Manyara: the phase of restriction and compression of elephants into ever smaller ranges. Their rapid concentration in the only safe refuges, the National Parks and Game Reserves, has undoubtedly been speeded up by the elephant's ability to learn which areas are safe and to move there.

One of the elephant's valuable attributes is for individuals to be able to pass on their experience to succeeding generations. In her long life a matriarch can accumulate experience of great value. An illustration is the way in which N'Dume in his first year learned to fear my Land-Rover by imitating his mother's response, which was one of circumspection. His first aggressive rush up to the wheel of the vehicle was never repeated.

Moreover the Torone matriarchs, who had probably been persecuted in the elephant massacres which took place in the mid 1950s in the south of the Park, showed their offspring by example how to react violently to human beings. In this way it is possible for elephants to perpetuate "traditions" within their family units.

Another example of their traditional learning comes from the South African National Park of Addo. Here, in 1919, at the request of neighboring citrus farmers, an attempt was made to annihilate a small population of about 140 elephants. A well-known hunter named Pretorius was given the job. Unlike Ian Parker's teams, whose rapid semiautomatic fire liquidated entire family units, Pretorius killed elephants one by one. Each time survivors remained who at the sound of a shot had witnessed one of their family unit members collapsing dead or in its death agonies.

No doubt the trauma was often associated with the hunter's smell, and danger arising from the presence of man had become deeply imprinted in the memory of those who escaped. Within the space of a year there were only sixteen to thirty animals left alive. It seemed that one final push would rid the farmers of their enemies, but by then the remaining elephants had become extremely wary and never came out of the thickest bush until after dark. On several occasions when the hunter ventured to pursue them, he in turn was hunted through the dense thickets and had to flee for his life. Pretorius eventually admitted himself beaten and in 1930 the Addo elephants were granted a sanctuary of some 8,000 acres of scrubby hillside.

The behavior of these survivors has changed very little, though they have been contained by a fence and are not shot anymore. Even today they remain mainly nocturnal and respond extremely aggressively to any human presence. They are reputed to be among the most dangerous elephants in Africa. Few if any of those shot at in 1919 can still be alive, so it seems that their defensive behavior has been transmitted to their offspring, now adult, and even to calves of the third and fourth generations, not one of which has itself suffered attack from man.

There seem to be two factors at work in the evolution of the escape responses and the defensive behavior of elephants: first, genetic selection arising from the predation of the large cats and other great animals of the early ages; and secondly, individual conditioning based on experience, which may be transferred from generation to generation.

Transmitted experience of course provides a much quicker means of adapting behavior than genetic selection, especially in animals with a long time between generations. It was interesting to note at Manyara that while family units such as the Torones remained implacable, others tamed rapidly after complete protection was introduced when the Lake shore was gazetted as a Park. Boadicea's family represented a conflict between these two extremes.

Boadicea herself probably had bitter memories dating from the colonial era when hunting was allowed on the western shore of the Lake. She gave vent to her feelings in frequent attacks on tourist vehicles which fortunately always stopped just short of collision, but often while she was making her impassioned displays other members of her family would stand quietly by as if nothing were happening.

Toleration of human beings was most strongly developed in Virgo. She was bold and independent but grew tamer and tamer. I became confident of moving openly around her on foot, while following Boadicea's family, but always provided the grand matriarch were not in sight. At first Virgo was aggressive and would shake her head or perhaps make a little rush in my direction but small tell-tale movements of her ears and trunk informed me of exactly what move she would make seconds before it happened. Mixed in with her aggression and apprehension there seemed to be intense curiosity. Gradually she learned that I was harmless and vice versa. She would stand watching me or even inquiringly wave her trunk in my direction. It was wonderful to see a wild elephant who had become used to the presence of the animal to whom her leader responded as a deadly enemy.

The other members of the family unit were much more suspicious. In particular Right Hook, Virgo's usual companion, would hover in the background while Virgo walked up to me, but in time even Right Hook slowly lost her fear and would carry on feeding while I walked on foot near her taking notes. Eventually the day came when Right Hook became so used to me that she could not be persuaded to extend her ears for the new photograph of her I needed for my photofile even though I approached on foot almost within a trunk's length of her.

Right Hook, Virgo and Virgo's calf eventually grew used not only to me but also to Oria and Mhoja, but if a stranger were present they would come nowhere near us.

For a brief period we fed Virgo with the fruits of

various plants, testing which she preferred, but I discontinued this at John Owen's insistence; he felt that feeding her might attract her to cars, and then if she were refused food she could become aggressive. In Murchison Falls this had actually happened with a fully grown bull called the Lord Mayor of Paraa. He learned to scavenge from dustbins and to raid people's cars for food. Unfortunately, in the end when he couldn't find the food he started to pick up the cars and shake them. For these crimes he was finally shot.

I assured John Owen that Virgo was an entirely different character, but on reflection I think he was right that I was mistaken in attempting these experiments. Although I knew that Virgo was harmless it was the principle of not feeding wild and potentially dangerous animals that mattered. My behavior though safe for me, might have tempted others to think they could do the same with another elephant, or with Virgo herself, and this could have been very dangerous. Several photographers who have injudiciously approached elephants on foot have been killed in other National Parks. For this reason I must emphatically warn any visitor to Africa not to walk up to wild elephants on foot. I am not trying to exaggerate the dangers but I do not want any fatal accidents to be blamed on the fact that some wild elephants have reacted in an understandably hostile way to their age-old enemy.

What we must realize is that, despite the efforts that have been made to set aside Parks for the animals, man still remains potentially the elephant's deadliest enemy. This is due primarily to the increase in human population, and the consequent conflict for space that compresses elephants into smaller and smaller areas. Without enough space they may not be able to survive. The compression has been reinforced by their own avoidance of man, itself the result of genetic and cultural evolution of timidity. Furthermore, their ability to learn where safety lies has speedily concentrated them within the protected National Parks.

This ever growing pressure of man on the elephants was just one facet of the problem that I was attempting to solve in Manyara, and in June 1970 I was to give the seminar in our camp on Ndala River to present my findings about the elephants. I could no longer postpone answering the question of whether or not the dense elephant population should be thinned by a calculated shooting program.

# 18

## Keys to Survival

By the middle of 1970 I had been at Manyara for four
and a half years, and not only was the seminar imminent but our final departure from Manyara was also
only a couple of months away.

It seemed a very long time ago when, for the first
time, and full of excitement, I had walked up to the
acacia tree near the waterfall, sat on one of the big
rocks that surrounded me, my thoughts full of tangled
impressions of wonder and beauty—and decided to
set up camp there. It was wild and practically untouched by man. Then had come the day when I first
brought Oria to share it with me. The idea of leaving
was very far away. Together we found a serenity in
Manyara, a sense of fusion with our surroundings and
harmony with the elements that other people seek in
high mountains or on the waves of broad oceans. We
had become absorbed in the problems and delights of
living and moving among the wild animals without disturbing them; of becoming harmless spectators of everything they did and, in Virgo's case, of eventually
being accepted by her.

I had changed a lot in that time. I had arrived alone
and as a scientist, but after Oria joined me, I saw things
increasingly through eyes opened to the importance of
individual and family relationships. Perhaps I was

made most aware of these changes by a vivid experience I had during those last weeks.

One day, short of equipment, with only one dart left in my gun, I tried to retrieve a defunct collar from a young bull in Sarah's family unit. I anticipated no difficulty, but an effective defensive circle soon shielded him from any approach, his mother tried to lift him, and the cross-tusked Sarah kept us at bay. Before long I realized I must inject the antidote by hand if he were to survive.

I drove in closer toward the elephants and all dispersed but for Sarah, who was probably the young bull's grandmother and who stood over him with one of her forefeet resting on his body. Nevertheless I took a risk, drove up and leaned over to give the injection. The needle went home, but at the same instant so did Sarah's crossed tusks, into the radiator. First she gave a little exploratory shove at the metal, and then with greater confidence dug her tusks well in and pushed. I let the brake out and we rolled backwards, like a pram being wheeled by a nurse. Mhoja fired a shot in the air, then we hit a tree and Sarah's tusks slid across the top of the bonnet straight at the cameraman on my left who was filming the operation. She swung across at me and I edged out of the door to keep beyond her range. Her tusks crashed against the steering wheel and then she swiveled around and went off.

It was the third time that my car had been struck by an elephant and I hated the whole business. It was not that I felt alarmed by Sarah, who was normally gentle and inoffensive, but I was loathe to cause her distress. At first I had found immobilizations enthralling, because they were exciting and showed me a touching side of an elephant's character, but I later became disenchanted with the undeniable anguish of the elephants struggling to save their loved ones. I did not like to think that they might visualize me as an attempted murderer, yet surprisingly they proved very forgiving. None of the elephants we drugged tried to charge us once they had recovered.

This coordinated group defense has been one of the elephant's keys to survival, effective for hundreds of thousands of years against a multitude of predators, but it is now obsolete. Conditions have changed. Man with a gun is a predator that can easily wipe them out, and the keys to the elephant's survival are now in the hands of man.

In June everyone arrived for the seminar in our camp at Ndala, as Oria has described in her chapter "Born in the Wild." If it was an ordeal for her to undergo the first pangs of childbirth, while ten fascinated conservationists discussed outside her window the consumption of *Acacia tortilis* seeds by elephants and their consequent dispersal and germination, it was equally difficult for me to marshal my thoughts on the management and survival of elephants when I knew that I might have to fly her to hospital any minute.

The primary problem of which we spoke that day, and the one from which all others stem, is space. Owing to the human population explosion, the Parks and Game Reserves have become the elephants' only safe refuge. The range of elephants is now confined to islands of wilderness lapped by seas of humanity. Not only are they prevented from wandering, but their numbers have also been swelled by the invasion of countless refugees fleeing from human persecution. This now causes wholesale woodland destruction as typified by the ill-fated *Acacia tortilis* of Manyara. What should the National Parks do about it?

There are two schools of thought, radically at variance with each other, about the correct answer. We touched on these briefly at the seminar, where they were relevant to Manyara, but did not have time to go into all the arguments which run as follows:

The first opinion holds that since man created the problem it is only rational that he should solve it, and that the elephants should be reduced by culling to counteract the excessive immigration. The aim is to restore a balance between the elephant and its habitat, where natural regulatory checks can once more operate. This school of thought holds that the woodland destruction is usually made irreversible by fire, which burns young trees growing up and unless drastic steps are taken may even lead to the ultimate extinction of elephants from lack of food and shade in the very areas set aside for their survival. Richard Laws and Ian Parker held these views and insisted that though shooting elephants was repugnant it was necessary, and preferable to thousands of elephants dying slow lingering deaths from malnutrition.

Apart from culling, other management options are also open, such as providing drinking places for animals, burning early or late, or even planting young trees and protecting them with firebreaks.

The second school of thought asserts that whenever man intervenes he tends to upset the balance of nature even further, and that culling within a National Park would subvert the fundamental aim of preservation. If only the elephants were left alone, this school argues, they would eventually reach a balance with their environment. This policy is based on the belief that the decline of the woodlands is not irreversible, but is part of a long-term natural cycle in which elephants have always played a role. The theory of natural cycles runs approximately and in its simplest form as follows: elephants knock down trees and bushes, establishing grasslands in their place, but then their numbers decline or they move away to where there are still trees. The grasslands now burn every year, preventing the regeneration of young trees, and establishing themselves even more permanently. This provides ideal conditions for grazing animals to increase; they may breed up to such an extent that the grass becomes threadbare. Patches of soil appear, denuded of grass, where the fire can no longer reach. Bushes and trees can sprout on these islands. With no browsers to suppress them the young woodlands proliferate, becoming the ideal habitat for elephants once more. Perhaps some hundred years after it began, the cycle comes full circle and the elephants begin their demolition once again.

It is cited in support of cycles that in Tsavo's fast-declining woodlands graves have been discovered which belong to the Galla tribe, who only inhabit open areas, and the elephants are therefore merely recreating the grasslands of a former epoch. David Sheldrick, the Warden, has also noticed a great build up in the numbers of grazing animals. Likewise, in Manyara, the presence of elephants was not remarked on by all the early travelers that explored the area, and the first German maps made in the 1890s only mentioned grasslands. My experiments showed that the *Acacia tortilis* tree is much faster growing than previously supposed, and many of today's woodlands, which are doomed to disappear in five to ten years, were probably only established within the last seventy-five years.

Of course the cycles cannot be as straightforward as this. The role of climate alone can upset any regular rhythms. Hugh Lamprey stressed at the seminar that I had only seen Manyara over a short spell of good rains, when the Lake had risen to unprecedented heights, but he remembered successive years of poor rains when animals became very thin and the whole Lake dried up to a shimmering salt pan.

Disease may also disrupt regular cycles, and man as hunter, firemaker, pastoralist and sometimes exterminator has always exerted a profound effect. The very adaptability of elephants makes accurate predictions impossible. They are found from sea level to the high altitude moorlands at 13,000 ft, and from lush tropical forests to burning deserts.

Yet even though the outline for a cycle which I have suggested may be a gross oversimplification, it is only by constructing models and testing them that scientists can get nearer to the truth. Essentially, this approach is the same as Vesey's progressive approximaion where he put up extreme hypotheses and worked inwards by a process of elimination. Any of the models for cycles that have so far been suggested are useful as a basis for discussion rather than as effective attempts to predict the future.

The paramount factor in examining the theory of cycles, which has direct bearing on whether we should shoot elephants to conserve them, is the increase of man, which has drastically and perhaps irrevocably restricted the movement of elephants, and worse than that has compressed them to unprecedented high densities. Consequently the key question which those who believe in noninterference must ask themselves is this: can the cycles continue to work in the confined areas of the present National Parks, or will they break down under the strain?

My main contribution toward unraveling this complicated puzzle was to demonstrate that provided food is abundant elephants do not regulate their own populations even when they are packed densely into a small area. The well-ordered family units I knew lived harmoniously together with overlapping home ranges and no territorial strife. When I finally came to balance all the births against all the deaths I had recorded I found that the population was even slightly expanding with a healthy proportion of young animals. The alarming implication is that the elephant numbers at Manyara may well remain excessively high until they have destroyed their food supply, when they may starve, unless some positive management action is undertaken.

Because the deciding factors are so difficult to evaluate and scientists cannot agree on their relative importance, I have come around to the belief that there is no simple answer to the correct management of elephants all over Africa but that each Park should be judged on its own merits according to its size, climate and the fluctuation of plant and animal numbers. Carefully controlled culling should be tried in some Parks and complete noninterference in others. In time, when all the pieces of the jigsaw have been studied sufficiently we may be able to be more precise in our recommendations.

Until we can do this we must study carefully the results of different policies. The culling undertaken by Laws and Parker in Murchison Falls where 2,000 elephants were shot is of fundamental interest. Equally the decision to let the massive feeding pressure of 20,000 elephants in Tsavo continue unchecked to its final conclusion is perhaps the most courageous example of noninterference anywhere, largely due to the determination of David Sheldrick who was among the first to realize that not all the changes caused by elephants are necessarily harmful.

At Manyara I had to admit that the elephants were gradually destroying the *Acacia tortilis* woodland faster than it could regenerate although the other trees and the Ground Water Forest were still just holding their own. Luckily I was able to suggest a unique solution which was to reverse the usually "irreversible"—to give the elephants more space. In 1955 the elephants living along the south-west shore of the Lake had been ousted from thirty square miles of their habitual range, when the area was made over to European farmers. By the time of the seminar many of these farmers were about to leave the country. I therefore proposed that the land, which would open up a corridor into the Marang Forest Reserve, should be returned to the elephants. Since the farmers had originally been given the land free, it should not prove too difficult to compensate them properly for their time, work, crops, stock and machinery. It would also be necessary to obtain the government's approval to the Marang Forest becoming a refuge for the elephants. Besides adding vital territory to their range, this would also have the important advantage of giving them safe access to the Marang Forest.

No one opposed this idea and indeed everybody at the seminar seemed relieved that there might be an alternative to decimating the Manyara elephants by shooting, and that the loss of the *Acacia tortilis* woodlands could be accepted with equanimity. Regenerating woodlands on the farms, not to mention the Marang Forest, would replace the trees destroyed in the present Park. I believed that when the elephants spread out and ranged through all three areas, there would be an overall balance as they moved from one patch of trees to another, each at a different stage of growth, the whole system acting as a dynamic mosaic.

There still remained the problem of what to do about the lions and their special trees. Most of the trees in which lions were seen sprawled were *Acacia tortilis,* but the lions were conservative in their habits and 80% of their tree climbing was confined to a mere seventeen favorite trees. These trees could be protected individually, and I recommended that they should be wrapped in wire, or surrounded by sharp stones which elephants dislike walking over.

These proposals were adopted as objectives of top priority by the National Parks, requiring both political and financial action. Oria and I hoped to use the film we had made to raise some of the money for the necessary compensation to the farmers.

As the seminar came to a close I was brought down to earth abruptly with the news that Oria's baby was to make its imminent arrival. Kix was waiting on the strip, but what would I do in such a small plane if the baby was born? Luckily John Owen rose to the occasion, as he had every time I was caught in a crisis, and offered to ferry us to Nairobi in his speedy and spacious Cessna 182. Oria has told of the flight and how we made it just in time. Five weeks later we returned to Manyara with our tiny daughter Saba, and enjoyed a united family life for just a few more weeks.

Our last morning at Manyara came all too soon. The day before, we had officially handed the camp over to Parks. Vesey was there to receive everything in good order. We sold him some of our belongings, and packed everything else into the Land-Rover which

John Owen had lent us for Mhoja and a driver to take our heavy kit to Naivasha. I was happy to know that this camp was going to be used by scientists, park people, and visitors, some of whom might give back something to the elephants: knowledge, love or money. Yet I could not forget Bernhard Grzimek's ominous remark when he had visited me. "You have a fine camp here, but you have introduced yet another human settlement into the wilderness. Your few houses may be the nucleus for a future town." Perhaps he was right and Ndala camp, however charming and beautiful, should have been pulled down after I left.

On that last morning the sun began to cast a pink glaze over the dark horizon. Oria took Saba in her arms, and sat on top of our rondavel, under the thatched verandah. The room was empty, apart from the bare table, the mattress on the rug, and a gaping cupboard. Time for takeoff was not to be later than 9 a.m. We needed the cool, heavy air to lift the loaded plane off our short bush strip. Full fuel tanks, three people, a baby and our kit was as much as Kix could carry.

Just before I got in the car to drive to the strip, I walked all around the camp. I wanted to have the feeling of seeing, touching and smelling the place one more time. The tree that Oria had planted beside the bathroom door was growing like an asparagus; all the plants were in flower; Biba, the goat, followed me or ran ahead. She was to find a happy home with the driver of the Land-Rover.

The plane sped down the runway, engine roaring. Oria's hand tightened around Saba, and then before we were half-way down Kix lifted off the ground, up and over the trees, and I banked around the camp. No elephants were in sight, the earth was brown and dry. Mhoja's green uniform and waving hand receded in the distance.

As the Great Rift Valley unrolled below us, my thoughts turned back to the elephants and their future.

The vital key to survival, for which we scientists still search, is how to conserve them properly within the arbitrary boundaries of the National Parks. The correct answers will depend on whether or not the Parks are spacious enough for cycles to work without the risk of extinction. In time we may know, but in groping for the details we run the risk of forgetting an even more serious aspect, that it is only man's fragile toleration that allows elephants to live at all in the modern world.

I fear that if hostile opinion armed with the devastating fire power of modern weapons ruled the fate of elephants, even temporarily, they could be exterminated on a national scale within a few years, rather than decades or centuries. Therefore, perhaps the most important key to survival is to gain the sympathy of the people with whom the elephants share the land and the politicians who represent them. This can only be done by awakening their latent interest and aesthetic awareness through the spoken and printed word, films, television and the opportunity to see the animals at first hand. From the enthuisastic response I have seen of Mto-wa-Mbu villagers to free trips around the Park, the outlook is encouraging. Perhaps also the Park's neighbors should be given greater economic benefits.

I realize that behind all the practical questions and our efforts to solve them lies a much more fundamental question. Why do we believe the survival of the African elephant, the wildlife, and the wilderness to be a matter of great importance? I have tried to sort out my ideas, to separate them from the ties of affection, which during our years at Manyara we had developed for the elephants among whom we lived.

Elephants are intelligent animals which resemble us in some of their behavior. They give an example of a society in which individuals behave with exceptional tolerance to their own kind, and even in times of distress and danger, hold fast to their family ties. As such they deserve our respect in the same way that human life deserves respect. This is why shooting elephants, to quote Richard Laws, "poses moral and ethical problems and cannot be undertaken lightly."

Also in trying to discover our own biological origins, it is of great interest to see how elephants, starting from entirely different beginnings, have evolved a social system fitted to cope with their problems, a society which shows parallels with and differences from ours that may be relevant to the study of our own social problems.

Other important considerations are that elephants and their wilderness are very beautiful and it is vandalism to annihilate anything of beauty and deprive others of the opportunity of enjoying it. I also believe that, with other wild animals, elephants fulfill part of man's deep need for the refreshment of his spirit. This is a need felt particularly by those who are obliged to live in highly industrialized surroundings. To some, in their power and irresistible need for space, elephants are symbols of freedom. Furthermore, they have lived side by side with man, in Africa, since the dawn of history and are an integral part of mythology and folklore; their disappearance would therefore diminish the cultural environment of the African people.

It would, however, be quite unrealistic in assessing the elephant's situation in today's world to confine oneself purely to ethical, scientific, aesthetic, psychological or cultural approaches. The economic argument too has its validity.

Elephants are a great tourist attraction and earn large amounts of foreign currency. Their ivory, hides and meat also fetch a high price. But one would, I think, have to be very limited in outlook to insist that their preservation can only be justified on commercial grounds. Economics are only one aspect of human ecology and though this approach is no less rational than the others, if adopted alone it is an impoverished philosophy which takes no account of the pleasure and interest which men can derive from elephants. It is like judging the artistic merit of the Mona Lisa by its current market value.

None the less, some would argue that at a moment in which the human race is approaching a global crisis of over-population, shortage of food and materials and possible economic breakdown, there is little hope left for the survival of the African elephant.

I am more optimistic. It is, I think, important to recognize that hardship does not inevitably crush the human spirit. Many of the greatest monuments to the genius of Greece, were created at a time when the Athenians were hard put to it to survive. In the same context, I believe that the people of Africa will, even though some sacrifice be involved, show the nonmaterialistic side of their nature by protecting their natural heritage, which is the richest in the world. President Julius Nyerere's Arusha Manifesto of 1961 is surely a confirmation that this is his country's intention, an intention which has so far been well borne out in practice.

## ARUSHA MANIFESTO

The survival of wildlife is a matter of grave concern to all of us in Africa. These wild creatures amid the wild places they inhabit are not only important as a source of wonder and inspiration, but are an integral part of our natural resources and of our future livelihood and well-being.

In accepting the trusteeship of our wildlife we solemnly declare that we will do everything in our power to make sure that our children's grandchildren will be able to enjoy this rich and precious inheritance.

The conservation of wildlife and wild places calls for specialist knowledge, trained manpower and money, and we look to other nations to co-operate in this important task—the success or failure of which not only affects the Continent of Africa, but the rest of the world as well.

# Postscript

For two years we lived in Oxford, a city of stone whose spires pierced the morning mist; during this time I was working on my thesis, analyzing our observations, and writing about elephants instead of living with them.

"Remember," Hans Kruuk had warned me "your examiners are not going to think of your elephants as lovely animals, they will expect you to write about them as dispassionately as if they were white mice in a laboratory."

Huddled around electric fires, pale-faced and wrapped in woolen clothes, we grappled with the simplicities of computers until evening came, the bells chimed and it was time to go home. Gone were the days of walking across the plains, darting away from elephants, scrambling up trees and racing through the skies. Out tight-muscled bellies and strong limbs turned soft as we buttered hot crumpets for tea and ate scones with cream and strawberry jam. Our second daughter Mara was born.

Then, at last, in 1972 my thesis was completed, accepted and deposited in the Bodleian Library.

Within a few weeks we were back in Africa and the day came when we drove in convoy with the children toward Manyara. The new Director of National Parks, Derek Bryceson, had given us permission to complete the film we had started in 1970 and Anglia Television were providing us with an experienced cameraman,

Dieter Plage. It was our hope that through the medium of a film we would be able to publicize the urgent need for an extension to the Park.

We arrived at the Rest House late at night with badly punctured tires. Here the new Park Warden, Benjamin Kanza, welcomed us and lent us his Land-Rover for the last eight miles of our long journey. As we drove into Ndala we saw Mhoja standing in the beam of the headlights.

Next day we woke to the sound of water running over the rocks, birds calling and the noise of branches breaking as some elephants ate behind the house.

The camp looked much as it had when we had left. It had a sort of Rest House look to it, practical, transitory and nearly empty. Bit by bit the bush around the house had crept back. One of the big acacia trees that shaded the house had died, perhaps of old age. If so it was one of the few to escape elephant tusks.

I walked along the scarred woodlands and found that only 40% of my marked trees were still alive; it was the proportion I had predicted, the trend had evidently remained consistent. At this rate, by 1980 at the latest, there would be none left.

Dieter Plage and his assistant, Lee Lyon, a tall, dark-haired Californian girl, arrived by plane. Together we quartered the Park to find out where all the elephants were and what had happened to them.

The Park looked healthy, the roads were well maintained. I examined the seventeen trees favored by the lions. They had been protected by fine chicken wire tightly wrapped around their trunks; it was surprisingly inconspicuous and for some mysterious reason the elephants had left it alone, although they could easily have ripped it to shreds with a few gentle pokes of their tusks.

Elsewhere in East Africa there had been a terrible drought. In Tsavo, where the policy was to let the elephants find their own level, at least 5,000 had died. On the other hand, in the Serengeti, after three years of field work, Harvey Croze was able to conclude that the elephant problem had been greatly exaggerated and that although in some places trees were being destroyed, in others they were sprouting up in spite of a similar elephant density.

Manyara had been spared the worst effects of the drought—no doubt because as soon as it became dry, the elephants had been able to retreat into the resilient Ground Water Forest or into the Marang Forest above the escarpment. There had now been some rain and the elephants looked in good condition.

I had no difficulty in recognizing any of them, since they had changed very little. I found that Sarah had exactly the same pattern of small holes in her ears as when I had first photographed her six years before. The only change was that her crossed tusks had grown a few centimeters.

Our daughter Saba slipped into camp life as though she had never left it. She went off to explore her surroundings, busily catching all the insects she could find. We had taught her that beetles were harmless but that scorpions must not be touched. She and Hadija, the little daughter of one of the Rangers, loved to play in the sand by the river. When elephants came to drink we explained that everyone must be silent so as not to scare them away.

After two weeks we moved out of the house into tents because Hugh Lamprey, who was writing up his work, needed peace and quiet and had booked the house some time ago for this purpose. In tents we felt even closer to the bush, better able to look up to the immensity of the sky and to hear all the night noises.

One evening we went over to the Lampreys to project some of Dieter's films. When we returned to our camp we found all our bedclothes lying in the sand outside our tent. I shone my torch over them and saw lion pugmarks everywhere. They had come into the tent, jumped on to the bed, pulled off all the bedclothes, ripped the sheets with their claws and chewed the blankets which they had left covered with saliva. The tent was an old "Manyara" type, lent us by Benjamin Kanza. The canvas was torn, one door was wide open where the zips had been broken, and there was sand all over the place.

Later that night we were woken by something hitting against the window of our tent and in the process knocking tins and bottles off the bedside table. Oria and I jumped up yelling, then I roared an imitation of a primate threat display that came out quite impressively—only to find that the cause of the commotion had been a dead acacia branch falling against the side of our tent. A few days later I saw a familiar head and ear outline that made my pulse race; they belonged to a large cow who tossed her head and swung around to face us.

"Watch this one Dieter," I said, "and you may get a good charge."

Torone Sister Number Three had come on one of her occasional forays to the northern end of the Park. The ground was flat so I turned in front of her and waited. She gave one outraged trumpet and then came in on a relentless charge, seeming to concentrate all her energy on overtaking the Land-Rover. Dieter was well prepared; he sat right at the back, holding his Arriflex camera at hip level with its wide angle lens pointing backwards. The elephant followed us for exactly three minutes, long enough for the film to run its full course, then she broke off exhausted and rejoined her family unit.

In contrast, the other elephants seemed completely oblivious to cars and tamer than ever. We found Radio Robert, the young elephant we had radio-tracked, ambling along the foreshore with M4/3, the first elephant I had immobilized. They passed within a few feet of us, never even looking at the Land-Rover. I was happy to see that both were plump and well rounded.

I was especially curious to see whether Virgo would remember us. When I found her I got out and called to her. She stopped and turned toward me, then slowly she came forward, extending her trunk to touch my hand and letting out her breath in a long whoosh. It was impossible not to be moved by her trust after our two years' absence. Our children, who had been conditioned from the earliest age to think of elephants as kind and gentle beasts, were longing to meet Virgo, so both were brought up to her to be introduced and sniffed at.

Losing their fear of man had, however, almost certainly brought disaster to some of the other elephants. When we came to check the family unit of the great matriarch, Boadicea, I was dismayed to find that four of the leading cows were missing. Boadicea herself was there, still standing suspicious and watchful, head and shoulders above the rest, but Giselle, who had been her closest associate, was gone, leaving her two young calves to Boadicea's uncertain care. Isabelle also was missing but I found her daughter Laila. She was now looking after not only her own calf, Bottlebrush, but Isabelle's calf as well. She allowed them to suck in turns; both had been born in 1969.

Leonora's family was in an even sadder state; both she and her daughter, Slender Tusks, had disappeared. The survivors were leaderless and the young teenager, Two Holes, was trying to take on the roles of both mother and aunt. I watched her mill around in hopeless confusion at some minor alarm that she was unable to assess, trumpeting loudly to her little adopted siblings and cousins. The orphaned N'Dume stuck to her like a leech.

The only solution for Two Holes was to attach herself to Boadicea's family and this is what she did, but, although she followed the older cows closely, she did not seem able to establish any close rapport with them. Still, she was able to shelter behind the threat charges which Boadicea made for the benefit of the whole kinship group.

The great matriarch's large, amalgamated group was something I had never seen before: an elephant social unit formed by a process of integration. This example completed the cycle. Now I realized that families, when enlarged by many births, would split up into independent family units, but when such family units were reduced by death, they would integrate once more into a coordinated group.

In many respects elephant society resembles some of man's tribal kinship systems, in which individuals are bound to look after each other according to ties of blood, thus overcoming the tribulations caused to the young by the death of their parents.

But what had killed these elephants? In my whole study period only one member of Boadicea's kinship group had died, and now four large cows, who had been in perfect health when I had left, were gone. I asked the Warden and the Rangers if they had observed any signs of illness. They said they had not. The only factor which could account for these deaths was the sharp increase in the price of ivory. Thanks to the world currency crisis, it had soared tenfold during our absence. As a result poaching had become such a problem that eventually the governments of both Tanzania and Kenya had introduced a total ban on hunting elephants: this meant that no fresh ivory could reach the market legally, although it continued to do so in unprecedented quantities on the black market.

Meanwhile, the Manyara Rangers assisted by the army had swept the Marang Forest, and here they found piles of ivory and rhino horn stacked in secret hiding places. Unfortunately such successes are droplets in contrast with the tide of illegal ivory traffic elsewhere. Unofficial slaughter of elephants is probably now worse in East Africa than it has been since the turn of the century. Elephants may well be wiped out of many areas outside the Parks, while the elephant problems inside the Parks may be made worse by fresh influxes of "refugee" elephants.

For Manyara, the problem is one of space. An extension of the Park seems the only reasonable solution. To do this it would be necessary to buy the farmland that forms the elephant corridor up to the Marang

Forest, in particular the farm owned by the Italian mentioned earlier in the book.

While we were filming, Professor Bernhard Grzimek visited us. I told him about the situation at Manyara and immediately he offered, on behalf of the Frankfurt Zoological Society, to raise money to buy the farmland.

With this encouragement, Oria and I set off to visit the Italian, driving to Maji Moto on a new road which had been cut by David Stevens Babu during his time as Park Warden. It ran across difficult terrain at the foot of the escarpment and was an important development, for now the hitherto inaccessible southern boundary would be open to Ranger patrols which would be able to deter would-be poachers.

In spite of the divergence in our aims, we found Signor Fiorotto a sympathetic character. He was a strongly built man who had a reputation among the Rangers for being able to lift a tractor engine in his arms. Arriving in 1958 he had cleared several thousand acres of bush and planted maize, but then he ran into trouble, for night after night elephants and rhino destroyed his crop. Unfortunately his defense of his maize resulted in the death of some 400 elephants. But now he was growing old and he was tired of shooting elephants.

"At night still they come, it was their land before I came and I cannot keep them away. I would be pleased if I could be paid a fair price by the National Parks. Then I would go back to Italia," he told us.

We conveyed the good news to Derek Bryceson that the one remaining farmer was willing to sell his land, that Professor Grzimek had offered to raise part of the sum required to buy him out, and that Survival Anglia Television too, producers of *The Family That Lived with Elephants,* would make a large contribution.

It therefore looks as though the crisis at Manyara which arose from overcrowding may be solved in the very near future. Already the Marang Forest has been promised to the Park, and if the regional authorities agree to the conversion of the corridor of farmland to wildlife conservation, the elephants will be able to return to much of the ranges that they enjoyed a hundred years ago.

Boadicea's Family Tree

Acknowledgments

Bibliography

Index

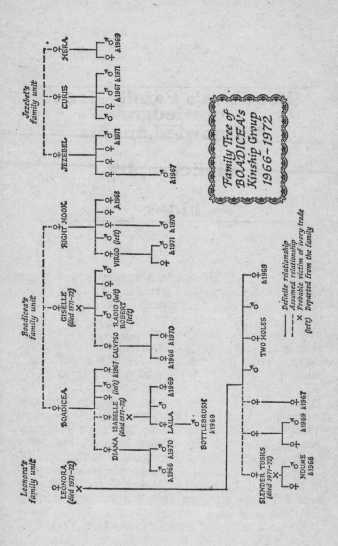

Family Tree of BOADICEA's Kinship Group 1966-1972

*Leonora's family unit* *Boadicea's family unit* *Jezebel's family unit*

——— Definite relationship
- - - Assumed relationship
× Probable victim of ivory-trade
(left) Departed from the family

# Acknowledgments

Without the help of many people the elephant study at Manyara could neither have been begun nor completed. Many of those who gave practical assistance or ideas are mentioned in these pages. To all of these we give our warm thanks and particularly to the following:

The President of Tanzania, Mwalimu Julius Nyerere and his Government who created in the Arusha Manifesto a climate of opinion whereby expatriate (foreign) scientists could come and work with Tanzanians to help conserve their incomparable natural heritage; the Board of Trustees of the Tanzania National Parks for permission to work in Manyara and for the great assistance we received from their administrative staff. We are specially grateful to the former Director, Dr. John Owen, who originally invited this study and supported it throughout; Dr. Hugh Lamprey and the late Desmond Vesey-Fitzgerald for invaluable advice on ecological matters; Myles and Kay Turner for much hospitality in the Serengeti; Mhoja Burengo our companion, instructor, and guide in all things concerning survival in the bush; and Jonathan Muhanga and David Stevens Babu, the Manyara Park Wardens, for unfailing cooperation.

We are also deeply grateful to the New York Zoological Society and the Royal Society of London who provided generous funds for the research; Professor

Niko Tinbergen who stimulated and guided Iain in writing his thesis; Iain's mother, Prunella St. Quentin Power, who gave unstinted help both with the manuscript and in looking after our children when we were writing; our children themselves, Saba and Mara we thank for tolerating the intrusion of "that horrible book" into their lives; and Diarmaid Douglas-Hamilton, Mike Norton-Griffiths, Patrick Scrivenor and David Western who read and criticized the manuscript; Oria's parents, Giselle and Mario Rocco, who gave us peace and quiet at Naivasha and Charles and Peggy Nichols who provided a refuge in Ireland for us to complete the writing.

We wish to thank our friends who have provided photographs: Lee Lyon for five photographs: a mother and three offspring, Boa's family inspecting bones, Boadicea and tusk, Boa's charge and Saba and Virgo; Peter Beard for the skeleton of an elephant; Peter Fera for the bull crushed by a falling baobab; Franz Hartmann F.R.P.S. for the portrait of Ahmed drinking; Mike Norton-Griffiths for taking the shot of Iain wading through the Lake toward some elephants; Alan Root for the calf dying in the Tsavo drought; and Simon Trevor for Boadicea's kinship group in front of our camp, Radio Robert and his transmitting collar, and the cow sitting on an immobilized bull; and Robert O'Meara for the kinship group drawing. We thank also Professor L. Van den Berghe for drawing our attention to the photograph of the man who ran in vain to save his life from a charging Congolese bull.

We owe much to our publishers and all who have helped us there; in particular we thank Sir William Collins for his infectious enthusiasm, and Adrian House and Marjorie Villiers whose patience and advice never failed us.

# Bibliography

ADAMSON, G. (1968) *Bwana Game.* Collins-Harvill.
(in U.S. *A Lifetime with Lions.* Doubleday, 1968)

ARENS, W. (1972) *On the frontier of change: Mto-wa-Mbu, Tanzania.* Unpublished manuscript.

BALDWIN, H. (1971) *Instrumentation for remote observation of physiology and behaviour.* Proc. Sym. Biotel. S.A. C.S.I.R. p. 137.

BAUMANN, O. (1894) *Durch Massailand zur Nilquelle. Reisen und Forschungen der Massai expedition 1891–1893* (+map). Berlin 1894.

BERE, R. M. (1966) *The African Elephant.*

BRYDEN, H. A. (1903) *The decline and fall of the South African elephant.* Fortnightly Review (n.s.) *79*:100–108.

BUSS, I. O. (1961) *Some observations of food habits and behaviour of the African elephant.* J. Wildl. Mgmt. *25*:131–148.

BUSS, I. O. and SMITH, N. S. (1966) *Observations on reproduction and breeding behaviour of the African elephant.* J. Wildl. Mgmt. *30*:375–388.

CALHOUN, J. B. (1962) *A behavioural sink* in Roots of Behaviour by E. L. Bliss, pp. 295–315. Harper-Hoeber.

CARRINGTON, R. (1958) *Elephants, a short account of their natural history, evolution and influence on mankind.* Penguin.

CROZE, H. (1974) *The Seronera Bull Problem.* E. Afr. Wildl. J. *12*:1–48.

DARWIN (1872) *The expression of the emotions in man and animals.* John Murray.

DOUGLAS-HAMILTON, I. (1967) *Report to Royal Society. Leverhulme Committee.* Typescript.

347

DOUGLAS-HAMLITON, I. (1969) *Lake Manyara elephant project.* S.R.I. Annual Report.

DOUGLAS-HAMILTON, I. (1971) *Radio-tracking of elephants.* Proc. Sym. Biotel. S.A. C.S.I.R.

DOUGLAS-HAMILTON, I. (1972) *On the ecology and behaviour of the African elephant.* D.Phil. thesis, Oxford.

DOUGLAS-HAMILTON, I. (1973) *On the ecology and behaviour of the Lake Manyara elephants.* E. Afr. Wildl. J. *11*:401–403.

FARLER, J. P. (1882) *Native routes in East Africa from Pangani to the Masai country and the Victoria Nyanja.* Proc. R. Geog. Soc. N.S. *4*: et seq.

FOSBROOKE, H. (1972) *Ngorongoro; the eighth wonder.* André Deutsch.

GLOVER, J. (1963) *The elephant problem at Tsavo.* E. Afr. Wildl. J. *1*:30.

GLOVER, P. E. (1972) *The Tsavo problem.* Africana *4*:10–11.

GORDON-CUMMING, R. (1850) *Adventures in South Africa.* Vol. 1. John Murray. (in U.S. *The Lion Hunter of South Africa.* Books for Libraries Press, Inc., 1972)

GOWER, SIR W. (1953) *The African Elephant in History* (*The Elephant in East Central Africa.* Ed. Hill, W.C.O.). Rowland Ward.

GREENWAY, P. J. and VESEY-FITZGERALD, D. F. (1969) *The vegetation of Lake Manyara National Park.* J. Ecol. *57*: 127–149.

GRZIMEK, B. (1956) *Ein merkwürdiges Verhalten von afrikanischen Elefanten.* Z. Tierpsychol. *13*:151–152.

GRZIMEK, B. (1960) *Serengeti Shall Not Die.* Hamish Hamilton.

HANKS, J. (1971) Ph.D thesis, Cambridge.

HANKS, J. (1972) *Reproduction of elephant, Loxodonta africana, in the Luangwa Valley,* Zambia. J. Reprod. Fert. 30.

HART, S. (1969) *Life with Daktari.* Bles-Collins.

HARTHOORN, T. (1970) *The Flying Syringe.* Bles.

HENDRICHS, H. (1971) *Freilandbeobachtungen zum Sozial-system des Africkanischen Elefanten, Loxodonta africana in Dikdik und Elefanten.* Piper.

HINDE, R. A. and SPENCER-BOOTH, Y. (1968) *The study of mother-infant interactions in captive group-living rhesus monkeys.* Proc. Roy. Soc. B *169*:177–201.

KÜHME, W. (1963) *Ethology of the African Elephant.* Int. Zoo. Yearbook *4*:113–121.

KURTEN, B. (1968) *Pleistocene Mammals of Europe.* Weidenfeld & Nicolson, and Aldine Publishing Co.

LACK, D. (1966) *Population Studies of Birds*, p. 296. Oxf. Univ. Press.

LAMPREY, H. F. (1964) *Estimation of large mammal densities, biomass and energy exchange in the Tarangire Game Reserve and the Masai Steppe in Tanganyika.* E. Afr. Wildl. J. *2*:1–46.

LAMPREY, H. F., GLOVER, P. E., TURNER, M. I. and BELL, R. H. V. (1967) *Invasion of Serengeti National Park by elephants.* E. Afr. Wildl. J. *5*:151–166.

LA PLUME (1911) *La Domestication des Elephants au Congo.* Bull. Afric. Congo Belge. 2:405–419.

LAWS, R. M. (1966) *Age criteria for the African elephant* (*Loxodonta africana*). E. Afr. Wildl. J. *4*:1–37.

LAWS, R. M. (1969b) *The Tsavo Research Project.* J. Reprod. Fert. Supp. *6*:495–531.

LAWS, R. M. (1970a) *Biology of African elephants.* Sci. Prog. Oxf. *58*:251–262.

LAWS, R. M. (1970b) *Elephants as agents of habitat and landscape change in East Africa.* Oikos. *21*:1–15.

LAWS, R. M. and PARKER, I.S.C. (1968) *Recent studies on elephant populations in East Africa.* Symp. Zool. Soc. London *21*:319–359.

LAWS, R. M., PARKER, I.S.C. and JOHNSTONE, R. C. B. (1970) *Elephants and habitats in North Bunyoro, Uganda.* E. Afr. Wildl. J. *8*:163–180.

LEOPOLD, A. S. (1970) *Research Policy in the Tanzania National Parks.* Tanzania National Parks.

LEUTHOLD, W. and SALE, G. D. (1973) *Movements and Patterns of Habitat Utilization of Elephants in Tsavo National Park, Kenya.* E. Afr. Wildl. J. *11*:369–384.

MAKACHA, S. and SCHALLER, G. B. (1969) *Observations on lions in the Lake Manyara National Park, Tanzania.* E. Afr. Wildl. J. 7:99–103.

MAUNY, R. A. (1957) *Repartition de la grande faune éthiopienne du Nord-Ouest Africin du Paleolithique à nos jours.* Proc. 3rd Pan-Afr. Congr. Pre-history (1955) pp. 102–105.

MORGAN-DAVIES, A. M. (1959–63) *Lake Manyara National Park monthly reports.* Tanzania National Parks, Arusha (typed).

PLINY, THE ELDER *Natural History.* trs. Bostock and Riley, 1855, and Harvard University Press.

RUSSELL, E. W. (1968) *Management Policy in the National Parks.* Tanzania National Parks. Extracts reprinted Oryx. 9 (6):404–406.

SCHALLER, G. B. (1974) *Golden Shadows, Flying Hooves.* Collins and (1973) Alfred A. Knopf, Inc.

SHELDRICK, DAPHNE (1972) *Death of the Tsavo elephants.* Sat. Rev. of Sci. N.Y. *1*:31.

SHELDRICK, DAPHNE (1973) *The Tsavo Story.* Collins-Harvill.

SHORT, R. V. (1966) *Oestrus behaviour—ovulation and the formation of the corpus luteum in the African elephant* (*Loxodonta africana*). E. Afr. Wildl. J. *4*:56–68.

SIKES, S. K. (1971) *The Natural History of the African Elephant.* Weidenfeld & Nicolson, and American Elsevier Publishing Co., Inc.

SIMON, N. (1962) *Between the Sunlight and the Thunder: The Wildlife of Kenya.* Collins.

TANZANIA NATIONAL PARKS (1959–1970) *Lake Manyara National Park monthly reports.* Typescript.

TINBERGEN, N. (1951) *The study of instinct.* Oxf. Univ. Press.

TINBERGEN, N. (1953) *The herring gull's world.* Collins and (1971) Harper & Row, Publishers.

TINBERGEN, N. (1968) *On war and peace in animals and man.* Science *160*:1411–1418.

VESEY-FITZGERALD, D. F. (1968) *An experiment in adapting an electric fence to elephant behaviour.* E. Afr. Agri. Forest. J. 185–190.

VESEY-FITZGERALD, D. F. (1969) *Utilization of the habitat by buffalo in the Lake Manyara National Park.* E. Afr. W. J. *7*:131–145.

WATERMEYER, A. M. and ELLIOTT, H. F. I. (1943) *Lake Manyara.* Tang. Notes and Records.

WATSON, R. M. and BELL, R. H. V. (1969) *Distribution, abundance and status of elephant in the Serengeti region of N. Tanzania.* J. Appl. Ecol. *6*:115–132.

WATSON, R. M. and TURNER, M. I. M. (1965) *A count of the large mammals of the Lake Manyara National Park: results and discussion.* E. Afr. Wildl. J. *3*:95–98.

WILLIAMS, J. H. (1953) *Bandoola.* Hart Davis.

WING, L. D. and BUSS, I. O. (1970) *Elephants and forests.* Wildl. Monogr. *19*:1–92.

WOODFORD, M. H. and TREVOR, S. (1970) *Fostering a baby elephant.* E. Afr. Wildl. J. *8*:204–205.

WYNNE-EDWARDS, V. C. (1962) *Animal Dispersion in Relation to Social Behaviour.* Oliver & Boyd, and Hafner Publishing Co., Inc.

# Index

## ABOUT THE AUTHORS

IAIN DOUGLAS-HAMILTON is a zoologist who has lived for several years in East Africa. His study of the elephants was supported by grants from the Royal Society in London and the New York Zoological Society.

ORIA DOUGLAS-HAMILTON is a photographer. She was raised in Kenya and taught to hunt by a Masai warrior at an early age.

# RELAX!
## SIT DOWN
## and Catch Up On Your Reading!

☐ BLACK SUNDAY by Thomas Harris (2100—$1.95)

☐ THE MONEYCHANGERS by Arthur Hailey (2300—$1.95)

☐ ASPEN by Burt Hirschfeld (2491—$1.95)

☐ THE EAGLE HAS LANDED by Jack Higgins (2500—$1.95)

☐ RAGTIME by E. L. Doctorow (2600—$2.25)

☐ THE ODESSA FILE by Frederick Forsyth (2964—$1.95)

☐ THE BELL JAR by Sylvia Plath (6400—$1.75)

☐ DRAGONARD by Rupert Gilchrist (6452—$1.75)

☐ FAMILY SECRETS by Rona Jaffe (6464—$1.95)

☐ THE DAY OF THE JACKAL by Frederick Forsyth (7377—$1.75)

☐ THE LOVE MACHINE by Jacqueline Susann (7970—$1.75)

☐ ONCE IS NOT ENOUGH by Jacqueline Susann (8000—$1.95)

☐ THE MANNINGS by Fred Mustard Stewart (8400—$1.95)

☐ BURR by Gore Vidal (8484—$1.95)

☐ JAWS by Peter Benchley (8500—$1.95)

☐ TINKER, TAILOR, SOLDIER, SPY by John Le Carre (8844—$1.95)

☐ THE DOGS OF WAR by Frederick Forsyth (8884—$1.95)

☐ THE HARRAD EXPERIMENT by Robert Rimmer (10357—$1.95)

**Buy them at your local bookstore or use this handy coupon for ordering:**

Bantam Books Inc., Dept. FBB, 414 East Golf Road, Des Plaines, Ill. 60016.

Please send me the books I have checked above. I am enclosing $_____
(please add 35¢ to cover postage and handling). Send check or money order
—no cash or C.O.D.'s please.

Mr/Mrs/Miss_____

Address_____

City_____State/Zip_____

FBB—9/76

Please allow three weeks for delivery. This offer expires 9/77.

# THE NAMES THAT SPELL GREAT LITERATURE

Choose from today's most renowned world authors—every one an important addition to your personal library.

**Hermann Hesse**

| | | | |
|---|---|---|---|
| ☐ | BENEATH THE WHEEL | 2509 ● | $1.50 |
| ☐ | MAGISTER LUDI | 2645 ● | $1.75 |
| ☐ | DEMIAN | 2944 ● | $1.75 |
| ☐ | NARCISSUS AND GOLDMUND | 6891 ● | $1.75 |
| ☐ | ROSSHALDE | 7370 ● | $1.50 |
| ☐ | STEPPENWOLF | 7979 ● | $1.50 |
| ☐ | GERTRUDE | 10060 ● | $1.95 |
| ☐ | THE JOURNEY TO THE EAST | 10136 ● | $1.75 |
| ☐ | SIDDHARTHA | 10266 ● | $1.75 |

**Alexander Solzhenitsyn**

| | | | |
|---|---|---|---|
| ☐ | AUGUST 1914 | 2997 ● | $2.50 |
| ☐ | ONE DAY IN THE LIFE OF IVAN DENISOVICH | 2949 ● | $1.50 |
| ☐ | THE LOVE-GIRL AND THE INNOCENT | 6600 ● | $ .95 |
| ☐ | STORIES AND PROSE POEMS | 7409 ● | $1.50 |
| ☐ | CANCER WARD | 8271 ● | $1.75 |

**Jerzy Kosinski**

| | | | |
|---|---|---|---|
| ☐ | BEING THERE | 2265 ● | $1.50 |
| ☐ | STEPS | 2597 ● | $1.50 |
| ☐ | THE DEVIL TREE | 7865 ● | $1.50 |
| ☐ | THE PAINTED BIRD | 8257 ● | $1.75 |

**Doris Lessing**

| | | | |
|---|---|---|---|
| ☐ | THE SUMMER BEFORE THE DARK | 2640 ● | $1.95 |
| ☐ | THE GOLDEN NOTEBOOK | 7747 ● | $1.95 |
| ☐ | THE FOUR-GATED CITY | 7937 ● | $1.95 |

**André Schwarz-Bart**

| | | | |
|---|---|---|---|
| ☐ | THE LAST OF THE JUST | 7708 ● | $1.50 |
| ☐ | A WOMAN NAMED SOLITUDE | 7880 ● | $1.75 |

Buy them at your local bookstore or use this handy coupon for ordering:

Bantam Books, Inc., Dept. EDG, 414 East Golf Road, Des Plaines, Ill. 60016

Please send me the books I have checked above. I am enclosing $_____ (please add 35¢ to cover postage and handling). Send check or money order—no cash or C.O.D.'s please.

Mr/Mrs/Miss_____

Address_____

City_____State/Zip_____

EDG—8/76

Please allow three weeks for delivery. This offer expires 8/77.